The Polish Dilemma

About the Book and Editors

Although much has been written about contemporary Poland, discussions that provide a balanced assessment of the current situation are in short supply. To correct that problem, this book offers a cross-section of intellectual opinion within Poland, including original research and works of synthesis that draw on Polish research and writing that have been, for the most part, inaccessible to scholars outside Poland. The contributors' views avoid the extremes of condemnation or defense of the system and make possible a more complete understanding of present-day realities. Their perspectives are moderated by the fact that, although the authors recognize the need for reform and change, they also take into consideration the great constraints facing all who would confront serious national issues. The discussions range from examinations of social structure and class to evaluations of the significance of the state apparatus in the analysis of policy and assessments of economic performance.

Lawrence S. Graham is professor of government at the University of Texas at Austin and coordinator of outreach programs at the Institute of Latin American Studies. He is the author of *Romania: A Developing Socialist State* (Westview, 1982). **Maria K. Ciechocińska** is associate professor in the Institute of Geography and Spatial Organization at the Polish Academy of Sciences.

The Polish Dilemma

Views from Within

edited by Lawrence S. Graham
and Maria K. Ciechocińska

LONDON AND NEW YORK

First published 1987 by Westview Press, Inc.

Published 2019 by Routledge
52 Vanderbilt Avenue, New York, NY 10017
2 Park Square, Milton Park, Abingdon, Oxon OX14 4RN

Routledge is an imprint of the Taylor & Francis Group, an informa business

Copyright © 1987 Taylor & Francis

All rights reserved. No part of this book may be reprinted or reproduced or utilised in any form or by any electronic, mechanical, or other means, now known or hereafter invented, including photocopying and recording, or in any information storage or retrieval system, without permission in writing from the publishers.

Notice:
Product or corporate names may be trademarks or registered trademarks, and are used only for identification and explanation without intent to infringe.

Library of Congress Cataloging-in-Publication Data
The Polish dilemma.
  (Westview special studies on the Soviet Union and Eastern Europe)
  Includes index.
  1. Poland—Social conditions—1980-   —Addresses, essays, lectures. 2. Poland—Social conditions—1945-   —Addresses, essays, lectures.
I. Graham, Lawrence S. II. Ciechocińska, Maria K. III. Series.
HN537.5.P5379 1987   306'.09438   86-1638

ISBN 13: 978-0-367-29482-3 (hbk)
ISBN 13: 978-0-367-31028-8 (pbk)

Contents

List of Illustrations ix
Preface xiii

Introduction, *Lawrence S. Graham* 1

Part One
Politics and the State

1 The Party System, Involvement in Politics,
   and Political Leadership, *Jerzy J. Wiatr* 13

2 The Contemporary Polish State: Structures
   and Functions, *Wojciech Sokolewicz* 37

Part Two
Social Structures and Attitudes

3 Change in Social Structure and the Increased
   Significance of the Working Class,
   Władysław Markiewicz 71

4 Polish Catholicism as an Expression of National
   Identity, *Władysław Piwowarski* 81

Part Three
Socioeconomic Change and Dislocations

5 Agriculture in Modern Poland,
   Ryszard Manteuffel-Szoege 95

6 Economic Development in Light of Regional
   Differences, *Jerzy Kruczała* 116

7 Rural-Urban Linkages and Change, *Andrzej Stasiak* 131

Part Four
The Sources of Tension Within the System

8   Problems in the Development of Social Infrastructure
    in Poland, *Maria K. Ciechocińska* 157
9   Sociopsychological Aspects of the Polish Crisis,
    Janusz Reykowski 180

Part Five
A Reassessment of the Polish Dilemma

10 Politics, the Economy, and Society: How
    They Interrelate, *Andrzej Rychard* 195
11 Some Lessons from the Historical Experience
    of Poland's Development, *Józef Pajestka* 214

About the Contributors 243
Index 249

Illustrations

Tables

1.1	Mass political and parapolitical organization membership	23
4.1	Overall attitudes toward faith among the adult population in Poland	85
4.2	General attitudes toward religion among youth in final year of secondary education in Poland	87
4.3	General attitudes toward religion among students	88
4.4	Frequency of religious practices among adults in Poland	89
4.5	Participation in religious practices among youth in final year of secondary education	90
5.1	Harvest of basic crops in Poland within present borders before and after World War II	96
5.2	Per hectare yield of basic crops in Poland within present borders before and after World War II	96
5.3	The growth of livestock population in Poland within present borders	97
5.4	Livestock population per 100 hectares of farmland	97
5.5	Land improvement projects	108
5.6	Overall farm production, production costs, and net production	108
5.7	Per capita consumption of basic food products in Poland	109
5.8	Structure of national income produced, 1980–1983	111
5.9	The share of the food complex in the national economy	111
6.1	Regional development, 1960–1978	120
6.2	Voivodships by size	122
6.3	Voivodships by population	122
6.4	Voivodships according to variations in living standards	127
7.1	The change in the number of towns in Poland, 15th to 17th centuries	135
7.2	The share of the population of towns of 10,000-plus inhabitants	136
7.3	Changes in Poland's class and strata structure in 1921, 1931, and 1938	139

7.4	Poland's population: Overall, urban, and rural, 1946–1983	141
7.5	Changes in the structure of employment in the years 1950–1980 in selected areas of the national economy	142
7.6	The relationship between natural increase in the countryside and the balance of migration from the countryside to towns, 1950–1983	146
7.7	The number of men per 100 women in the 20–34 age group, 1978	150
8.1	The number of units in the territorial organization of the country, 1960–1980	168
10.1	The desirable type of authority, according to selected groups	206

Figures

7.1	Natural increase in the countryside and the balance of migration between towns and countryside, 1952–1983	147
8.1	National income produced in 1970–1982	166
8.2	National income distributed in 1970–1982	167
11.1	Diagram of the economic system	225

Maps

6.1	Poland's territorial division into regions (voivodships)	121
6.2	Industrial development by voivodship	123
6.3	Intensity of farming production by voivodship	124
6.4	Standard of living of the population by voivodship	128
6.5	Strong, medium, and weak regions	129
7.1	The average size of a village according to voivodships, 1978	133
7.2	The proportion of nonagricultural population of the countryside according to voivodships, 1950	143
7.3	The proportion of nonagricultural population of the countryside according to voivodships, 1978	144
7.4	The share of the population aged 60 and above in the countryside, according to voivodships, 1978	149

7.5	Voivodship indicators of masculinization of the rural population in the age group 20–24, 1978	151
7.6	Change in the rural population according to voivodships, 1950–1978	152
7.7	Change in the rural population according to voivodships, 1970–1978	153
8.1	Service center according to delivery level	169
8.2	Accessibility of regional centers from local centers in 1978–1979: Time required by the most convenient means of public transportation	173

Preface

Ideally a volume designed to give readers outside of Poland insight into Polish social science research should use the proper diacritical marks for all Polish words. However, the circuitous route this manuscript has taken in getting from first drafts in Polish into a final acceptable English language edition has taken an extraordinary amount of time. The manuscript was completed in late 1984, and more than two years have elapsed since then due to problems in preparation and publication. In recognition of the need to speed up this process and to prepare the final manuscript for typesetting by electronic conversion of the word-processor disks, I made the decision to omit diacritical marks because each mark would require separate coding and even then the final copy would have omitted the Polish "l," which requires a slash. The diacritical marks have been inserted manually on contributors' names in the Table of Contents, in chapter headings, and in the "About the Contributors" section at the end of the book.

This is only the last in a series of problems related to finding the proper "space" within which to negotiate a book of this type and locating an appropriate publisher outside Poland. My coeditor, Maria K. Ciechocinska, understands these difficulties even better than I. Throughout this project her collaboration has been superb. In mentioning her name, it is most appropriate to acknowledge institutional support—on my behalf, from the Advisory Committee on the USSR and Eastern Europe of the National Research Council for a short-term grant to go to Poland, and on her behalf, from the International Research Exchanges Board for a collaborative research projects grant that brought her to the United States. Without the support this project could not have taken place.

There are two individuals without whose cooperation the completed manuscript would never have seen publication: Jerzy Wiatr and Ning Lin. It is Wiatr who consolidated the final publishing arrangements with the publisher at the 1985 meeting of the International Political Science Association in Paris, and it is he who devoted many hours during his subsequent semester in the United States, while teaching at Southern Illinois University, to correct errors in Polish in the typed manuscript. The second person, Ning Lin, has had the thankless task of transcribing the typed manuscript on to word-processing software—first to prepare camera-ready copy and then to code it for electronic conversion. A research assistant from the Chinese Academy of Social Sciences who is completing advanced work on Latin America here at the institute, he has devoted countless hours to entering, reentering, and correcting final copy with me. I am truly grateful for his assistance.

Finally, I would like to acknowledge the cooperation received from all the contributors to this volume. I would never have guessed that a short-term visit to Poland, intended to provide a comparative perspective on work I had been doing in southeast Europe, would lead to additional visits, first by Ciechocinska to the United States, later by me to Poland, and finally to this book. If this cooperative venture can make a contribution to a better understanding of the very complex social, political, and economic reality that is modern Poland, we will all indeed feel most gratified.

Lawrence S. Graham

Introduction

Lawrence S. Graham

It is no understatement to say that the Polish crisis of 1980–1981 has evoked worldwide interest and an outpouring of writing assessing the significance of these events. Even more abundant is the literature on the whole postwar Polish situation—the repeated political and economic crises, the continued problem of legitimacy for a regime imposed from outside and maintained from within essentially by force, the dichotomy between the rulers and the ruled, the anomaly of a workers' state with limited worker support, and an unofficial labor movement in solidarity with the Polish people that in a matter of months shook the regime to its foundations. Additional insight comes through discussions of a church that is the receptacle of nationality and how it has maintained institutional autonomy— not to mention analyses of the aftermath of the 1980–1981 events: first military rule and then the return of a shattered party to the center, with no greater capacity than before to institute any of the fundamental changes needed to extricate the country from what has become its most severe postwar political, economic, and social crisis.

In the discourse that has ensued, one is confronted frequently with a literature that is skewed between the extremes—accounts published abroad, which dramatize the actions of Solidarity and resistance, and statements from within, which evince images of reform and response to crisis. In the midst of all this controversy, however, some very solid and balanced assessments have appeared. One is Neal Ascherson's *The Polish August: The Self-Limiting Revolution,* which deals specifically with the events surrounding the rise of Solidarity and the imposition of martial law, as well as with the wider attempt to create a Polish road to socialism. Another is Leopold Unger's "The People versus the Party" in the Spring 1983 *Wilson Quarterly,* an article what succinctly outlines the reasons for the repeated crises of regime and for the absence of an alternative to the present situation.

The present book differs from these assessments and others written to date in that it constitutes a search for a middle ground that scarcely exists.

It seeks to give representation to the labors of intellectuals who have opted to face harsh realities by remaining within Poland, rather than emigrating—to bring together into a single volume men and women who have sought to confront that reality directly by searching for ways to ameliorate present conditions. None is unaware of the choices available, of the benefits and the costs behind each concerted action. These are the voices of scholars writing about their own society within the context of severe constraints. The perspectives presented here are to a certain degree uncommon outside Poland because they all are essentially those of people in the middle who with varying degrees of intensity accept as a given the existence of a socialist state and view that state as the only viable option for the foreseeable future. The opinions range from extreme caution, born of years of confronting the realities of power, among those whose life experiences reach back to the war years, to a more aggressive insistence that a greater pluralism be accepted by the authorities as the indispensable basis for a reconstituted polity and economy.

The materials contained herein are selective in yet another sense, for they are the product of a specific set of circumstances. The common thread tying these chapters together is shared interest in presenting to people outside Poland the essential ingredients for understanding the present situation from the standpoint of what is rather than what might have been had external forces shaping postwar Polish reality been different. Even the most conservative of these chapters—"conservative," that is, in the sense that it takes the status quo as a given—seeks to communicate a vision of how the polity (the political world and its economic correlates) functions and what its dynamic is. The core of this reality is to be found no longer in the primacy of the party but in the primacy of the state apparatus—or what a number of these authors refer to as "the system for exercising power." The policy outcomes discussed in subsequent chapters are the consequences of the actions of that apparatus in terms of producing a desired set of socioeconomic conditions adjusted to the limits imposed by the people and constrained by the bureaucratic structures created by the authorities themselves.

These materials also have in common the fact that they are the result of continued scholarly contacts between academics in the United States and Poland and of the desire to maintain the exchange of research in the social sciences. When virtually all other communication had ceased at an official level at the height of the crisis, academic contacts continued; visas were issued, and scholarly visits proceeded apace. All the contributors to this volume have participated in one way or another in the academic exchange programs sponsored on the Polish side, through the Polish Academy of Sciences, and on the U.S. side, through the National Research Council of the National Academy of Sciences and the International Research and Exchanges Board.

The origins of this book thus lie in the dialogue encouraged through the interacademy exchange agreements among the Soviet Academy, the

Eastern European Academies, and the U.S. National Academy of Sciences. More specifically, it is the outcome of professional visits conducted under the auspices of these programs. It began first simply as a meeting of two academics when Maria K. Ciechocinska, a Polish geographer with an interest in regional planning, requested that the Section on the Soviet Union and Eastern Europe in the National Research Council arrange a series of visits to U.S. campuses for her while she was enroute to the University of California at Los Angeles where she was to teach during the fall 1980 semester. Several years then elapsed during the course of which Ciechocinska and Graham maintained professional contact. The outcome of these contacts was the invitation for Graham to make a one-month visit to Poland coinciding with the second official visit of John Paul II in June 1983. The purpose of Graham's visit was to meet a cross section of the Polish academic community in the social sciences and law. Arrangements made through the Polish Academy of Sciences and the Catholic University at Lublin provided entrees not only in Warsaw and Lublin, but also in Gdansk, Poznan, Cracow, and Wroclaw. In the course of these visits, because much of the discussion focused on recent research done by Polish scholars on Poland, the question arose as to whether or not it would be appropriate to compile some of this information in the form of general, overview-type articles, focused around identifying the primary factors that have gone into shaping the postwar state and economy, the playing out of this dynamic, and the resultant dilemmas contained within the present situation. The result of these discussions was the selection of twelve scholars with established reputations in their own particular fields and with access to substantive empirical research in Poland on politics, economics, and society.

One should have no illusions about the limitations on this work. June 1983 made possible an initial dialogue in the first real thaw that had occurred in the country since the declaration of martial law. A number of people opted not to participate from the outset because of the constraints imposed by the current situation. Others indicated initial interest but for one reason or another declined to deliver a finished manuscript. Then too there was the problem of how to analyze the current polity objectively if the contributors were to come exclusively from within Poland and each currently held an established position. To do so entailed excluding the extremes: those who were quite openly apologists for the regime and whose stances impinged upon their academic work as well as those whose criticism of the government had been so direct as to preclude objectivity. At the same time, it should be understood that the general thrust of these contributions comes largely from the center, individuals whose careers and commitments have involved them in the negotiated search for greater space in the current system.

In selecting these chapters the criterion used was this: the degree to which the scholar could communicate to readers outside Poland information, research, and perspectives developed in Poland in the debate over where public policy should go from here. The basic point to be communicated is that the current situation involves a fundamental structural crisis in the playingout of the Leninist development model that has dominated postwar Poland. This larger sustained crisis goes far beyond the political crisis. Yet the constraints, international as well as national, preclude very clearly any basic departure from the commanding position occupied by the Polish Communist party—the Polish United Workers' party (PZPR).

There is a very great internal debate going on within Poland over where the authorities should move from here. The past record is clearly known and understood; the constraints are obvious, and yet there is recognition that action must soon be taken if only because the other option is to accept solutions imposed by circumstance and from outside. The search is, in short, for a middle ground in which a modicum of autonomy can be established in order to defend the interests of a national community, much of whose history has been saddled with a state it could not call its own. But who is to define those interests and to create a set of policies designed to take the form of specific programs—without confronting head-on the dilemmas of power that have faced each postwar government and ultimately brought about its displacement by another?

The chapters that follow provide no clear-cut answer because there is none at the present moment. What they do provide is insight into the dynamics of the Polish polity, the changes that have been occurring in national society, and the options that are being explored by the current government. The prospects are not great that the results will be very different from those of any previous postwar government. But the attempt goes on in the search for the acceptance of a greater pluralism than has been possible until now. Still, one should not forget in approaching the Polish polity that previous conditions and outcomes have produced more of an acceptance for a plurality of social forces—albeit a very limited one—than has been possible any place else in Eastern Europe. These social forces are reflected in the acceptance of private ownership as the dominant pattern in Polish agriculture, the recognition of institutional autonomy for the Roman Catholic church, and tolerance of access to information sources independent of those controlled by the official state—through the tacit agreement not to jam certain radio broadcasts from the West, the availability of the Western press in reading rooms in the major cities, and lack of effective control of the underground press. What has not been acceptable until now is the concept of an independent labor movement by those responsible for what might by termed "the system for exercising power," when theoretically they are already acting on behalf of the working class, but according to what the authorities define as best for working-class interests whether or not those the workers agree.

These chapters have been organized in such a way as to carry the reader though the current Polish polity from its initial structuring to the present. The point of departure is the primacy of politics and the apparatus of power over all other factors, be they social or economic. The structuring of the contemporary polity is the consequence of the political forces that moved to the foreground in postwar Poland. Hence, the first chapter begins with a discussion of the evolution of the Polish political party system. Critics of the regime have always denounced the alleged plurality of parties. But that commitment to maintain a multiparty system—albeit a controlled one—when in other socialist states that possibility is never even entertained shows that there is a difference to be encountered within the Polish regime, when compared with those of the rest of Eastern Europe.

The preoccupation of people within system with the legitimacy of the state is the most difficult component for those outside Poland to accept when contrasted with the fact that for vast components of Polish society, if not the majority, the state is conceived to be illegitimate. Thus rather than reject the second chapter as an outright apology for the regime, the reader should search between the lines for the underlying dilemma faced by those who would reform or alter the state apparatus: that is, how to achieve legitimacy when the existing dichotomy between state and society precludes such legitimacy by the very course taken so persistently since the war. The unanswered question here concerns the attempt to return the Sejm—the historic Polish parliament, which antedates socialism—to the center of the policymaking system: Is it simply another charade? Or does it represent an attempt at arriving at a lawmaking institution that will involve a wider range of forces than just the PZPR and hence begin a de facto experiment to create an opening without challenging the official forms dictated by the Soviets?

The second section discusses Polish society from the vantage point of two major groupings. First there is a brief, summary discussion of the social transformations imposed by the outcome of World War II, the consequence of which has been—so say the authorities—the primacy and the privileged position of the urban working class. Following that is a discussion of religious identity as the source of a national consciousness that covers the whole state and exists independent of the wishes of the authorities to impose crosscutting cleavages that would limit, if not curtail drastically, that sense of social solidarity. Although not explicitly spelled out, the implications of this discussion are that the great resource of the church in its ability to maintain autonomy and to act independently within Poland is its mass-based support and its legitimacy as a Polish institution responsive to, yet shaping, the wishes of the people.

Socioeconomically speaking, Poland is a diverse country—with quite decided differences among its regions, between rural and urban areas, among groups within the citizenry in their differential access to social services and benefits that theoretically are supposed to be open to all equally. In dealing with Poland as a social system in the midst of change, one should begin with the countryside. The great postwar change to be encountered in Poland in social terms is the movement from a rural-based society to one that is now predominantly urban and industrialized—but without having changed the peasantry's fundamentally strong commitment to private ownership of land. The policy implication of Chapter 5 lies in the acceptance of the peasantry's tie to the land concurrent with the concentration of resources for increased productivity in collectives (with privileged access to mechanization, agricultural services, and markets). Because these arrangements have not been successful in resolving Poland's needs and 75 percent of the land still remains in private hands, despite official actions, and because statistics show greater yields when minimally advantageous incentives are created for this sector, is it not appropriate—asks Manteuffel indirectly—for the state to accept the possibility of credits for private producers?

Agriculture, however, is only one area of the social changes characterizing postwar Poland. The movement of Poland's borders westward has entailed immense population relocation and resettlement independent of the stimulus to move from rural to urban areas. Chapter 6 gives the necessary background information to understand these developments—what the sources of regional differentiation are and what their impact on the formation of contemporary Poland has been. Chapter 7 complements 6 by looking at the linkages between city and countryside. It provides a panorama of the Polish social landscape as we know it today.

Against this background one must next set current social tensions within the system and the mass psychology that has developed as a consequence of the very process by which national identity has been maintained independent of, if not in spite of, state structures. This section of the book demonstrates that the very ideology of equality, which stands at the core of socialist rhetoric, has been undercut by the state itself in building its own apparatus of power. At the time when mass expectations were being raised in the context of improved living levels for all, equal access to basic social services (contingent upon realizing that commitment to equality) was being undermined by the authorities themselves who were bureaucratizing the social services system and centralizing its decisionmaking. The new technocratic structures substituted technical categories of service delivery for concern about the mass clientele that these systems were designed to serve originally.

The final section contains a reassessment of the Polish dilemma. This is twofold: the emergence of a pluralism within Polish socialism that fits neither standard and accepted concepts of monolithic power derived from Soviet practice nor the pluralism identified with Western political systems. This new plurality of interests within state socialism, argues the author, requires first a recognition of the facts supporting the emergence of the new social, political, and economic reality and second, the movement away from formulas of monolithic control. The final chapter hones this insight not by discussing politics further but by reexamining the performance of the Polish economic system. This author's conclusion is that there is no solution possible other than to permit the market to function once again independent of the political wishes and priorities of the authorities. Thus, he would reserve questions of state authority largely to the political leadership and move to the foreground solidly trained technocrats with a knowledge of economics and market incentives to elicit a favorable response on the part of workers engaged in productive enterprises.

It is in arriving at this point that readers will find that they have come full circle. In returning to the theme of the priority of politics over markets, the final author points out that the goal of accelerating economic growth to bring about transition from an agriculturally based to an industrially based economy has now been achieved and that the concept of a command based economy was an essential part of the success achieved in laying the foundations for mass industry. But in a context where increased quality, greater competition internationally, and continual access to new changes in technology have become paramount, decentralization, the relaxation of political control, and experimentation with economic incentives to improve performance are essential ingredients for moving out of the current impasse.

In short, the possibilities of further development under the current model have become exhausted, and there is no alternative to stalemate and ultimately to collapse without acceptance of basic economic reforms. Thus the last author's conclusion is that if real and meaningful change in economic policy is not currently possible for political reasons, long-term prospects argue for a fundamental readjustment on the basis of sheer economic need—a need that is above all the determination to avoid complete economic breakdown. The same dilemmas are present today as in the past. But for all these authors there is a common meeting ground in the articulation of the view that the larger crisis is not specifically political but economic, in the failure and breakdown of command-economy concepts as the best means to achieve sustained socioeconomic change and growth in Polish society. The ultimate irony in a Marxist-Leninist political world is to rediscover the primacy of economics in determining political structures that are congruent with reality when the authorities argue that political considerations must first receive attention in the defense of state interests.

PART ONE

Politics and the State

The intent of this first section is to lay out for the reader the current structure of the Polish state and the forces that have given shape to it, as understood by those working within the system. Crucial to the structuring of a socialist state in postwar Poland is the leading role played by its reconstituted Communist party—the Polish United Workers' party (the PZPR). For this reason, before the book deals with the state apparatus per se, the first chapter provides an overview of how the political party system now dominant in Poland took form, of the framework within which all subsequent political involvement has operated, and of the patterns of collective political leadership.

Jerzy Wiatr is eminently qualified to provide an overview of the postwar Polish political party system. A prolific writer on Polish parties and political behavior, he agreed to prepare for this volume a chapter that would synthesize his previous scholarship and establish an overview of the Polish political party system. The crucial concept that he introduces here is that of a hegemonic party system in which one party clearly dominates and exercises a leading role. Of course, in a socialist state that political organization is the Communist party. But whereas in other socialist states the only legitimate party is the duly constituted national Communist party (which is, in turn, frequently matched by some form of a socialist unity front designed to mobilize mass sectors of society), in the Polish case, mobilization of a mass constituency has taken the form of reshaping the historic parties and granting them the exclusive right of representing the various recognized sectors of Polish society.

There are four major party groupings. The official organization for representing the peasant sector is the United Peasant Alliance (ZSL). That representing urban labor is the Polish United Workers' party (PZPR), which because of its vanguard role as a national Communist party, dominates and sets the parameters for the actions of the other party organizations. The third is the Democratic Alliance (SD); its roots lie in the liberal-democratic movement of the prewar era, and it is the official organ representing the middle sectors of Polish society. The fourth alignment consists of the Catholic associations; these number three—the PAX Association, the Christian Social Association (ChSS), and the Polish Union of Lay

Catholics (PZKS, sometimes referred to as ZNAK. Attention to the performance of these Catholic associations and their relationship to the Catholic community, however, should not lead one to conclude necessarily that they are representative organizations. The same could also be said of the SD and the degree to which it really gives representation of the middle sectors of Polish society. The more appropriate organizing concept, one that comes from nonsocialist systems, is that of corporatism, whereby the state organizes and sanctions the official organizations representing the various interests in society. It is here that the concept introduced later in this book, of "the system of exercising power," becomes most appropriate. These organizations are an extension of the state and must be viewed as distinct from any one particular social sector that may be identified in the larger society.

With this political party background set, Wojciech Sokolewicz's discussion of the functions and the structures of the contemporary Polish state becomes most appropriate. Generally speaking, most Western political scientists—especially those trained in the traditions of comparative politics—accord minimal importance to the state apparatus. Likewise, those trained in political science in Eastern Europe rarely consider the category "public bureaucracy" to be an appropriate part of the political domain. Yet no discussion of Polish politics aimed at an assessment of the consequences of political action can ignore the presence of the state and organizational structures that clearly define the limits of action. My own way of dealing with this phenomenon comparatively is to speak of the division between state and society and of the alignment between prosystem and antisystem forces.

The Sokolewicz chapter, then, offers a detailed account of the state apparatus, subdivided according to its major components. It is these components, in turn, that define the arenas in which the government of Poland acts and implements its policies. In order to deal with the administrative state phenomenon, which is such an important part of the evolution of all modern governments, one frequently has to go to those trained in law for understanding the continental systems, in Eastern as well as Western Europe. A major part of the Sokolewicz chapter concerns the Polish parliament, the Sejm. In order to place this discussion in proper context, I would like to suggest that the richness of detail contained here is best understood as a problem in the analysis of the administrative state under socialism, in the context of prior practices centered around executive supremacy (in which political and governmental control has been fused in the person of the premier and the first party secretary) and present desires to bring about political reform by revitalizing the legislature. This, then, is the setting in which one finds discussion taking place of how to achieve a greater amount of pluralism within socialism as a corrective to bureaucratism and reliance on single-person leadership. There is likewise preoccupation with legalism and constitutionalism in recognition of the power vacuum that has emerged as the consequence of major sectors of society regarding the current state as illegitimate. Many argue that to achieve legitimacy it is essential to permit the Sejm to reemerge as the decision-making center of the governmental system. Whether or not that will come to pass cannot be determined here, but what I would suggest is that the Sokolewicz chapter can be read with profit by anyone interested in understanding the structure within which policy is made and implemented in contemporary Poland as well as the current dilemmas of power and authority.

1

The Party System, Involvement in Politics, and Political Leadership

Jerzy J. Wiatr

The political system of People's Poland, shaped after World War II, has been based on a durable system of cooperation among political parties, which nevertheless has undergone change from time to time. This system is an expression of the political involvement of the citizenry and serves as the means for the selection of both national and local political leadership. The stability of the whole political and socioeconomic leadership depends in a great measure on the extent to which the actual functioning of the party system corresponds to its theoretical assumptions. The political events of 1980 and 1981 demonstrated powerfully how a weakening of a party system brings in its wake profound disturbances in the functioning of the state as a whole, including the economic area. The reconstruction of the system, embarked upon after the imposition of martial law in December 1981, signified also the reconstruction of the party system, a process that did not amount to a return to the past but was a critical continuation instead, containing as it did a germ of political reform.

In this chapter, which refers to my earlier publications on the subject, albeit enriched by more recent experience and ideas, it is my intention to

1. give a synthesis in outline form of the historical evolution of the party system in postwar Poland, from 1944 to 1980;
2. trace back the ideological assumptions legitimizing that system in the period in question;
3. consider the mechanisms and effects of political mobilization within the political system in force then and now against this background, the essential features of which involve the selection and operations of the political leadership;
4. present those aspects of the sociopolitical crises of 1980-1981 that are directly related to the operation of the party system and analyze

the new processes of political mobilization and selection of leadership groups in that period;
5. outline the direction of the essential political reforms of 1982-1983 in regard to the operation of the party system, the mechanisms of political involvement, and the selection of leadership groups.[1]

The only way such a broad range of objectives can be fulfilled is by presenting a synthesis of the conclusions that follow from sociological-political studies, including ones I carried out myself and ones I carried out with the help of my associates, as well as the conclusions coming from observations while participating in the political life of People's Poland. Detailed empirical material can be found in the literature mentioned in the notes.

The Evolution of the Party System in 1944-1980

The party system of People's Poland is based on the cooperation of the workers' party, the peasant party, and the party representing the intermediate urban classes, as well as political groups that combine a Christian philosophical orientation with the political option of participation in the building of a socialist system. The party system is the consequence of history, especially the history of the Polish people's struggle for liberation during World War II. It took root in the alliance of radical left-wing forces in a country occupied by Nazi Germany. The emergence of this alliance signified the abandonment of the "historical parties" of the prewar Second Republic, which had their political successors in the emigre groups supporting the Polish government in London (led by General Wladyslaw Sikorski until his death in July 1943 and afterward by the leader of the Peasant Alliance [Stronnictwo Ludowe—SL], Stanislaw Mikolajczyk). The Polish government-in-exile enjoyed, in contrast, the support of underground political organizations operating in Polish territory, which claimed to be heirs to the prewar political parties; it also controlled the biggest military organization of the Polish political underground, the Home Army (AK).

The split between the Left and the historical parties did not occur all at once. Until 1942 the radical Left existed only in the form of scattered underground groups set up by Communists and radical Polish socialists, especially the "Hammer and Sickle" group, the Association of Friends of the USSR, and the Union of Liberation Struggle. This was so because the Communist Party of Poland (KPP) had been dissolved by the leadership of the Communist International, with which it was affiliated, on the basis of false accusations that were not rescinded until 1956. Despite the absence of a Communist party, the radical left nevertheless joined the struggle; the Left combined a program of national resistance against Nazism with slogans of a revolutionary social reconstruction in postwar Poland.

The Polish Workers' party (PPR) was formed underground on January 1, 1942, by members of the left-wing organizations listed above. Its military arm, set up at the same time, was the People's Guard (GL), later renamed the People's Army. The PPR was headed by Communist activists of prewar times: Marceli Nowotko, Pawel Finder, Malgorzata Fornalska, Wladyslaw Gomulka, Boleslaw Bierut, and others. The party attracted the youth in particular; a major part of its members during the war were people who were too young to have acquired any political experience before the war. This was political mobilization through underground armed struggle, which made the PPR a new party, with a membership and experience distinctly different from that of its predecessor, the KPP. As for ideology, the PPR pointed to its Communist heritage and accepted Marxism-Leninism as its ideology.

The foundation of the PPR accelerated the radicalization of other left-wing parties. At the time, Poland's socialists acted through two clandestine parties, one of which—the more radical one—sought deeper revolutionary transformations (the Polish Socialists, founded in September 1941 and renamed the Workers' Party of Polish Socialists [RPPS] in April 1943). The left wing within the RPPS was inclined to establish close cooperation with the PPR, up to the point of forming a joint political representation of the whole Polish Left. The same path was taken by the leftist group of peasant activists associated with the underground bulletin *Wola Ludu* (The Will of the People), who later formed the Wola Ludu Peasant Alliance. Finally, the road of cooperation with the PPR was taken by the activists of the progressive-liberal group set up in 1937 and known as the Democratic Alliance (Stronnictwo Demokratyczne—SD).

Initially, the PPR sought to build a broad national front for the anti-Nazi struggle and did not rule out cooperation with the government-in-exile. However, negotiations on such proposals produced no results in view of the London-camp historical parties' decidedly negative attitude toward the PPR. This led to the decision to set up the underground National Home Council (Krajowa Rada Narodowa—KRN). Established on December 31, 1943, it was made up of representatives of the PPR, radical socialists, peasant leaders, and nonparty patriotic activists cooperating with all the others. At a time when the first bits of Polish land were being liberated by the Soviet army and the Polish socialist armed forces set up in the USSR in 1943, the KRN assumed the responsibilities of an interim parliament and established the Polish Committee of National Liberation (PKWN), whose July Manifesto (issued in Chelm on July 22, 1944) laid the cornerstone for the building of a new state system in the liberated country. The PKWN was headed by one of the leaders of the RPPS left wing, Edward Osobka-Morawski.

The reactivation of the political parties of the radical Left occurred between August and September of that year; they then became legally acting elements of the new party system. The RPPS congress held on September 10-11, 1944, revived the Polish Socialist party (PPS) under its traditional name, albeit without a majority of the activists who, whether in exile or at home, supported the London government-in-exile. The Wola

Ludu group started to act as the revived Peasant Alliance (SL), and the Democratic Alliance (SD) resumed activity on September 24, 1944, selecting its delegates to the National Home Council. In this way, the rebuilt party system became a system of cooperation of four parties and alliances: the PPR, PPS, SL, and SD.

This alliance of four parties took up the challenge of organizing the state authorities, building the armed forces, and representing Poland in its relations with the anti-Nazi coalition countries. By taking the reins of power, the alliance of the Left departed from constitutional legalism on which the existence of the London government was based. From the formal and legal point of view, this departure took place in the form of the rejection, as null and void, of the April 1935 constitution, whose adoption shortly before the death of Marshal Josef Pilsudski was the constitutional culmination of the military coup d'etat of May 1926 and whose legality was debated from the very beginning.

The situation of the left-wing alliance and of the state authorities established by it was extremely difficult. A considerable part of Polish society supported the London government and its underground structures. After it was set up in July 1944, the PKWN enjoyed the support of only a minority of Poles and had to overcome the distrust or often simply the passiveness of the majority. The PKWN sought to attain that goal through radical socioeconomic reforms (beginning with the September 1944 agrarian reform in which large landed estates were divided among small landholders and farm laborers), the organization of the armed forces (at the end of the war, Poland had the fourth largest armed force of all the countries of the anti-Nazi coalition in Europe), and the reconstruction of the economy, culture, and education. The success of those undertakings is attested to by the fast growth in membership of the political parties, notably the PPR and the PPS.

The diplomatic situation of the nascent state was also complicated. Only the Soviet Union recognized the new Polish authorities right from the start and granted them assistance. Yugoslavia was the one other member of the anti-Nazi coalition that accorded diplomatic recognition to the socialist government. In contrast, the Western powers continued to support and recognize the government-in-exile in London. This situation was the subject of Soviet-U.S.-British negotiations in Yalta (February 1945), when it was decided to broaden the political base of the provisional government (set up on December 31, 1944, by transforming the PKWN) by bringing in domestic and emigre democratic activists associated until then with the London government. This took place in mid-1945; the ex-premier of the London government Stanislaw Mikolajczyk then became one of the vice premiers of the National Unity Government. Edward Osobka-Morawski remained the prime minister and the four parties of the left-wing alliance retained a clear supremacy in the new government. Two new parties appeared on the political scene: the Polish Peasant Alliance (PSL), led by Mikolajczyk, and the Labor Alliance, headed by Karol Popiel, which claimed to be heirs to the tradition of Christian Democrats. The National Unity Government was recognized by the United States, Britain, France, and other member states of the anti-Nazi coalition.

In the years 1945–1947 Poland had a limited multiparty system. It was a multiparty system inasmuch as among the six legally operating parties and alliances there were some that although represented in the government, opposed de facto its principal policy line. The number of parties participating increased further as a consequence of two groups of activists breaking away from the PSL, who leaned toward an understanding with the left-wing alliance. The nature of the multiparty system was limited because groups supporting the emigre and the domestic underground structures of the London government were denied the right to operate legally. The political underground continued to exist and for several years engaged in an armed struggle for power. This struggle took a toll of several tens of thousands of lives; it was, therefore, a limited civil war.

This system of cooperation among the four left-wing parties was present also at the time of the limited multiparty system. In 1946, the four parties took the initiative in launching an agreement before the parliamentary elections scheduled for January 1947. This initiative was rejected by the PSL, whereas the Labor Alliance accepted it only in the "Regained Territories." The elections took place in an atmosphere of fierce political struggle, with an occasional resort to armed struggle as well. As a result of the elections, the Bloc of Democratic Parties won indisputable superiority and was able to set up a government on its own. Boleslaw Bierut, who was the president of the National Home Council until then, became president of the Polish Republic. The government was headed by Secretary General of the Polish Socialist party Jozef Cyrankiewicz, while its members hailed from the PPR, PPS, SL, and SD. After acting as parliamentary opposition for a brief period of time, Stanislaw Mikolajczyk and a group of his associates fled to the West, while a group of PSL activists who were in favor of cooperation with the government gained control of the PSL. The era of limited multiparty system was drawing to an end.

Its final episode was the unification of both working-class parties and their merger into the Polish United Workers' party (PZPR) in December 1948, the merger of all the peasant parties into the United Peasant Alliance (ZSL), and the incorporation of the remains of the Labor Alliance into the Democratic Alliance in 1950. The result was the emergence of the tripartite system of cooperation among the PZPR, the ZSL, and the SD, which forms the core of the political system of People's Poland. In subsequent years, three political organizations of a Catholic nature came into being: first the PAX Association, then the Christian Social Association (ChSS), and lastly the Polish Union of Lay Catholics (PZKS), which was preceded by the "Znak" (Sign) Sejm Deputies' Club. They are represented in the Sejm (parliament) and are elected from a joint ballot, together with representatives of the three political parties and independent candidates.

No formal changes in the structure of the party system occurred between 1950 and 1980, with the exception of an increase in the political representation of Catholics in 1956. However, the way in which the system operated changed with the passage of time.

The years 1948–1956 saw, on the one hand, a huge consolidation of the position of the PZPR and a weakening of the role of the smaller alliances, plus a decline in membership. It was sometimes said that the alliances in question were a transitional phenomenon, doomed to disappear in the end. These views were rejected in 1956. With the democratization of many areas of political life, the ZSL and the SD obtained broader opportunities for action. Their prestige began to grow and so did their ranks. In subsequent years, the position of the political alliances evolved in step with the evolution of the overall political situation. The periods of curbs on democracy, especially the second half of the 1960s and then the latter half of the 1970s, were accompanied by limitations of sovereignty and of the freedom to exert significant political influence by the ZSL and the SD. On the other hand, the importance of the ZSL and the SD increased in times of democratizating reforms (especially after 1956 and to some extent also in the beginning of the 1970s). A similar situation obtained with regard to the Catholic associations. However, the changes were rather limited, occurred behind the scenes, and were often not disclosed to the public. These changes did not alter the principal characteristics of the party structure, shaped as a durable system of interparty cooperation and political hegemony of the PZPR as the strongest and leading party in this alliance.

The Hegemonic Party System in Poland

I have termed the system dominant in Poland ever since a hegemonic party system, and this term has become accepted in the specialized literature, not only in Poland but outside.[2] Let me recapitulate the principal features of this system as they are expressed in program documents and theoretical elaborations.

The first characteristic of the hegemonic party system is the special, leading role of the working-class party (in Poland—the PZPR) whose political leadership is recognized by other parties forming the ruling coalition. In some respects, this party fulfills the same role the Communist party plays in one-party political systems, while in other respects its situation is different precisely because it operates in alliance with political organizations that, although recognizing its hegemony and bound by lasting bonds with it, retain their autonomy and ideological and political identity. The special powers of the PZPR, acknowledged by other members of the left alliance as signs of its leading position, are the following:

1. Defining strategic aims of the building of socialism and the fundamental ideological values lying at the basis of this building;
2. Filling state posts of special political significance, in particular the position of prime minister, as well as a majority of government posts and top positions in the local administration, etc.;

The Party System

3. Exercising especially close and direct control over the armed forces, in which the PZPR in the only political organization authorized to operate;
4. Organizing the participation of members and supporters of the party in state activities, both within the structures of executive power and in various representative or self-government bodies, as well as within the programming of propaganda and education activities.

The second feature of the hegemonic party system is the existence of political differentiation within that system. The Polish United Workers' party is not the only political party—it cooperates at present with two political alliances and three Catholic political organizations. This socialist pluralism within the party system sets the system of hegemonic parties apart from one-party systems. However, this system differs substantially from the multiparty systems in the West.[3] In a hegemonic party system, pluralism is limited to those political formations that agree to act within the alliance and recognize the leading role of the PZPR.

The third feature of the hegemonic party system is the lasting nature of the ruling coalition, which is governed by long-term rather than by short-term interests. As distinct from the coalitions formed sometimes by political parties in Western parliamentary systems in order to secure a majority, the coalitional nature of government in the Polish system is built into the system itself a priori. Despite the fact that it holds an absolute majority of seats in the Sejm, the PZPR does not rule on its own but in a coalition with its allies. Those allies influence government decisions not through voting but through a process of negotiation and search for compromise solutions. Their strength does not stem from the number of seats in parliament but from the awareness of all the members of the coalition, the PZPR included, about the supreme need of preserving the alliance of the Left. This implies that the alliance's policy must be the product of interparty coordination of policies rather than a decision of the hegemonic party itself. In this manner, the hegemonic party system is based on the mechanism of policy coordination among allies whose aim is to ensure the broadest possible support for the policies of the whole ruling coalition.

As I have mentioned before, the practical implementation of this principle varied in different periods. In the years 1980–1981 there was much criticism of the policies that had de facto limited the participation of the ZSL, the SD, and the Catholic associations in policymaking, especially in the late 1970s. As a result, the coalitional character of government had became to some extent a front. But even those errors should not obscure the fact—important from the point of view of future transformations—that the accepted principles of the party system urged a coalitional approach combined with the continued recognition of the special leading role of the PZPR by all the parties in the alliance.

The fourth feature of the hegemonic party system is that fact that all the members of the alliance—and not only the hegemonic party—are a source of top state administration. This applies to the filling of government posts, local administration jobs, the diplomatic service, and so forth. Some state jobs are considered to be within the regular domain of one of the parties (e.g., the Sejm speaker is always an activist of the ZSL).

Finally, the fifth feature of the hegemonic party system is that the elections to representative bodies (the Sejm and people's councils) are based on voting regulations that rule out political struggle among rival parties. A vital part of the electoral process is the preparation of joint lists of candidates by all the members of the ruling coalition.[4]

The hegemonic party system is based on triple legitimization. It is based in the first place on the vision of a socialist development of Poland accepted by the whole coalition and the theoretical precepts of Marxism-Leninism that are connected with that prospect. Although not all the forces in the coalition profess a Marxist ideology, all of them recognize the Leninist principle of the leading role of the working-class party in the process of building socialism. In this sense, the Marxist-Leninist conception of the Communist party and of its role in the building of socialism constitutes the ideological legitimization of the system.

The hegemonic party system is also legitimized by the history of joint struggle. The more than forty-year-old history of the left alliance, first in the struggle for power and afterward in power, furnishes arguments legitimizing the continued maintenance of that system. The ruling coalition naturally points to the accomplishments of the whole period and the historical legitimizing argument.

Finally, the third element legitimizing the hegemonic party system is the national idea, that is, the argument that the broad political unification within the alliance of the Left is in the national interest of Poland and the Poles, ensuring the optimum conditions for the country's development, the consolidation of its existence as a sovereign state, and its international standing.

The individual elements of ideological legitimization of the hegemonic party system have different appeal in various social milieus. For this reason this legitimization is a political process abounding in internal contradictions. The legitimacy of the system has differed from one period to another. The very strong degree of legitimization demonstrated in the 1957 elections to the Sejm can be contrasted with the crisis of legitimization that became evident in 1981.[5]

The relegitimization of the hegemonic party system, combined with political reforms that strongly modified that system in some respects, is one of the most important accomplishments of in the years 1982–1983 insofar as civic consciousness is concerned. In general, it can be said that any party system—hence also the hegemonic party system—is not only a set of institutions and legal norms governing their operation but also a system of internalized norms belonging to the realm of political tradition. The legitimization of the hegemonic party system was part of political traditions and was connected with the internalization of socialist principles.[6]

However, the political crisis that erupted in the summer of 1980 undermined this legitimization, especially because the hope for a harmonious implementation of the promises of a rapid increase in general prosperity proved to be unfounded. The consequences were dangerous for a whole political system.

A side effect of the crisis was the increased awareness of the fact that the legitimization of the party system must be based on more solid foundations than uncertain economic programs. The sense of the democratic reforms, which will be mentioned in a later part of this paper, follows the conviction that the hegemonic party system must be based on the citizen's deeper and more genuine experience of participation in the political process.

Political Mobilization and Political Leadership Prior to 1980

Among the features considered to be desirable for a political system, Marxist ideology lists the involvement of citizens in political life or, in the jargon of modern political science, a high degree of political mobilization. Political mobilization fulfills a number of roles with regard to the socialist political system. It constitutes the path through which political socialization consistent with the aims and values of the socialist system takes place. This mobilization is also a form of legitimization of the system because by participating in political activities (e.g., joining political parties and alliances, youth organizations or other political associations; taking part in elections; consenting to being elected to representative bodies, etc.), citizens demonstrate their recognition of the legitimacy of the political system of the socialist state. Political mobilization also creates conditions for citizens to participate in exercising power to the extent authorized by the binding legislation and political customs.

In the initial postwar years, the Polish political system aimed at maximizing the scope of political mobilization, especially—although not only—for youth. This concerned in particular the socializing and legitimizing functions of mass mobilization; these were especially important in a situation when the new political system still had to win public acceptance. The rapid, significant growth of political mobilization in the years 1944–1956 was, to some extent, the result of pressure exerted by the state authorities, but it would be an oversimplification and a half truth to reduce everything to that pressure. History has shown that even much more powerful pressure than that exerted by the authorities in Poland cannot break resistance to political involvement if that resistance is spontaneous and based on strong emotions. Therefore, even if the political conditions in which mobilization during the first postwar years took place are borne in mind, the value of political mobilization as evidence of the new socialist political system gaining ground in Polish society cannot be questioned.

After 1956, the attitude of the authorities to political mobilization changed in one subtle way. The ideal of mass involvement in political activities remained in force, but its pursuit was freed from previous pressures. The change was the most pronounced with respect to youth organizations, which never again obtained the degree of political mobilization of the younger generation recorded by the Polish Youth Union (ZMP) prior to 1956. With the exception of participation in elections, to which official propaganda did attach a great deal of importance, it was really left to the individual to decide whether he or she wanted to join a political organization or take part in other political activity. It is true that in Poland—as in most other countries, both socialist and nonsocialist—membership in a political organization could make life easier, especially for people choosing careers in which political criteria were of greater relevance and for those seeking promotion within the hierarchical structures of power and subordination. But it is also a fact that in Poland people who did not join any political organizations did not automatically deprive themselves of any chance of success in their careers and, in a broader sense, in their lives. Most professors in universities and research institutes, including an overwhelming majority of the most prestigious body of scholars—the Polish Academy of Sciences—did not join the PZPR, other political alliances, or any other political organizations. In general, it can be said that political participation was not a precondition of professional advancement in post-1956 Poland.

This is not to say, however, that the involvement or lack of involvement in politics made no difference at all. Throughout the postwar period, albeit with varying intensity, there were demands for creating broader opportunities for nonparty people. There was also criticism of the existing political practice that introduced discrimination against nonparty people, especially in entrusting them with responsible top posts. This must be borne in mind in evaluating the effects of political mobilization during the years 1956-1980.

Progressive political mobilization resulted in the emergence of mass political and parapolitical organizations in Poland. This is illustrated in the statistical data in Table 1.1 for the end of the period in question.[7]

In terms of numbers, the degree of political mobilization in the 1960s and 1970s was considerable, although it did not nearly match the figures recorded for other socialist countries. Approximately one-fourth of the adult population were members of the party or political organizations and over half of the whole population of employable age (i.e., including private farm owners and other self-employed people as well as people without employment) were members of trade unions. Outside of agriculture, virtually the whole work force was unionized.

However, a different picture is obtained if one looks at the quality of that mass participation. With the trade unions, the matter is simpler. Although membership in the unions was optional, social mechanisms were in force that made this membership almost automatic. The unions had at their disposal funds that helped them offer union members benefits such as cut-rate holidays and interest-free loans. In practice all employees were automatically entered on the list of members unless they expressly refused to join the unions. Although the unions did have many dedicated and

Table 1.1
Mass Political and Parapolitical Organization Membership (thousands of members)

	1960	1970	1979
Polish United Workers' party (PZPR)	1,154.7	2,320.0	3,079.2
United Peasant Alliance (ZSL)	258.7	413.5	458.6
Democratic Alliance (SD)	n.a.	88.4	109.4
Trade Unions	6,122.8	10,101.7	13,626.4
Polish Socialist Youth Union (ZSMP)[a]	976.1	2,361.1	2,591.2
Socialist Union of Polish Students[b]	83.0	225.0	228.2
Union of Fighters for Freedom & Democracy[c]	159.4	329.5	659.0
Poland's population	29,795.0	32,658.0	35,414.0

Notes: a. In 1960 and 1970, the Socialist Youth Union (ZMS) and the Rural Youth Union (ZMW).
b. In 1960 and 1970, the Polish Student Association (ZSP).
c. An association of veterans of armed struggle and underground activity before and during World War II.
Source: Author's compilation from official Polish sources.

energetic activists, the main body of members was largely passive toward union activities. This became quite evident in 1980, when in the face of the alternative provided by the dynamically growing Solidarnosc union, the old union began to lose rapidly the support of their members, many of whom defected.

Political mobilization in the parties, youth unions, and other political organizations was of a more selective nature. As a result, the degree of members' identification with their organization was higher than in the trade unions. However, the 1970s saw a drive to increase rapidly the number of members in the PZPR and youth organizations. During that period the number of party members increased by over a million people, adding more than 50 percent to the original number. It is not irrelevant that it was mostly those new PZPR members, admitted in the 1970s, that left the party after August 1980. Out of the almost one million people who quit the PZPR ranks in 1980 and 1981, half had fewer than five years of seniority in the party. To some extent, this could be connected with the fact that they were younger and that the sociopolitical crisis took the most acute form among the youth. However, the defections were also the consequence of the lowered requirements the party had for new members in the 1970s. Similar phenomena occurred in that period in youth organizations.

A special feature of political involvement is the fact that it creates conditions for the selection and training of cadres for various levels of political leadership. In Polish conditions, this applies first of all to the PZPR and, to a lesser extent, to the two political alliances, youth unions, and other political organizations.

Over the four postwar decades, it is possible to distinguish four basic kinds of careers that led to the emergence of a cadre of political leaders.[8]

The first road was revolutionary activity in the Communist, socialist, or radical peasant movement before the war and participation in the struggle of the left-wing resistance movement during the Nazi occupation of Poland or in the Polish armed forces set up in the Soviet Union during the war. People who became politically involved in one way or another, even before the left-wing coalition took over power, formed the core of the leading political cadre for the first quarter of a century after the war. Some of them were still members of the political leadership in the early 1980s. This was possible due to the fact that they had been relatively young when the left wing established itself in power. When the war ended, most of the top activists of the left-wing camp were not even forty years old, while leaders above the age of fifty were an exception (one was Boleslaw Bierut, who was born in 1892). At local levels it was possible to come across representatives of the apparatus who were barely twenty years old. In terms of their political biographies, the political leaders of that period belonged to one of two generations: The older ones were the generation of prewar revolutionaries, while the younger were resistance fighters and excombatants. Both had a history of underground activity involving personal risk and sacrifices. They represented the heroic kind of leader.

The second path to a political career was promotion within the local structures of power shaped after the war. As a result of the scarcity of experienced politicians, combined with the mass participation in political life, the new authorities had to rely on people who had started their political activity only after the war. They were rapidly advanced to top positions at local levels in the state administration and in the political parties and mass organizations. These people formed a reserve pool for the leadership cadre. As early as the 1960s, some of them made it to the level of central political authorities (the PZPR Politburo and Central Committee Secretariat, the Council of Ministers), but they appeared in the national leadership in greater numbers only in the 1970s.

The biographies of the people who joined the top political cadre in the third way were somewhat similar. They began with work in the central political and administrative apparatus and were promoted to ever higher levels within the hierarchy of authority. This kind of political career is most typical of people active in the state administration, although it can also be found in the PZPR and the political alliances.

Finally, the fourth type of political promotion is cooptation into the leadership cadre of already seasoned people who held posts of importance outside the structure of authority (e.g., university professors). Their cooptation or election is based on their professional prestige gained outside the realm of politics, although in most cases these people have had some experience in political activity anyway. This type of political career was not infrequent prior to 1980 but became much more commonplace from 1981 onward as a result of the democratization of the system of leadership selection in the PZPR and the political alliances and the desire to bring outstanding specialists into the government.

Polish sociological-political studies of local leaders have made it possible to collect much empirical material concerning their careers, the values they profess, their political behavior patterns, and their relations with the people.[9] The most characteristic features of local leaders, examined many times in the 1960s and 1970s, are their strong attachment to the concept of material, economic, and cultural progress (even at the price of giving up other goals and values), a sense of their own responsibility for the duties entrusted to them coupled with a striving to obtain greater autonomy in relation to higher authorities, low level of acceptance of the demands of citizens for greater participation in decisionmaking and of the values of socioeconomic egalitarianism, the desire to avoid conflicts, and a conviction about their own political competence. In general it can be said that the sociological-political studies done in the 1960s and 1970s showed the local leaders to be a vanguard conscious of its mission but attaching little weight to the views and behavior of fellow citizens. However, this was also coupled to other phenomena.

Our studies have shown that especially in the 1970s, the views of the leaders and the population on the desirable goals of the development of a community differed considerably. They also demonstrated that again in the 1970s rather than in the 1960s, the social prestige and financial situation of the local leaders were distinctly better than the average living conditions in the milieus in which they operated. Although these studies did not point to the existence of large-scale conflict between the local leadership groups and the population, they did reveal some characteristic symptoms of the alienation of local leaders. This alienation was one of the factors that aggravated relations between local authorities and citizens in many parts of the country when the crisis erupted in the summer of 1980.

The conflicts that emerged then were sometimes the outcome of errors committed by the local leaders. There were also some cases of corruption among political activists, which contributed to the notorious scandals of that period. More often, however, the problem was of a different nature. The local activists operated within a highly centralized system, which even they themselves deemed to be too centralized because it left them too little freedom of action for the benefit of the local community. But operating as they did within that system, they had to adapt to the rules it imposed on them. Even the best local activists, who were capable of doing a great deal for the benefit of their community, had to identify themselves in public with the whole policy pursued within the centralized system. In this way they were denied an opportunity to form an individual political image of themselves. There were exceptions to this rule, but they were few and far between. As a result, when the political system found itself in a crisis and became the target of widespread public criticism, the local leaders became local symbols of the whole system of exercising power, whether they deserved it or not. They had to bear the consequences—often exaggerated and unjust—not only of their own actions but also of their identification with the entirety of the official policies of times past.

In this sense, the crisis of 1980 can be regarded as a crisis of political leadership among other things. The upsetting of political stability, which had survived the previous quarter of a century despite the political tremors of 1968, 1970, and 1976, resulted in a profound change in the mechanisms of mobilization and political leadership, both in 1980 and in subsequent years.

The Party System During the Crisis of 1980-1981

It would take a separate treatise to explain in detail the origin of the sociopolitical crisis that arose in Poland in the summer of 1980. In this chapter I will only outline the principal causes. As there is already ample—and growing—literature on the subject, such a synthesis of the problem appears admissible.[10]

The direct reason for the tide of strikes that swept Poland in summer 1980 was the collapse of the overambitious plans for accelerated economic growth and rapid improvement in the living standard of the population—in other words, of the economic program formulated by the new political leadership (with Edward Gierek as PZPR first secretary and Piotr Jaroszewicz as prime minister) after the riots and bloodshed in Baltic coast towns in December 1970. The 1970 workers' protest had been successful in the sense that it forced the replacement of the former leadership (ousting Wladyslaw Gomulka, the first secretary, and Jozef Cyrankiewicz, the prime minister); the other reaction to the protest was a revision of the economic policy. The new economic policy was a peculiar brand of "welfare socialism," to borrow a term used by a friendly if not uncritical Western Marxist.[11] Within that policy, the rule of the new team was to be legitimized by the implementation of a program of continuous and rapid improvement in levels of living. Both scientists social and party activists cautioned that this kind of legitimization by the authorities could quickly collapse if the far-fetched economic promises misfired.[12]

That is exactly what happened. The recession in the West caused more hardship to Poland than to other socialist countries because Poland's economy had strong ties with Western economies. The overambitious industrial development program meant that the country had embarked on projects that exceeded its capacity. As a result of borrowing in the West—

also to finance actual consumption—Poland became one of the most heavily indebted countries in the world. Its export revenues were too low to ensure regular debt servicing. Because Poland had abandoned structural reforms of the economy, not even the importation of modern technology could produce the acceleration needed for its economic growth. All of this led to the economic crisis, spreading market shortages, and a decline of the purchasing power of the population. The working class was the hardest hit by the crisis. As it had done in 1956, 1970, and 1976, it began to press for change again.

However, the working-class protest of 1980 occurred in a political situation different from that of the previous decade. Organized political opposition, centered around the Workers' Defense Committee (KOR), which was set up in 1976, operated in Poland openly—albeit in contravention of the existing laws. By the end of the 1970s its organizational and propaganda structures were already well established. The activities of this opposition were tolerated de facto by state authorities, although some rather mild harassment was occasionally applied to the oppositionists. As a consequence of this relative tolerance toward its activities, the opposition managed to join in what was—at least in the initial phase—a spontaneous strike movement with a great measure of efficiency. It began to exert a considerable influence on that movement. Well-known activists of the KOR and other opposition groups formed a large proportion of the advisers to the strikers and later to the Solidarnosc union.[13]

Finally, it is impossible to ignore the fact that the events in Poland were watched intently right from the start by Western political propaganda centers. From the beginning of the 1980 strikes, the sociopolitical conflicts in Poland were the subject of not only commentaries but also political enunciations through which Western political centers tried to exert an influence on the evolution of the situation in Poland. A special role was played by Polish-language broadcasts (notably Radio Free Europe, the Voice of America, and other Western stations). Their tenor was decidedly hostile to Poland's political system and the state authorities' moves at a time of the deepening crisis. The political line of that propaganda was summed up in the motto "The worse it gets, the better."

The strikers' demands in the summer of 1980 and the next few months centered on three groups of topics. The first of them concerned financial matters. In particular, this meant wage increase demands, and shorter working hours. In the second group were the principles of social justice directed first of all against the large-scale corruption of the 1970s and the many kinds of privileges enjoyed by various people in positions of authority.[14] Finally, in the third group were demands for participation, especially calls for new independent trade unions. It is this third kind of demands and the consequences of their implementation that fall within the scope of this chapter.

The Independent Self-Governed Trade Union "Solidarnosc" was set up in the autumn of 1980 on the basis of agreements signed by strike committees with government representatives at the end of August and the beginning of September 1980. These agreements provided for the establishment of new trade unions that would observe the principles of the binding constitution and would recognize the leading role of the PZPR. From the point of view of the law, the foundation of Solidarnosc did not constitute a change of the political structure within the hegemonic party system.

However, before long political reality began to differ from the accepted obligations and legal norms contained in the statutes of the new union. Already in the autumn of 1980 Solidarnosc had begun to undertake political actions far surpassing the normal limits of trade union activity. By 1981 it had established itself as a political force clearly opposed to the government and the party. As time went by, its political position became increasingly radical, a development acknowledged even by impartial Western observers.[15] There were various reasons for this radicalization. One was the poor and deteriorating economic situation and the resulting frustration of society. Moreover, there was the political propaganda of opposition groups, which were establishing ever closer ties with the organizational structures of the new union, and that propaganda was drifting toward an incessant escalation of demands. The ostentatious support Solidarnosc received from influential forces in the West—including some national leaders, especially in the United States—gave many inexperienced Solidarnosc leaders a false sense of strength and of the possibility of having even their furthest-reaching demands accepted. The indecision of the PZPR leadership and the government in the first months following the strikes of summer 1980 also encouraged the radicalization of Solidarnosc. This development is seen in the fact that the government and party acted only in response to pressure, making concessions to demands but failing to take the initiative with regard to economic and political reforms. The death of the aged primate of Poland, Stefan Cardinal Wyszynski (in May 1981), who was in favor of moderation and compromise right from the beginning of the crisis, weakened the influence of the Catholic Church, which, incidentally, was not at all united with regard to the attitude it should adopt toward the rising tide of antigovernment radicalism.

In addition to these phenomena was the factor that I have termed an "explosion of mobilization."[16] It received less attention but was nevertheless quite important. Before long, Solidarnosc organized about nine million people, most of whom having had no experience of political activity. It is true that they were union members before, but those unions did not engage in political activity and their members were for the most part quite passive. Solidarnosc was also joined by one million PZPR members, but from the beginning they were—with few exceptions—barred from occupying leading posts in the union and were therefore not able to influence in any significant measure the course the developments took.[17] Within Solidarnosc's executive leadership, and more especially among its advisers rather than the elected authorities, opposition activists played a part, but their number was very small indeed. There is good reason for saying that the main body of Solidarnosc activists were newcomers to politics who got their first taste of it in 1980–1981.

This political (as well as biological) juvenility of the new leaders was an important factor in the political radicalization of the Solidarnosc ranks, and in this way, it contributed to worsening of the political crisis. The youthfulness of the Solidarnosc leadership was conducive to the union's radicalization in three ways: First, because young people are naturally more inclined to radical actions, less likely to seek compromise, and more easily carried away by emotions; second, because with the political "youthfulness" of Solidarnosc executives went a lack of experience and political knowledge that contributed to overestimating their own strength and underestimating the opponent and misinterpreting the international situation;[18] third, because the people who grew up after World War II tended to dismiss the historical experience of their elders—those who had survived the war and remembered how high a price Poland had to pay for the unrealistic policies of its prewar and wartime leaders, in their uncritical reliance on Western "guarantees," or in the anti-Soviet edge of official Polish policy prior to 1939 and during the war. To use terms introduced by Adam Bromke, the generation of "realists" who were in power was opposed by representatives of the generation of "idealists."[19] As the latter were at the same time newcomers to politics, the explosion of political mobilization produced a radicalization of the crisis situation that was headed for a confrontation.

The radicalization of Solidarnosc led to the questioning of the foundations of the hegemonic party system. Although the system continued to exist de jure, its actual existence was questioned by the strong, aggressive, and self-confident political movement, which, particularly after the First Congress of Solidarnosc held in Gdansk in September 1981 was no longer just a labor organization. In retrospect, it could be said that the struggle to keep the August 1980 accords alive—including the principle of the leading role of the PZPR and cooperation in the spirit of national agreement—was essentially the struggle to allow the hegemonic party system to keep functioning in a reformed manner (notably, with a much broader array of political forces authorized to operate legally). The radicalization of Solidarnosc resulted in its proclamation of a program amounting to the replacing of this system by a different one, patterned after pluralistic Western systems. As has often happened in history, the more radical demands made it impossible to implement a more moderate and potentially very important reform. The imposition of martial law in December 1981 and the suspension of and subsequent ban on Solidarnosc activity were a crushing defeat of that movement and the plans to change totally Poland's political system, as formulated by trade union leaders. Nevertheless, these actions did not signify the end of reforms within the existing party system.

In order to understand this aspect of the problem it is necessary to focus attention on another aspect of political change occurring in Poland between August 1980 and December 1981—namely, the changes within the coalition of the Left itself.

The changes that were taking place in Poland after August 1980 were by no means limited to the emergence of Solidarnosc and its activities, although this situation did receive the most attention from numerous Western commentators. Considerable changes were taking place both within the PZPR, ZSL, and SD, consisting first of all in the democratization of intraparty relations. These processes occurred in all three political parties. All of them held national congresses and elected new authorities. The executives of the PZPR, ZSL, and SD, elected in a truly democratic vote, were largely made up of people who joined the national leadership teams only during the crisis. The process of internal democratization of the PZPR, crowned by its Ninth Extraordinary Congress (July 14–20, 1981) was particularly pronounced.[20] No fewer than 91 percent of the membership of the new Central Committee of the PZPR were people who had been elected to the supreme party body for the first time. Of the fifteen new Politburo members, only four had been on that body before the congress. No previous PZPR congress had witnessed such a sweeping change of the top party cadre.

The democratization of the system of intraparty elections in the PZPR, the ZSL, and the SD consisted first of all in the introduction and observance of the following principles:

1. an unlimited number of candidates for all elective posts,
2. strict observance of the secrecy of voting,
3. determination of voting outcomes by simple majority.

The election campaign held in the PZPR up to the voivodship (regional) level in the end of 1983 and beginning of 1984 was based on similar principles. Although the degree of turnover of party authorities was lower than in 1981, the candidates nevertheless had to pass a genuine electoral test and obtain support in a difficult political struggle. This testifies to the preservation of the more democratic norms in intraparty life that had been introduced in 1981.

The democratization of intraparty life means that the role of political parties in the entire political system is growing. The party as a whole, and not only its leadership and apparatus, acts in these circumstances as the political force determining the direction of the binding policy.

The post-August changes in the operation of the hegemonic party system found an expression in the evolution of cooperation between the PZPR and other members of the left coalition. Interparty relations have been based on respect for the autonomy of the PZPR's coalition partners and an increase in their participation in government. In the cabinet formed by General Wojciech Jaruzelski, who assumed the post of prime minister in February 1981, two positions among deputy prime ministers have been held by representatives of the Democratic Alliance and the Catholic PAX Association, among other vice-premiers representing the PZPR and one from the ZSL. The number of ZSL and SD members and representatives of Catholic associations in various state posts also increased. Significantly, the non-Communist parties and organizations began to exert a greater influence on the shape of government policy. In this sense the hegemonic party system got nearer in practice to the theoretical assumptions on which it was based and that in the preceding years had been curbed or indeed had existed only in theory.

At the end of 1981, the political situation in Poland had deteriorated seriously. The plans to find a way out of it, presented to the Sejm on October 30, 1981, by Jaruzelski, who earlier that month had been elected PZPR first secretary and had combined that post with that of head of government since, called for national understanding of all the patriotic forces. In the crucial passage of that speech, General Jaruzelski declared:

> I propose . . . the establishment of the Council of National Reconciliation, which would get down as early as possible to drafting and agreeing upon the program of the front, its role, structure and principles of operation in the socio-political life. I invite the United Peasant Alliance, the Democratic Alliance, the trade unions, public organizations, scientific and artistic associations to join this Council. I shall ask citizens who enjoy high prestige among the society to take part in the Council's work. I expect that the initiative will get the support of the Church hierarchy.[21]

This was an offer of broadening the coalition of the forces ruling Poland, especially by enlisting the new force that had emerged in the form of Solidarnosc. The acceptance of this proposal would signify a significant broadening of the scope of political diversity within the front of national understanding. Yet it would also make it possible to avoid a showdown and an open struggle for power.

At that time there was a chance of finding a solution to the political crisis. Such a solution would have the virtue of making it possible to preserve the continuity of the original set of political institutions and the existing constitutional order while also preserving the principle of the leading role of the PZPR in the state, although at the same time adding Solidarnosc to the organized forces coresponsible for the state and cogoverning it. Only the rejection of the proposal by the Solidarnosc leadership and Solidarnosc's call for political demonstrations aimed at taking over power ended that phase of the search for new solutions by way of understanding and compromise. This led to the army taking charge, the establishment of the Military Council of National Salvation, and imposition of martial law (which was lifted in July 1983).

The Prospects of Political Reforms

The introduction of martial law and the accompanying curbs on political freedoms signified a considerable reduction of political participation. A ban was imposed on the operation of all trade unions—that is, both Solidarnosc and the "branch" (old) unions as well as the new autonomous unions whose attitude toward the government was more constructive than Solidarnosc's. In October 1982 the government passed a new trade union law that dissolved all the previously existing labor organizations and authorized the establishment of new ones from scratch.

The founding of new unions encountered considerable difficulties. By the end of 1983 the new unions had organized just under four million employees—that is, not even one third as many as in 1979. The meaning of membership in a trade union changed. Under the influence of the political crisis, the former automatic enrollment in a union gave way to a conscious choice. At the same time, the dissolution of Solidarnosc and the other unions was an unpopular move, and as a result, many ex-members were illdisposed toward the new unions that were formed instead. Characteristically, this kind of reaction could be observed among former members not only of Solidarnosc but also of the other unions.

The PZPR, the ZSL, and SD, and the Catholic associations incorporated in the ruling coalition did not suspend their activities, but in the initial phase of the martial law period they were seriously limited. Slightly less than a million members and candidate members quit the PZPR between August 1980 and the beginning of 1982. There were many reasons for the decline in membership, connected with both opposition to party policies and disillusionment and with the lack of psychic strength so badly needed in the very difficult political situation. Similar defections occurred in the Polish Socialist Youth Union and the Socialist Union of Polish Students. However, one new union was formed, the Rural Youth Union (ZMW), which together with the other youth organizations, constitutes a form of political mobilization of the younger generation.

Generally speaking, however, 1982 and 1983 were years of an ebb in political activity. This appraisal is not affected by the survival of underground political structures taking root in the disbanded Solidarnosc, the Independent Student Union banned in 1982, or older political opposition organizations such as KOR, the Confederation for an Independent Poland, and other associations. By its very nature, underground activity could not become the platform of mobilization of significant numbers of people. As time went by, the impact of the underground groups began to diminish, if one were to judge, for example, by the number of people engaging in street demonstrations. Nevertheless, there was continued resistance of a considerable part of society to any form of participation in the activity of legal progovernment political and social organizations, especially among younger workers and the intelligentsia. The peak of political involvement of the years 1980 and 1981 gave way to political absenteeism.

The meaning of the political absenteeism displayed by a large part of Polish society after 1981 is not unequivocal. In the most general terms, there are three distinct kinds of postures manifested in political absenteeism.

First, absenteeism may be a sign of a lack of interest in politics in general. Some of these apolitical people had been carried along by the huge whirlpool of political animation in 1980–1981. But after the imposition of martial law, they returned to their normal apolitical position.

Second, absenteeism may be a manifestation of disillusionment with all the political variants available in Poland, whether progovernment or opposition. The political tension of the closing months of 1981 and the failure of the efforts to reach understanding contributed to the emergence of this type of absenteeism, irrespective of whom a given person blamed for that state of affairs.

Third, absenteeism may be a form of demonstrating one's displeasure with the options of political participation that remained available after the dissolution of Solidarnosc and other opposition organizations. In this instance politically passive people are in favor of alternative political solutions and demonstrate their support for such solutions through their ostensible "passiveness."

We lack sufficient data to estimate the extent of each type of political absenteeism. Besides, widespread political absenteeism is not so much a symptom of a lack of interest in politics as it is a consequence of the political divisions that occurred in Polish society under the conditions of the crisis.

From this follow the fundamental conclusions for political reforms. The reconstruction of political stability and legitimization of the socialist system cannot be attained through socioeconomic policies of the kind that had appealed fairly effectively to the political consciousness of the nation at the beginning of the 1970s. After the experience of 1980–1981, it is obvious that besides economic recovery resulting in gradual improvement in the standard of living, there is a need to introduce political reforms broadening the possibilities of citizens' effective participation. These reforms had been initiated back in 1981, but the political tensions prevailing then made it impossible to develop them fully. However, the important thing is that they were not abandoned after the introduction of martial law. Although under martial law the introduction of political reforms proceeded at a slower pace, they were nevertheless continued; the lifting of martial law made it possible to accelerate the reforms.

Of the political reforms introduced so far, the following are the most important from the point of view of the participation of citizens in political life: the law on trade unions, the law on workers' self-management, the law on the people's councils, the organizational principles of the Patriotic Movement of National Revival (PRON), and the changed electoral law.

A legal foundation for the representation of workers' interest is provided by the legislation broadening the powers of worker self-management bodies in factories and the considerable powers and guarantees of autonomy of trade unions. The broader powers of people's councils and residents' self-government introduce more elements of "local democracy." The revision of the electoral law, largely as a result of public consultation on the draft submitted to public discussion in December 1983, goes in the same direction; it increases the democratic character of voting (particularly through the introduction of the principle of having two candidates for each seat and of broadening the democratic mode of proposing candidacies).

It was expected that the emergence in 1982 of PRON, whose first congress was held in May 1983, would broaden considerably the coalition of forces involved in cogoverning the country and would permit them to base their mutual relations on cooperation and partnership. However, from the beginning PRON's growth encountered considerable difficulties, which reflected the absence of participation in political life analyzed above. Even so, PRON has more autonomy as an element of political life than the coalition structures it succeeds (the National Front and the National Unity Front) once had. For example, the movement proposed new legislation, advocated political amnesty for persons serving prison terms or awaiting trial for violations of martial law regulations, and submitted proposals regarding major changes in the electoral law draft presented by the Council of State. In its activities, one may perceive the germ of a new role of coalitional forms of cooperation.

All of this is only the beginning. The political reforms carried out thus far constitute an essential step toward such a broadening of participation in political life. By so doing they would make it possible to eliminate gradually political absenteeism and boycott and in this way create conditions for political stabilization and a relegitimization of the system. The success of the program of democratic reforms, planned for a number of years, is a precondition of overcoming political alienation and of basing the party system on democratic cooperation of a wide array of patriotic and pro-socialist forces. Polish leaders are aware that the process of such reforms is a difficult one and that it has to take time. In an address to the Sejm on October 9, 1982, General Jaruzelski said:

> Already today we are laying foundations for the structures and patterns that shall develop in Poland after a full normalization of the situation. Our aim is a strong and efficient state, the crowning of national life, which will enjoy the firm support of a society organized in a democratic manner. The society will be guaranteed an influence on the way the state is being run.
>
> This is a prolonged process and it has to take time. But a reform is an occupation for the patient and persistent. It also takes patience to appraise its results.[22]

The experience accumulated by socialist Poland until now suggests that the implementation of reforms conceived in this way will indeed call for patience as well as perseverance. However, these reforms are a political necessity. Unless they are carried out, it will not be possible to satisfy the citizens' desire to participate in governing the country, hence to eliminate their alienation toward the state—an important factor of tensions and conflicts in previous years.

Notes

1. I am referring in particular to the following works: "The Hegemonic Party System in Poland," in *Mass Politics: Studies in Political Sociology*, eds. Erik Allardt and Stein Rokkan, (New York: The Free Press, 1970, pp. 312-321), and "Political Parties, Interest Representation and Economic Development in Poland," *The Amer-*

ican Political Science Review, 64:4 (December 1970), pp. 1239–1245. Both papers were reprinted in my book *Essays in Political Sociology* (Wroclaw: Ossolineum, 1978).

2. At the Sixth World Sociology Congress in Evian in 1966, together with the Indian scholar Rajni Kothari, I presented a paper entitled "Party Systems and Political Pluralism: Comparisons Between India and Poland." In it, we classified the existing party system into the following categories: alternative party systems, national agreement party systems, hegemonic party systems, one-party systems, limited party systems, and "nonparty" systems. This typology departed from the customary division of party systems (e.g., into multiparty, two-party, and one-party systems). India was given as an example of the system of parties of national agreement, whereas Poland was a representative of the hegemonic party system. Giovanni Sartori, *Parties and Party Systems* (New York: Cambridge University Press, 1976), pp. 273–282.

3. Some Polish authors refer to the Polish party system as a multiparty one, usually qualifying this assertion somehow (e.g., by pointing out that the system relies on the cooperation of the parties). This was done by Adam Lopatka, *Kierownicza rola partii komunistycznej w stosunku do panstwa socjzlistycznego: Zasady leninowaskie* (The Leading Role of the Communist Party in Relation to a Socialist State: Leninist Principles), (Poznan: n.p., 1963), p. 205; Wieslaw Skrzydlo, "System partyjny PRL i jego wyraz w ustroju politycznym panstwa" (Poland's Party System and its Articulation in the Political System of the State), *Panstwo i Prawo*, no. 7 (1959); Witold Zakrzewski, "W sprawie klasyfikacji systemow partyjnych" (Regarding the Classification of Party Systems), *Studia Socjologiczno-Polityczne*, no. 10 (1961). However, I do not think it is correct to stretch the term "multiparty system" to include the Polish and similar systems because the mutual relations between the parties in this system are totally different from those in multiparty systems based on the rivalry for power among a formally unlimited number of political parties.

4. Jerzy J. Wiatr, "Elections and Voting Behavior in Poland," in *Essays on the Behavioral Study of Politics*, ed. Austin Ranney (Urbana: University of Illinois Press, 1962), pp. 235–251.

5. With regard to the 1957 elections, a well-informed British scholar wrote: "A basically Communist government thus sought, and obtained, a genuine mandate to govern the country—at least for the time being," Zbigniew A. Pelczynski, "Poland 1957," in *Elections Abroad*, ed. D. E. Butler (London: MacMillan, 1959), pp. 119–166. I therefore do not accept the assertion, made by some Polish authors, to the effect that the postwar political system was never legitimate. Cf. for example, Jacek Kurczewski, "The Old System and the Revolution," *Sisyphus —Sociological Studies* (Warsaw) 3 (1982), pp.21–32.

6. This problem is approached in an interesting manner by George Kolankiewicz and Ray Taras ("Poland: Socialism for Everyman?," in Archie Brown and Jack Gray, *Political Culture and Political Change in Communist States* [London: MacMillan, 1977], pp. 101–130).

7. *Pocznik Statystyczny 1980*, pp. 23, 29.

8. I discussed this problem in greater detail in the article "Przywodztwo polityczne w swietle badan socjologicznych" (Political Leadership in the Light of Sociological Studies), *Studia Socjologiczne*, 93:2 (1984).

9. Cf. in particular: P. E. Jacob et al., *Values and the Active Community: A Cross-National Study of the Influence of Local Leadership* (New York: The Free Press, 1971), which presents the results of a comparative study of local leaders in India, Poland, the United States, and Yugoslavia in the second half of the 1960s,

and also: Krzysztof Ostrowski and Adam Przeworski, "Local Leadership in Poland," *The Polish Sociological Bulletin*, no. 2916 (1967), pp. 53-71; Renata Sieminska and Jacek Tarkowski, "Polish Local Leaders and Fulfilling Community Needs: Politicians or Administrators?," *International Political Science Review*, 1:2 (1980), pp. 245-246; Aleksandra Jasinska and Renata Sieminska, "Attitudes of Local Authorities Prior to the Crisis of 1980," *Sisyphus-Sociological Studies* 3 (1982), pp. 161-171; Renata Sieminska, "Local Party Leaders in Poland," *International Political Science Review*, 4:1 (1983), pp. 127-136. The results of empirical studies were presented in two collective works of which I was the editor: *Wladza lokalna a zaspokojenie potrzeb* (Local Authorities and the Satisfaction of Needs), (Warszawa: Instytut Filozofii i Socjologii PAN, 1981), and *Wladza lokalna u progu kryzysu* (Local Authority on the Eve of the Crisis), (Warszawa: Instytut Socjologii Uniwersytetu Warszawskiego, 1983).

10. A broader outline of my views regarding the sources of the political crisis in Poland can be found in my article "The Sources of Crisis," *Polish Perspectives*, 25:4 (1982), pp. 9-21.

11. Sten Tellenback, *The Social Structure of Socialist Society: The Polish Interpretation* (Lund: Studienlitteratur, 1975).

12. I wrote about it in 1978 in a paper then distributed as a script "Problematyka zaspokajania potrzeb ludnosci a funkcjonowanie polskiego systemu politycznego" (The Satisfaction of Society's Needs and the Functioning of the Polish Political System). It was later included in my book *Nauki polityczne a potrzeby praktyki* (Political Sciences and the Requirements of Practice), (Warszawa: Ksiazka i Wiedza, 1982), pp. 55-120.

13. The significant role of KOR activists during the 1980 summer strikes and later on in the Solidarnosc leadership was noted, among others, by Neal Ascherson, *The Polish August: The Self-Limiting Revolution* (New York: Penguin Books, 1982).

14. Cf. Jacek Tarkowski, "Patronage in a Centralized Socialist System: The Case of Poland," *International Political Science Review*, 4:4 (1983), pp. 495-518.

15. Jerry F. Hough, *The Polish Crisis: American Policy Options* (Washington, D.C.: The Brookings Institution, 1982), p. 40.

16. Jerzy J. Wiatr, "Mobilization of Non-participants during the Political Crisis in Poland, 1980-1981," a paper read at the 12th World Congress of Political Science, Rio de Janeiro, 1982, and later published in *International Political Science Review*, 5:3 (1984).

17. This means that the hopes of those who thought that the PZPR members who joined Solidarnosc would be able to act as a kind of a bridge and help achieve some compromise proved illusory. Cf. Stanislaw Ehrlich, "Rebellion in Polen 1980-1981," *Journal fur Sozialforschung* (Vienna), 22 Jg. (1982), Heft 1-2, pp. 33-43.

18. The same processes of misperception that have been described in detail in relation to other situations, especially ones concerning international relations by Western scientists, could be observed in the behavior of Solidarnosc leaders. Cf. especially Robert Jerwis, *Perception and Misperception in International Relations* (Princeton, N.J.: Princeton University Press, 1976).

19. Bdam Bromke, *Poland's Politics: Idealism vs. Realism* (Cambridge: Harvard University Press, 1967).

20. More on the subject: Jerzy J. Wiatr, "Poland's Party Politics: The Extraordinary Congress of 1981," *Canadian Journal of Political Science*, 14:4, pp. 813-826.

21. Wojciech Jaruzelski, *Przemowienia 1981-1982* (Speeches), (Warszawa: Ksiazka i Wiedza, 1983), pp. 181-182.

22. Ibid., p. 469.

2

The Contemporary Polish State: Structures and Functions

Wojciech Sokolewicz

The Polish state today is a socialist state. As a result of revolutionary transformations, its internal functions have expanded and become more complex in the process. The nationalization of the basic branches of industry, the gradual growth of the role of the public sector in farming, the expansion of the state-owned retail trade network, and in particular, the introduction of a planned economy coupled with the limits placed on the market economy have resulted in a significant growth in the economic role of the state. The expansion of social insurance and various forms of assistance for handicapped people as well as the introduction of free health care have led to an increase in the welfare function of the state. The dissemination of primary and secondary education and access to universities for all strata of the population, along with state control of publications and the mass media, have resulted in imparting a new quality to the educational and ideological roles of the state.

The assumption of responsibility for all the most important areas of collective life by the Polish state makes it possible, on the one hand, to ensure a more just division of goods and services along egalitarian lines. But it has produced, on the other hand, negative side effects. I shall mention but two of them: the tendency of people to blame the state for shortcomings occurring in any of the many domains that it controls and the growth of a bureaucracy, which tends, according to the sociological laws of large organizations, to generate its own interests up to the point of having autonomous goals.

Contemporary Poland, as a socialist state, is obliged to act for the benefit of workers, whose interests are best and most fully articulated by the working class. This signifies a clear preference for one type of goal, shared—or so it is theoretically assumed—by a majority of society. Furthermore, it means a lower place in the hierarchy of group social interests for those of the strata that do not live off their own work. Finally, it formulates the general interest as harmonious with the interest of the working classes, even though that belongs to only one sector of society.

The purpose of this chapter is to examine the changes that have occurred in the institutions and structures of the contemporary Polish state, paticularly developments connected with the crisis of the years 1980-1981, and especially the reform programs formulated at that time. I shall be examining these changes from the perspective of law, but also looking at practical applications of the law. From this point of view it will be most convenient to adopt a broad definition of the term *state* as all the bodies and institutions taken together (irrespective of the voluntary or professional nature of the work conducted by their personnel executing state power), which are organized hierarchically in accord with binding legal requirements and, more generally, with principles contained in the supreme legal act, the constitution.

The System of State Organs

Through mutual relations, subordination and superiority, control and cooperation, coordination, and creation, all the state organs and institutions taken together (which execute state power and implement the functions of the state through legal organization and hierarchy) form a coherent system. General functions are implemented jointly through various detailed powers and are executed through various legal forms ascribed to component parts of the state.

There are four main binding agents of this system. The first is the principle of the rule of law, subordinating all state organs to the rule of law in general and to the principles and provisions of the constitution in particular. From the rule of law follows the requirement of proper legal title, preferably constitutional or at least a legislative one, for forming state organs equipped with appropriate powers. It is also the duty of all state organs to operate on the basis of legal foundations when this action is to be effected "outside" state organizations. The requirement of the rule of law gives great significance to legal relations occurring between individual state organs and institutions. The practical importance of this requirement depends, among other things, on the guarantees that make possible the process of law—also in relations between state organs and institutions—should the law be infringed upon. Until recently, this set of guarantees was not complete, as it turned out, because it was assumed that—given the identity of class interests and the political essence of all state bodies—conflicts between them were unlikely. Should they occur, it was assumed, they would be resolved exclusively on the political, rather than the legal, plane.

The second binding agent of this system of state organs has been their constitutional classification.[1] In its original 1952 shape, the constitution differentiated between organs of state power and state administration organs. First, the organs of state power include the Sejm, the Council of State, and the people's councils. Of these, the Sejm and the people's councils were representative bodies that constituted the foundation of the whole system of state organs and were considered to be a source of their democratic legitimization. The Council of State was classified as an organ of state power that was and remains an emanation of the Sejm. Even though it is made up wholly of deputies, it does not have a representative character according to the views accepted in the literature on the subject. Second, there are state administration organs—the government and the presidia of the people's councils, the ministers and heads of departments subordinated to the presidia of people's councils. The government and the presidia of people's councils were treated separately as a subgroup of executive bodies that differed from the remaining administrative bodies through: (1) their direct subordination to organs of state power; (2) their executive and coordination power vis-a-vis other administrative organs; (3) their general powers in the domain of state administration; (4) their status as collective bodies; (5) their role as general and special law courts as organs of the administration of justice, with the Supreme Court at the top of the hierarchy; and (6) their function as prosecuting organs with the prosecutor general as their superior.

During the first twenty-five years in which the 1952 constitution was in force, the pattern of state organs outlined above underwent only small corrections: The category of state control bodies was expanded in 1957 with the introduction of the Supreme Chamber of Control and its local agencies; the 1972–1975 reform of the system of people's councils and reorganization of their administrative organs did away with the division of administrative organs into executive and governing ones and the remaining ones. The former presidia of the councils were then replaced by monocratic organs that in a given unit of territorial division of the country, were the only administrative bodies. Administrative departments in the council lost their status as autonomous bodies; they became instead parts of the bureaucratic apparatus fully subordinated to the aforementioned monocratic bodies.

This classification of state organs is important for the coherence of the system because it creates a clear definition of relations both between individual groups of organs and within each group.

The third binding agent of the system is the hierarchy of state organs envisaged by the constitution, which puts the organs of state power above all other bodies and in particular above the administration. The constitution also envisaged the independence of the prosecuting agencies from the administration and recognized the sovereignty of the courts in passing verdicts. The undisputedly, highest place in the constitutional hierarchy of state organs was (and still is) occupied by the Sejm. It is the "supreme articulator of the will of the working people of towns and countryside" that "effects the sovereign rights of the nation" (Article 20, paragraph 2 of the constitution). By establishing the supremacy of the Sejm over all the other state organs, the constitution avoided any division of power among state authorities. It abandoned the idea of balance of power and referred to the radical and revolutionary principle of unity and homogeneity in state power, a concept the authors of the constitution were quite proud of. As power is to be exercised by a sovereign working people, its supreme representative is entitled to exercise this sovereignty also in relation to other state organs. However, it should be admitted that the practical implementation of this constitutional model of a hierarchy of state organs encountered various obstacles right from the start for many reasons. In contrast, demands for strengthening the position of the Sejm and bringing it closer to what it should be in line with the constitution resurfaced during each consecutive political crisis, be it October 1970 or August 1980.

The fourth and possibly the most important binding agent of the system of state organs is the uniform political leadership exercised with regard to the whole system and its individual component parts by the Polish United Workers' party (PZPR) and its coalition partners, the United Peasant Alliance (ZSL) and the Democratic Alliance (SD), together with members of lay Catholic associations represented in the organs of power. According to socialist constitutional theory, political leadership is responsible for: (1) the formulation of the general goals of state activity; (2) control over the operation of state organs making it harmonious with these goals; (3) the nomination of candidates for deputies and councillors and the filling of leading posts in administrative bodies. Political leadership should also be exercised mainly through party members working in state organs and institutions and especially through deputies and councillors. As thus conceived, political leadership of the state by the party and its allies was confirmed by the 1976 constitutional amendment stipulating that "the PZPR is the leading force of society in the building of socialism" (Article 3, paragraph 1).[2]

In practice, the exercising of political leadership was not perfect. The general nature of targets and control gave way to preoccupation with details. And instead of influence exerted through deputies and councillors, there was the *direct* influence of state administration by the party apparatus. This led to a parallelism between the two structures that limited the responsibility of state organs and institutions for their work, undercut the actual subordination of the state administration to representative bodies of state power, and was conducive to the emergence of bureaucratic attitudes among party apparatchiks. This was one of the reasons why representative bodies did not play the role entrusted to them by the constitution, a shortcoming that distorted the constitutional hierarchy of state organs.[3]

An attempt to remedy this situation was made in 1975 with the introduction of the principle that the first secretary of a local party committee also held the post of chairman of the local people's council. However, instead of strengthening the local representative body in its relations with the administrative body at the same level, the change actually contributed to the subjection of the elected body to even more intense and direct influence of the local party apparatus, which in most cases identified itself with the local bodies of state administration.

The Crisis and the Constitution

During the crisis the constitution was regarded as the mainstay of the stability of the political system. All the legally operating political forces, the Solidarity union included, declared faithfulness to its principles, as confirmed in the so-called social contracts signed in August 1980. For this reason one had to be rather cautious in contemplating the introduction of any amendments to the text of the constitution.

However, the crisis demonstrated the inadequacy of the state and political practice in light of the constitutional pattern set for this system of state organs, insufficient cohesion of this system in practice, and consequently insufficient capacity of the channels connecting the system of state organs with the public—thereby ensuring low social effectiveness in the work of state organs. The shortcomings justified a program of reform of the system of state organs, at the practical level as well as at the legal level, although in such a way as to introduce as few changes as possible in the text of the constitution, which played an important stabilizing role.

As a result of the crisis, the constitution was amended three times. The first occurred in 1980, when the Supreme Chamber of Control (NIK), subordinated to the government from 1976, was again put under the Sejm. The second took place in 1982, when martial law was already in force. At that time new institutions guaranteeing constitutional rule of law were introduced in the form of the Constitutional Tribunal and the Tribunal of State. Finally, the third was in 1983, when the constitution was amended by the introduction of provisions concerning the Patriotic Movement of National Revival (PRON). These dealt with political management of the system of state organs modifying it.

The changes introduced new institutions into the system: The Constitutional Tribunal and the Tribunal of State together with the Supreme Administrative Court, established in 1980 but not yet anchored in the constitution, form a new group of judiciary organs of public law. The provisions also consolidated the existing ones: The NIK today constitutes a separate category of state organ. And they increased the importance of the political leadership as the real binding agent of the constitutionally defined system of state organs.

The legislative changes introduced during implementation of the slogan "reconstruction of state life" were formulated as a result of the experience with the crisis and as an attempt to prevent another crisis in the future. These changes were not limited to constitutional amendments. The slogan was developed in the most important political document of the period, one that still remains valid: the resolution of the Ninth Extraordinary Congress of the PZPR, in July 1981.

The PZPR resolution took into account the urgent need to oppose "deformations of a technocratic or bureaucratic nature that could lead to a continued domination of the executive and administrative bodies over representative bodies, the lowering of the effectiveness of democratic institutions and the maintenance of the rubberstamp character of social self-government bodies." It promised new legislation concerning people's councils, based on the idea of decentralization and of increasing the rank of representative bodies, the development of various forms of social self-government, and the implementation of the PZPR's political leadership of the state. This was to be done "within the framework of strict observance of the binding laws, with safeguarding of the full constitutional role of representative and executive bodies of state power, self-government, and the administration." Additional promises included consideration of institutional control ensuring that the laws conform with the constitution, abandoning the system of appointing the Supreme Court for a specified term of office, and changes in the mode of appointing the prosecutor general and the first chairman of the Supreme Court.

In keeping with the resolution of the ninth congress of the PZPR as well as other programmatic political directives, the following changes were made in state structures, the system of state organs, and the legal regulations governing the organization and functioning of individual organs:

1. New electoral regulations governing the people's councils were enacted. They fit within the legal framework defined by the constitution but incorporate many novel solutions (1984).[4] The earlier voting regulations for elections to the Sejm and the people's councils (of January 17, 1976) remain in force only for Sejm elections, and even that is considered to be a temporary state of affairs.[5]

2. A number of changes were introduced in the inner regulations governing the work of the Sejm.[6] The aim of these changes is to facilitate the Sejm's discharging its supervising powers in relation to other state organs.

3. A number of detailed laws broadened and specified the control duties of the Council of State vis-a-vis those state organs whose activity is especially closely connected with the area of human rights (e.g., censorship).[7]

4. Efforts have been begun (not finished yet) to adopt a law—the first one in the history of constitutional rule in Poland—regulating the structure and forms of activity of the Council of Ministers. For the time being, a number of legal acts introduced changes whose common objective is overcoming the pursuit of narrow interests by individual ministries and strengthening the leading and coordinating powers of the government as a superior body for the whole state administration. This entails establishment of specialized committees and councils attached to the Council of Ministers, the elimination of some ministries that were in charge of too narrow areas of activity, and the restructuring of other ministries.[8]

5. A law regarding the system of people's councils and local self-government, in line with the recommendations of the ninth PZPR congress, was passed in 1983.[9] It was based on conclusions drawn from the dual role of the people's councils as organs of state authority and of local self-government at the same time.

The renewed subordination of the Supreme Chamber of Control to the Sejm and the awarding of relatively large autonomy to the latter, along with the establishment of the Supreme Administrative Court, the Constitutional Tribunal, and the Tribunal of State have already been mentioned. The provisions concerning the chamber and the two tribunals follow the same principles. Chapter IV of the constitution has led some authors to argue that, as a consequence, all these bodies form one common class of state organs, characterized by extensive powers of exercising broadly understood control. However, in view of the differences in these bodies' legal situation, such an approach is debatable.[10]

As the crisis grew worse, the political authorities decided that the situation had become so dangerous to the normal functioning of society as to warrant the resort to extraordinary methods of exercising state power, envisaged by the constitution. In December 1981, the Council of State proclaimed martial law—the constitution did not then encompass a milder form of an extraordinary situation, for example, a state of emergency. Because regulations for the imposition of martial law were lacking, the Council of State found it necessary to pass a decree filling the gap.[11] But whereas the right of the Council of State to proclaim martial law was unquestionable from the constitutional point of view, this was not true about the decree, as it was issued while a Sejm session was in progress. Therefore, shortly afterwards, the contents of the decree were approved in an appropriate Sejm law.[12]

Martial law meant a restriction of constitutional civil rights that was gradually eased as time passed. It did not, however, signify the takeover of state power by bodies not envisaged in the constitution. The Military Council of National Salvation (WRON), set up simultaneously with the imposition of martial law, in principle acted with the help of the constitutional state mechanisms. The supreme state organs—the Sejm, the Council of State, the government—all kept working. After a brief hiatus, the people's councils also resumed their activities as local representative organs of state power. The state could be said to be run on constitutional principles. The WRON limited its activity to directing and controlling the constitutional organs of state power. When martial law was lifted, the council was disbanded.

Nevertheless, it is worth noting that the legal problems that emerged during the introduction of martial law in 1981 led to legislative changes. The constitution was amended by the introduction of regulations that distinguished martial law, which could be proclaimed in the event of an external threat to the state, from a state of emergency, which could be declared in case of an internal threat.[13] The requirement of defining the terms and the legal consequences as well as the mode of imposing a state of war, martial law, and a state of emergency through Sejm law was passed along with other pertinent legislation.[14]

As can be seen, in overcoming the crisis, the authorities recognized the general value of constitutional provisions. At the same time, however, the crisis demonstrated the weaknesses of individual regulations contained in the constitution and was an incentive for amending it. Be that as it may, the further stabilization of the political situation may well prompt the question whether the crisis is not a reason for drawing farther-reaching conclusions concerning the adequacy of the constitution to meet existing conditions and requirements. The need for more profound changes in the constitutional provisions governing the structures of the state cannot be ruled out.

Elections to Representative Bodies

In a socialist political system there is no room for organized opposition. There is no rivalry for power among parties representing different programs and competing visions of the future. The constitutions of socialist states—Poland being no exception—as a rule state that the decisive influence in the exercising of power is permanently held by the Communist (Marxist-Leninist) party, sometimes cooperating with other political forces, but always only with those that recognize its ideological and political supremacy. If elections therefore do not determine the political composition of state power, what is their role in public life then?

First of all, elections are meant to supply state authorities with "democratic" legitimization; participation in elections is regarded as a sign of support for the existing system of exercising power and as a way in which the voters vest in the authorities the right to exercise that power. Second, the election campaign, in which there is much public involvement, influences the selection of the candidates who are to seek the seats on the councils. Although campaign discussions about the proposed candidatures and the elections themselves cannot influence the political alignment of forces on representative bodies, they can—and do—influence the personal composition of the representation of these forces. Third, the election campaign also helps shape the programs of action of the bodies elected.

In various periods, the Polish electoral system has taken these three election goals into account to a varying degree; that is, the stress on one or more of these goals has differed from one period to another. During the crisis, the point was raised that previously there was too much emphasis on the legitimization of the authorities (manifested in efforts to achieve a turnout as close to 100 percent as possible), with too little attention to the selection of individual representatives and to the formulation of programs. Actually, in the 1970s the presentation of separate political programs was abandoned altogether, and party programmatic documents were submitted instead. The changes that have been or are going to be introduced in voting regulations are aimed at balancing all three tasks in elections. In other words, the objective is a democratization of electoral procedures without abandoning the canons of a socialist political system.

The basic electoral principles in Poland are identical for elections to the Sejm and to the people's councils. The constitution guarantees that elections are general, equal, direct, and secret. Members of the Sejm and the people's councils are elected to four-year terms, which is not to say that these elections must be held simultaneously.[15] In this respect, practice varies: There have been periods when elections to all representative bodies were held on the same day, periods when elections to the Sejm were coordinated with elections to voivodship councils and held separately with regard to other councils, and periods when elections to the Sejm were held separately from elections to the people's councils at all levels. At first, there were separate regulations governing elections to the Sejm and those to the councils; joint voting regulations for the Sejm and the people's councils were only adopted in 1976, but even those regulations did not stipulate that elections be held on the same day. Based on the 1976 regulations, elections to the Sejm were held together with elections to voivodship people's councils, with local elections organized on another date.

The regulations concerning elections to the people's councils were redefined in the law of February 13, 1984, on the basis of which new councils were elected on June 17, 1984.[16] These elections tested the practical value of the new legal solutions contained in the February law. The 1984 voting regulations governing the people's councils reduced the emphasis on legitimizing the authorities. One aspect of this approach was restricting participation in the elections of local authorities to people permanently residing in the area in question. This was in keeping with the demands voiced by legal scholars for a long time, but it met with an unexpected objection on the part of a segment of the public and the charge of contravening the constitutional principle of universality of election. It should be remembered that along with other political reasons, these new regulations were also responsible for the fact that the turnout in the June 17 elections, although exceeding 75 percent of all the people eligible to vote, was lower than the turnout in the 1970s, which as a rule was above 90 percent.

The 1984 voting regulations put more emphasis on programs, making the preparation of local electoral programs a legal obligation and requiring that these programs refer to the tasks contained in socioeconomic plans and take into account "real" civilian initiatives.[17]

However, the most significant novelty from the point of view of the whole electoral system is the emphasis on the selection of candidates. In brief, voters now influence who will hold specific seats on a council. It is true that only those candidates may be elected whose names are included in the one officially registered list. This list is drawn up by a new collective body called the electoral selection committee, representing political forces participating in the Patriotic Movement of National Revival (PRON), led by the PZPR. However, the selection committee is obliged to submit all the candidatures to prior approval of the voters at pre-election meetings, which have been nicknamed "primaries" by some journalists, although this is clearly an exaggeration. Once this list is officially registered, the list of candidates is submitted to voters again during the second round of pre-election meetings.

As previously, elections are held in constituencies, each of them having several seats to fill (three to six); but within the constituency there must be two candidates contesting every seat. In practice, the two candidates must be from the same party or organization. This mode of voting "in pairs" to some extent broadens the voters' choices. They can of course cross out the name of one or even both candidates, but if they leave their ballot without deletions, this means that they are voting for the first candidate in each pair. This puts the first-placed candidate in a privileged position as many voters either vote without deletions to show their civil loyalty, or leave the ballot untouched because they do not know the candidates well or do not see much difference between them. In the June 17, 1984, elections, the instances of candidates placed second in a pair winning the contested seat were very rare indeed.[18]

The 1984 voting regulations considerably expanded the system of court control over the course of elections and the counting of returns. The Supreme Court examined a number of protests lodged by the voters.[19] In addition to that, in some constituencies repeat elections were held as the turnout was lower there than required by law, which stipulates that for the voting to be valid, at least half of those eligible to vote must actually do so.

Parliament

The Position of the Sejm in the Political System

All 460 deputies to the Sejm are elected in general, equal, and direct elections, by secret ballot. In this manner, the Sejm is a representation of the whole nation (all the voters), which entitles it to act, in keeping with the constitution, as the "supreme articulator of the will of the working people of towns and countryside," embodying the sovereign rights of the nation. True to its "democratic" principles and given this particular shape, the Sejm occupies unchallenged the highest place in the constitutional hierarchy of state organs, with all other state organs either directly or indirectly subordinated to it.

An important problem is the influence of the Sejm's relations with political parties (and especially a hegemonic Communist party) on the practical implementation of the constitutional patterns envisaged by the lawmakers. The PZPR both influences the composition of the Sejm and guides its activity, which is fully consistent with the logic of this political system. However, in some periods this influence on the composition of the Sejm resulted in too many Sejm seats being filled with party apparatchiks and thereby reduced the legislative role of Sejm to rendering political decisions in a predetermined fashion. But the political crisis of the years 1980–1981 created an atmosphere in public life such that the Sejm could fulfill its constitutional role to a greater extent than previously.

It should be obvious that in a socialist political system it is difficult to define an inviolable boundary between the area of interests of the party and the parliament; the difference largely consists in the form of the decisions adopted. The parliament also deals with major political problems, while the party does not remain indifferent to parliament's actions concerning socioeconomic problems or current affairs of the state but having also a clear political dimension. However, the problem of establishing a lasting division of labor should not lead to a limitation of the role of the Sejm and to the takeover of its duties by party authorities, as happened in the past.

Such practices are now being abandoned. A resolution adopted by the PZPR political bureau in 1980 increases the role of the PZPR caucus in the Sejm and limits the independence of PZPR Sejm deputies by party discipline in their activities within the Sejm. But deputies' statements in parliamentary committees need not reflect the position of the caucus, only the views of individual deputies. Also in only some of the matters discussed and put to a vote at plenary Sejm sessions are the PZPR deputies expected to act in a uniform manner and to obey party discipline. This is imparting a more genuine and creative character to the Sejm debates.

More changes are now being introduced in the draft laws submitted to the Sejm, and the outcome of voting in the Sejm on the laws proposed— or changes in cabinet posts, for that matter—is far from unanimous. It can be said that the Sejm is gradually gaining its own identity in the political system. Practice has gotten nearer to the pattern envisaged by the constitution.[20]

This is confirmed by the actualization of Sejm supremacy over other supreme state bodies, particularly the Council of State and the Council of Ministers. The Sejm approves the decrees of the Council of State only after careful consideration, as witnessed by the procedures concerning the confirmation of the decree on martial law, and more closely follows the activity of the Council of State in various areas. However, it should be admitted that not all possibilities in this respect have been exhausted already. The proposal for examining the annual reports submitted by the Council of State at a plenary meeting of the Sejm has not yet been carried out in practice.[21]

The changes in the Sejm's relationship with the government are more pronounced. Cabinet changes are decided upon by the Sejm only after first consulting the appropriate Sejm committee on the nominee proposed by the chairman of the Council of Ministers. The opinion of Sejm committees, introduced by amending the Sejm's internal regulations, is often sought in practice, and it has already happened that a proposal that was not approved by the appropriate committee was subsequently withdrawn. I have already mentioned the very critical approach of the Sejm in the drafting of laws submitted to it, mainly by the government. This is another sign of the growing independence of the Sejm in the system of exercising power, especially at a time when the government is headed by a person who also acts as the leader of the party.

Changes in the Internal Structure of the Sejm

The Sejm has retained its unicameral structure, even though it has set up a rather large, separate consultative body, composed of 150 members: the Socioeconomic Council. The council is a unique experiment that is to be put to a test during the Sejm's present term of office. For this reason its existence is for the time being based not on the constitution or an ordinary law but on the Sejm's internal regulations, enacted in 1982. It can be expected that if this new institution confirms its value in practice, it will receive a more solid legal foundation. The council is the representation of various social and professional groups on whose behalf it is supposed to pass judgment on matters that are being examined by the Sejm. So far the council's members have been appointed by the house itself by voting en bloc for a list of proposed names. A link with the leading Sejm bodies was ensured by the adoption of the provision that the chairman of the council becomes ex officio a member of the elders' convention, which is made up of the Sejm speaker and deputy speakers and the chairmen of the individual caucuses. Time will show whether the council will become a permanent feature of Polish parliamentary practice and, if so, whether it will remain a Sejm advisory body or, as some people suggest, will evolve toward becoming a second chamber of the parliament, representing various self-governing institutions (workers' self-management; professional, farmers, or local self-government).[22]

Another sign of "democratic" tendencies in the Sejm has been the increase in the number of deputy speakers to four.[23] In this way, two out of the five members of the Sejm presidium now are people with no party affiliation.

For a long time it was believed that the growth of the number of Sejm committees was conducive to the activity of the parliament. Finally it was decided, however, that excessive splintering of committees, which resulted, turns their attention to problems that may be important from the point of view of a given industry or ministry but are only of secondary significance from the point of view of state policy. Therefore in 1984 it was decided to decrease the number of specialized committees corresponding to "branches" of the economy to fifteen and to broaden the scope of their interests. At the same time, five standing committees, whose juridictions are broader than the branches of the economy regulated by individual ministries, were retained: the mandates committee, the legislative procedures committee (which sees to the formal side of all the laws adopted by the Sejm), the constitutional accountability committee (which examines motions for bringing senior state officers before the Tribunal of State, a rough equivalent of the impeachment procedure), the committee for enterprise self-management (set up in connection with the economic reform to oversee the correct implementation of the provisions for workers' self-management), and the committee for suggestions and complaints (set up to improve the guarantees of civil rights).[24] The last three committees were established only in the 1980s.

Broadening the Scope of Sejm Activity

The legal and potential possibilities of Sejm activity are very broad, and in the period of the political crisis the Sejm made use of these opportunities more often than before, making them a reality. In part, this was due to the Sejm's actively joining in the mediation between the various political forces involved in the conflict, which in practice amounted to attempts to facilitate agreement between the Government and Solidarity. Although it was elected at the beginning of 1980, before the outbreak of the crisis, the Sejm, as the supreme representative of the nation, enjoyed a measure of moral and political authority. In part, this wider use of its powers was due to the fact that the Sejm spoke on difficult political issues in order to support the line of reform and agreement proclaimed by the party. The activity of the Sejm was also broadened as a result of the desire to endorse legislatively the changes occurring in the economy and state.

The Sejm's involvement in the solving of social conflict was expressed, among other things, in the establishment of a special Sejm commission for the implementation of the social accords, signed by the government with representatives of striking workers in Gdansk, Szczecin, and Jastrzebie.[25] This commission, headed by the sociologist and independent deputy, Professor Jan Szczepanski, tried with varying degrees of success to mediate disputes arising from differences in the interpretation of these accords. Its mission ended when martial law was imposed and the Solidarity union was banned.

The Sejm statements on current policy matters were usually made in the form of resolutions. The constitution says that the Sejm not only passes laws but also adopts resolutions defining the basic directions of the activity of the state (Article 20, paragraph 3).[26] In the situation that existed in Poland these resolutions dealt much more often than before with important problems of a political nature. For example, in a resolution passed on January 25, 1982, the Sejm deemed the introduction of martial law to have been indispensable and a "lesser evil," but at the same time it declared that martial law should not stay in force any longer than necessary and that the "great task of socialist renewal must be and will be carried on" while "national agreement invariably remains our objective."[27] The Sejm resolutions I am mentioning here not only constitute a declaration of political intentions but are binding for the organs subordinated to the Sejm—hence for all state organs, the government included. Although much more could be said about the Sejm's legislative activity, at this point what needs to be emphasized is that through its laws the Sejm provided legislative foundations as well as guarantees for the reforms taking place. As required by the social accords, the Sejm also passed in 1981 the important law on the control of publications and entertainment (specifying the limits of activity of the censors) and then, after some delay, the law on trade unions.[28] An especially important package of laws also passed in 1981 dealt with the operation of the national economy in the context of economic reform. These replaced earlier government decisions, perpetuating the new economic mechanisms and making it difficult to depart from them.

The Council of State

In the constitutional hierarchy of state organs, the Council of State places second, right behind the Sejm, which is its only superior. The council, made up of seventeen members, is elected by the Sejm from among the deputies. For this reason it is sometimes referred to as an offshoot of the Sejm. In view of the role the council fills in the structure of the state, some writers refer to it as the collective presidency, but this is not very accurate because the council carries out not only the duties traditionally reserved for the head of state but also ones connected with the functioning of the Sejm and also partially deputizes for it between plenary meetings. In addition, it has exclusive powers granted to it by the constitution and other laws, regarding supreme state leadership, they are executed, as it were, parallel to the work of the Sejm.

As the head of state (the collective presidency), the Council of State confers orders, awards, and honorary titles (including the title of honorary professor); can offer clemency (to individual convicts, whereas a general amnesty can only be passed by the Sejm); fills some civilian and military posts; ratifies and terminates international agreements; appoints and recalls Polish ambassadors to other countries, and receives the credentials of foreign ambassadors accredited in Warsaw. The Council of State is the supreme representative of state authorities in external and internal relations and a distinctive symbol of these authorities. As collective representation is often impractical if not completely impossible, the council fulfills its ceremonial duties through its chairman.[29] However, a majority of the decisions falling within the powers of the council are adopted collectively, at meetings held at regular intervals.

The powers of the Council of State connected with the functioning of the Sejm or with deputizing for it include the announcing of Sejm elections and the convening of its sessions. In both instances, the freedom of action of the council is considerably limited: It is obliged to announce new elections to the Sejm not later than a month before the expiration of the Sejm's term of office, and it is obliged to convene a session of the Sejm at least twice a year. It should be noted that the dates of individual plenary meetings within the session convened by the Council of State are determined by the Sejm itself. In between Sejm sessions, the Council of State may pass decrees equivalent to Sejm laws, but these must be approved by the Sejm at its next meeting; and the council also may introduce changes in the cabinet at the request of the chairman of the Council of Ministers; such changes must also be subsequently approved by the Sejm. Finally, when the Sejm is not in session—not only in the periods between its sessions but also between individual plenary meetings—the Council of State is the body to which the government answers for its actions. Also under the same circumstances the Council of State is authorized to strip Sejm deputies of their immunity and to agree to penal proceedings being instituted against them and/or to their arrest.

The significance of the council's powers in this area is modest and appears to be diminishing. Both the announcement of the elections to the Sejm and the convening of its sessions are really formalities. Besides, misgivings have long been voiced whether such relics deserve to be preserved and the Sejm should not receive these powers instead. As for the right to issue decrees, the Council of State has availed itself of this power with utmost restraint and only in exceptional and emergency cases. The reason is simple: to avoid limiting the legislative role of the Sejm and transforming its decrees into a rival source of legislation. Likewise, the council rarely uses its powers of introducing changes in the cabinet, leaving this task for the Sejm to carry out.

The Council of State has always treated with restraint its supervisory powers with regard to the government, trying not to interfere in current state administration or becoming a cogoverning body. The practical possibilities of the Council of State using its supremacy over the Council of Ministers depend on the actual political prestige enjoyed by each of these organs. After 1980 and especially after 1981, the head of government became the leader of the PZPR as well, while the leaders of the remaining two parties were incorporated into the cabinet as vice-premiers. At that point, when the government included representatives of other sociopolitical groups and together began to work out the coalition formula, the supremacy of the government's political authority became obvious. In this situation, the implementation of the constitutional supremacy of the Council of State over the Council of Ministers would be problematic, if only because few progressive political changes occurred in the membership of the Council of State, which had been elected in early 1980, at the beginning of the tenure of the eighth Sejm. The changes in the leadership of the PZPR and its coalition partners were not always quickly reflected in the composition of the Council of State. As a result, the constitutional supremacy of the Council of State over the government did not correspond to the actual position of the two bodies.

Therefore it is quite paradoxical that precisely at a time when the government was elevated to a higher place in the political system, the Council of State obtained new powers in the area of supreme state leadership, most of which could well have been entrusted to the Council of Ministers. They could have been, but they were not, and the reason was the resentment directed against the council of ministers. In the 1970s the government had become the supreme "representative" of an excessively developed state, of economic administration, and an overly autonomous organ, making itself the real center of all actions connected with running the state and the national economy. The immense activity of the government overshadowed other supreme state organs, including the Sejm and the Council of State; the latter two, especially the parliament, lacked sufficient control, while the government overemphasized bureaucratic and technocratic values and underestimated the importance of social ones. The strongly autocratic personality of the former prime minister added to the irregularities taking place in relations among various institutions. The critical appraisal of this state of affairs subsequently led to the awarding of new powers to the Council of State, rather than to the government and to the subordination of newly established bodies to that council. However, it should be understood that this transfer of powers concerned only those responsibilities specifically transferred to it instead of the government. This is because even before 1980, the constitution and other laws had entrusted the Council of State with supervision over those central and local state organs that did not fit into the structure of the administration but that actually supervised or controlled them. Therefore the council could not be subordinated to the government, which was coresponsible with it for work of the state administration. It was also recognized that it would be wrong to entrust the Sejm with controlling these various supervisory organs falling outside direct state administration, as this would require systematic performance of specialized work. Nevertheless, this matter remains controversial and is still debated to this day.

The Council of State appoints and in instances specified by the laws recalls all judges, including the judges of the Supreme Court and the Supreme Administrative Court. The Council of State also appoints and recalls the prosecutor general and examines his reports on the activity of prosecuting agencies. If one adds up the council's supervising powers vis-a-vis the Supreme Court, the Supreme Administrative Court, and the prosecutor general, and its partial powers over the Supreme Chamber of Control, it will be apparent that it is precisely the Council of State that coordinates the complicated mechanism of ensuring the rule of law in the state and the control over the observance of the law by state and economic administration agencies. This function of the Council of State explains why it is authorized by the constitution to make the interpretation of laws that is binding on all the state organs applying that law as well as on citizens and organizations whose behavior is regulated by that law.[30]

The local people's councils are representative organs of state power and are at the same time units of local self-government, supervising the work of local administration. Therefore they are themselves supervised by the Council of State rather than by the government. The highest sanction the Council of State has at its disposal—though it has never used it—is the right to dissolve a people's council and order new elections. Since the new law of July 20, 1983, on the system of people's councils and local self-government, the Council of State has been also able to dissolve the presidium of a people's council.

I have already said that in the period of the political crisis, the powers of the Council of State were enlarged. One sign of this was the subordination to it of the Main Office for the Control of Publications and Entertainment, under a law passed in 1981—thereby entrusting it with supervision over the very delicate matters of preventing state censorship.[31] Prior to the reorganization of the main office and in keeping with the regulations that were in force until 1981, censorship was within the scope of the government, although even in 1980 censorship decisions could be and indeed were occasionally subjected to court control. This possibility has, of course, been retained.

On the strength of detailed regulations, the Council of State played an important role in the restructuring of the trade union movement, first in 1980, and then again in 1982, when new unions began to be set up after the dissolution of all previously existing ones.[32] In order to help the budding unions, the Council of State set up social consultative commissions and local councils to supply legal and organizational advice to them.[33] The Council of State also supervises the state labor inspectorates, which see to the observance of labor law in individual enterprises, with special emphasis on safety and hygiene. An auxiliary public labor inspectorate, formerly attached to trade unions, was also reinstated under the aegis of the Council of State because the new unions lack experience and are not sufficiently strong yet.[34] At the same time, efforts are being made to make the inspectors independent of state economic administration.

The Government

By the government I mean executive state power. While its core is the Council of Ministers, it also covers—in addition to auxiliary and advisory bodies to the Council of Ministers—such integral supreme state organs as the government presidium, the chairman of the Council of Ministers (also referred to as premier or prime minister), and individual ministers who act on their own, not as members of any collective bodies.

It is commonplace in probably all socialist states for some people to combine government responsibilities with membership in the supreme party bodies. In this way, some cabinet members obtain additional political authority. As a rule, this obtains for the ministers of foreign affairs, internal affairs, and national defense, as well as for some of the vice-premiers and the prime minister. In Poland since 1981 the chairman of the Council of Ministers has also been the first secretary of the PZPR. This signifies a far-reaching integration of the party and state leadership. This practice leads to party authorities exercising direct political control over the work of the government and to the government occupying an independent political position in relation to other state organs, even those that are placed above it in the constitutional hierarchy.

The symbiosis of the party and government leadership, which has now actually reached an even higher level, does not signify a merger of the duties and a lack of division of responsibilities between the two leaderships.[35] Joint meetings of the government presidium and the PZPR Politburo, formerly quite frequent, are now rare. The practice of adopting joint resolutions has virtually been abandoned. It is true that the party authorities do examine the political aspects of the matters falling within the scope of responsibilities of the government, but the government also deals with purely political questions, especially through its Sociopolitical Committee.[36] Only government decisions are binding on state organs and citizens, although it is a fact that, for obvious reasons, they are often inspired by earlier resolutions of the Politburo.

An important attempt to prevent the personal fusion of party and government leaderships and the transformation of them into a functional unity, becoming a germ of some monolith party-state executive (which would only formally be divided into various party and state segments) was the establishment of the Tribunal of State. It was set up to pass verdicts on senior state (and only state!) officials charged by the Sejm with infringing the constitution and laws in their official actions. Party officials are exempted from this kind of constitutional accountability; therefore, it has been recognized that the whole system, by depriving state officials of the possibility of shifting blame to directives received from the party and to their authors, ensures that these directives will conform to the binding laws. One can only be held accountable for his own actions and his own judgment of what is legal or what is a violation of the law.

The Council of Ministers is a superior body for all the central and local organs of state administration. On this account it coordinates the activity of ministries and defines the directions of their work. With regard to matters of nationwide importance ("centralized" ones), it guides the work of the *voivods* (provincial heads), town presidents, and *gmina* (or borough) heads, while with regard to local ("decentralized") matters, it supervises their work. The forms and intensity of government control over the work of the administration vary, depending on the weight of the matter and the branch of the administration.

The government exercises its influence over administrative bodies involved in managing the economy primarily through its duties fulfilled in socioeconomic and financial planning. The Council of Ministers prepares the drafts of long-term plans, as well the drafts of medium-term, five-year socioeconomic plans and annual state budgets. It also sees to the implementation of the tasks specified in these documents.[37] On the basis of the socioeconomic plan and upon consulting public opinion and social organizations, the Council of Ministers adopts a central annual plan, but it cannot alter the targets and directions of the policy specified in the national socioeconomic plan passed by the Sejm. It can merely state these tasks in greater detail and develop them. The law on planning adds further precision to the directive contained in the constitution. Whereas the constitution puts the Council of Ministers under the obligation to "see to" the implementation of the socioeconomic plan (Article 41, paragraph 5), the law on planning orders it to "arrange the execution" of this plan. This may be interpreted as a sign of the strengthening of the government's position in planning and management of the national economy, although by itself the change only confirms a practice that became consolidated long ago.

Of all the branches of state administration, the constitution selects three areas that the government should approach with particular attention: foreign policy, the country's defenses and organization of the armed forces (over which the Council of Ministers is to exercise "general leadership"), and protection of public order, traditionally referred to as internal affairs. The establishment of a special committee of the Council of Ministers as an auxiliary and consultative body on internal affairs in 1983 was a sign of the government's concern about this area.[38] State management of national defense matters was reorganized in a more complicated manner.

The National Defense Committee (KOK), which was formerly situated in the system as one of the committees of the Council of Ministers—albeit with a special composition, a special scope of powers, and special relationship toward other state organs—has obtained considerable autonomy from the government. The chairman of the KOK is appointed and recalled by the Sejm, while the deputy chairmen (except for the defense minister, who is ex officio one of the deputy chairmen) are appointed by the Council of State.[39] It is also the Council of State that defines (upon consulting the Council of Ministers) the principles and mode of appointing the members (other than the chairman and deputy chairmen) and the secretary of the KOK as well as the principles and mode of work of the committee. Although the respective law says that the KOK is to carry out its task "in conformity with the decisions of the Council of Ministers made within the framework of its general leadership, with regard to the country's defenses and the organization of the armed forces of the Polish People's Republic"—doubts may emerge about the division of powers between the KOK and its chairman, on the one hand, and the government, on the other. The KOK chairman is the supreme commander of the armed forces of the PPR and on this account enjoys considerable powers (including, for example, approving the prime minister's nominee for the post of defense minister). So long as the chairman of the Council of Ministers is also KOK chairman, such doubts are unlikely, but although the combination of the two posts in one person is not required by any law, it is hard to say whether or not it might become a permanent practice. At any rate, the reorganization of the KOK was based on the experience gained by the Military Council of National Salvation, which operated during martial law (1981-1983).[40] To this extent then it institutionalizes a broader participation of the armed forces in political life and their greater responsibility for the security of the state, including internal security.

Ever since the 1952 constitution came into force, the position of the chairman of the Council of Ministers has in reality been stronger than that of a person presiding over the debates of a collective body. However, whereas until 1976 this actual position was hardly justified by the provisions of the constitution, the amendments introduced that year deal separately with the premier. They state that he directs the work of the Council of Ministers and the government presidium (rather than merely presiding over their debates) and that he may be authorized by laws to issue executive orders on their implementation. The chairman of the Council of Ministers is the highest superior of all civil servants. Therefore it was his decision that led to the adoption and publication of a document called "The Code of Duties of Civil Servants," which specifies their duties toward the state and the citizens.[41] The assumption by the chairman of the Council of Ministers, General Wojciech Jaruzelski, of the duties of first secretary of the PZPR in 1981 considerably increased the prestige of the head of government and strengthened this position in the political system.

The 1976 amendments to the constitution also included a clause on the government presidium. It is composed of the premier and the deputy premiers, as well as several ministers appointed by the Council of Ministers itself. The government presidium acts within the constitutional powers of the Council of Ministers. With its help, the Council of Ministers coordinates the work of individual ministers. The government presidium also makes preliminary analyses of the proposed decisions of the Council of Ministers. The government presidium works regularly, meeting at least once every two weeks. However, as an institution it is as energetic as it is controversial. Some authors point to the vagueness of the division of powers between the government presidium and the Council of Ministers and perceive the activity of the former as a threat to the principle of collective decisionmaking in the activity of the Council of Ministers itself.[42] Such views are especially typical of those who would be inclined to emphasize the "political-executive" nature of the government, while weakening its "administrative" functions.

A characteristic feature of the evolution of the system since 1980 is the fact that the government has surrounded itself with a number of auxiliary collegial bodies (committees) and consultative bodies (councils). These include, among other organs, the Sociopolitical Committee, which has been working very energetically, the Committee for the Observance of Law, Public Order, and Social Discipline (which is subdivided into subcommittees in charge of individual aspects of law and order), and the Committee for Youth Affairs.[43] Among the various councils, especially great prestige is enjoyed—next to that of the Legislative Council—by the Consultative Economic Council, led by the economist, Professor Czeslaw Bobrowski.[44]

There are so many councils that it is sometimes said that this multitude may lead to diluting the powers of the government and to crediting it with responsibility for decisions over which it does not have influence. However, the committees and councils attached to the Council of Ministers reflect the attempt to increase society's say in governing and to optimize decisions on the basis of a more diversified input independent of the administration.

The Council of Ministers, its chairman and deputy chairmen of the government presidium, and the committees and councils attached to the Council of Ministers or the prime minister have at their disposal expert advisers and administrators. The latter form the Office of the Council of Ministers. This apparatus is led by the chief of the Office of the Council of Ministers, who is assisted by under secretaries of state. A research institute called the Opinion Research Center (CBOS) was set up in order to gauge the opinion of society on matters of interest to the government, and the Government Press Office was established to shape public opinion about government policies and actions.[45] It is an internal organizational unit of the Office of the Council of Ministers, and is headed by a government spokesman with the rank of an under secretary of state.

Ministers are in charge of individual sectors of state administration, while at the same time being members of the collective organ, the Council of Ministers. The hybrid character of the office of minister place the occupant in the center of a never-ending dilemma: Should the minister represent the government in dealing with the branch of administration entrusted to him and see to the implementation of government policies by the administrative apparatus subordinated to him, or should he articulate instead the interests of his branch in the government and seek to ensure that they are taken into account? The proponents of a "political-executive" government will certainly opt for the former variant, while the supporters of an "administrative" government will tend to favor the latter option, at least tacitly. The idea that the minister should try to reconcile both approaches, representing the government in his branch and his branch in the government does not solve many practical problems coming from the hybrid situation of the minister. In practice, most ministers tend to identify themselves with the needs and interests of the branch of economy or administration that they represent, occasionally reaching or even surpassing the boundaries of egoism. This phenomenon is to be prevented by the coordinating role of the government presidium and the activity of the specialized committees of the Council of Ministers.

The division into ministries is based on laws passed by the Sejm. The efforts to rationalize this division that have been undertaken thus far have yielded very modest results, as the attempts to dissolve one ministry and entrust its duties to another often encounter resistance on the part of not only the ministry bureaucrats, but also the appropriate Sejm committee, which shares the views of those employed in a given branch of the administration. Such pressure prevented the proposed merger of the ministries of farming and forestry into one body. The opposition of the forestry lobby proved effective and blocked the proposed change.

In recent years, efforts have been made to define with greater precision the powers and structure of individual ministries. One such act that was important from the point of view of the protection of civil rights was the law governing the Office of Minister of Internal Affairs.[46] Work is underway on a draft law for the Council of Ministers, which should solve many of the problems outlined above, such as the "integral" resolutions of the Council of Ministers, the system of committees and councils in the Council of Ministers, or the division of powers between the Council of Ministers and the government presidium.[47]

State Authorities in the Provinces and Local Self-Government: The People's Councils

The development of various forms of self-government, supported by the state, was envisaged and indeed required by the constitution in its 1976 shape. However, the stimulus for the practical implementation of this constitutional provision was provided only by the developments of the summer of 1980. The institution of self-government then began to be perceived as a remedy against bureaucratic ailments plaguing state administration. Self-government was supposed to arrest the autocratic tendencies occasionally demonstrated by the links of this system of exercising power. In fact, self-government was supposed to become one of the ways of socializing the state. Overcoming the inconsistencies between the state conceived of as a system of organs and the institutions exercising this power in society, it is the state as a general organization of society that controls, inspires, and also executes the power of self-government.

Although it is true that attempts were made then to use self-government as a platform of expression for the opposition forces and to set self-government against the state, the predominant idea was that the institution of self-government can be used for a genuine and legally guaranteed decentralization of some functions of the state. Therefore, after the proclamation of martial law on December 13, 1981, work on the development of various forms of self-government and the preparation of the necessary legislative acts was not abandoned but was actually accelerated. Laws were passed on the establishment of worker self-management bodies in state-owned enterprises, private farmers' self-government, self-management of universities and of some professions, for example, defense counsels or legal advisers.[48] The idea of setting up self-management bodies was dropped only with regard to institutions where their operation might clash with the fulfillment of the tasks of the state, for example, courts of law. The same tendency is reflected in the July 20, 1983, law on the system of people's councils and local self-government. This law envisages the introduction of the most common form of self-government—local self-government.[49]

Local self-government is made up of groups of organs: people's councils and residents' self-government in the form of neighborhood commissions. They are united by shared concern about the satisfaction of the needs of local communities. Differences between them include the scope of their activity, the amount and nature of the financial means that are at their disposal, and their rights as well as their legal nature. People's councils are elected at every level in the territorial division of the country—in voivodships (provinces) as well as towns, big districts, and *gminas* (boroughs). There is a two-tiered administrative division of Poland: The country is divided into forty-nine voivodships, which in turn are divided into towns and *gminas*. Exceptions from the two-tier rule are certain cities (e.g., Wroclaw) that do not constitute separate voivodships (as Warsaw, Cracow, and Lodz do) but have a population over 300,000 people and are divided into districts. In those special cases, there is a three-tiered structure, where the voivodship council is above the town council, while the latter is above district councils. A unique feature is the practice in these cases whereby a common council is elected for a town and the surrounding *gmina*. In contrast, residents' self-government bodies operate in smaller areas. Within a *gmina* they operate in individual villages, while within towns (or districts in the case of larger cities) they function in individual housing "estates" developments. Only in this sense can it be said that in the system of local self-management people's councils there is a specific form of superstructure over residents' self-government bodies.

However, in comparison to residents' self-government, people's councils have many greater opportunities for actual work. The councils' revenues, the part of the State Treasury revenue that is directly and, as it were, automatically put at the councils' disposal, have been considerably augmented. The councils supervise many local enterprises and other institutions, such as hospitals, museums, or schools, whose activity meet local residents' needs.[50] What is no less important, the councils now have at their disposal more effective, one might say stronger, legal means than in the past that make it possible to implement their decisions, with regard to both citizens and state-run units. For the councils—unlike residents' self-government bodies—are not only organs of local self-government but also local organs of state power. This puts them above the local state administration and is related to the councils fulfilling the function of uniform state power. Along with the duties of local self-government, the councils carry out tasks of nationwide significance. As local organs of state power, the councils take part in shaping and executing state policy in the regions. It is still difficult to say whether the fact that the councils combine the duties and responsibilities of a self-government body with those of a uniform state power will enhance both lines of their activity or result instead in a relative weakening of one of them. Nevertheless, this design was deemed to be the optimum one as it serves both the socialization of the state and the tying of local self-government to the state. Separate development and greater autonomy for local self-government might ultimately lead to a destabilization of state power.

As a result, the scope of powers of people's councils was defined very broadly. It embraces all the problems connected with meeting the needs of local communities except for those that by law fall within the powers of other organs. This is the principle of the general competence of the people's councils and their assumed competence in doubtful cases. In addition to self-government duties, people's councils are to fulfill many tasks of uniform state power, for example: environment protection, fire prevention, the handling of natural disasters, national defense, and the preservation of public order and security. In the last domain, people's councils exercise control over local militia units.

People's councils, acting in a dual role as organs of local self-government and of state authority, plan the socioeconomic and cultural development of their area. The changes in recent years consist of lengthening the time span of the plans, with all local planning now based on a five-year comprehensive socioeconomic plan supplemented by a five-year financial plan, rather than on one-year plans, as was the case heretofore. These changes also call for broader participation by representative bodies and the public in decisionmaking with regard to planning. This practice is often referred to as the socialization of planning. Nowadays the people's council is obliged to examine not one but at least two variants of the plan prepared by expert planners and to submit the proposals to public discussion.

The implementation of the plans takes place with the help of enterprises and other local economic organizations—those bound by the local plan and budget passed by the people's council. Local enterprises, like all other state-owned enterprises, operate according to the principles of autonomy, self- management, and self-financing introduced by the economic reform. In order not to infringe upon these rules, a council may exert its influence on enterprises mainly through the use of economic instruments (e.g., taxes) rather than through administrative methods (orders, bans, and commands). (The only exception are emergency cases listed in the laws.) The enterprise's plan is coordinated with the local plan. The category "local enterprises" includes a distinct subgroup of nonprofit organizations whose main purpose is the satisfaction of the inhabitants' specific needs. The influence of the councils over this group of enterprises is somewhat larger than over the remaining local enterprises.

The legislative acts issued by the people's councils and their organs, as well as by local administrative bodies not subordinated to people's councils (e.g., maritime offices), are collectively termed "local law." The overwhelming majority of local legislative acts, however, are originated by the people's councils and their organs. They issue these acts in one of two situations: either when they are authorized or required to do so by laws or executive orders (i.e., acts adopted at the central level), or when a nationwide regulation is missing and yet the issuing of a legal act is indispensable to protect the "lives or the health of citizens or to protect property or ensure security, order, peace, and public order." This means that the local law specifies and supplements a general legal order. Of course, acts of local law are only binding in the area of operation of the people's councils that issued them.[51]

A people's council exercises its rights directly through its sessions, or through intermediary organs: the presidium, the commissions, and the local administration. The people's council of a *gmina,* town or town district may delegate some of the matters falling within its powers to the residents' self-government to decide.

Sessions of people's councils are convened at least twice a year, but this legal requirement is easily exceeded in practice by all the councils. The presence of at least a half of all the councillors is required for the session to be valid. The council itself defines the procedures of the debates. The atmosphere at the sessions depends on the general political atmosphere in the country, which may encourage or discourage the councillors from presenting their views. In general it can be said that since the autumn of 1980, discussion at these sessions has become more authentic and councillors are more willing to present their views and opinions, even if they clash with the position of the administration. The discussion of basically every issue ends with the adoption of a suitable resolution by the council. The resolution is signed by the chairman, while the more important resolutions (including all the resolutions of a lawmaking nature) are published in an official voivodship gazette that appears in every voivodship.

The presidium of a people's council initiates and organizes the work of the council.[52] It prepares sessions and controls the implementation of resolutions. The presidium is composed of the chairman of the council, the deputy chairmen, and the chairmen of all the standing commissions of the council. All the presidium members are elected by the council from among the councillors. By 1980 the earlier practice of combining the post of chairman of the council (and also of its presidium) with the duties of the leader of the local PZPR organization had been abandoned. The new law on local self-government gave the presidium the right of passing guidelines that are binding on the local administration. This means that when the council is not in session, its presidium is the organ that controls the administration and is a superior body to it.

The standing commissions of a people's council are organized by the council in a basically independent manner, according to individual branches of the administration and local economy. One commission that must be set up by every council is the standing commission for self-government, whose duty it is to maintain ties with different self-government bodies on behalf of the council. The commissions are auxiliary organs of a consultative and control character. In addition to councillors, the commissions may include people from outside the council, but the latter must not exceed half of the overall membership of the commission. The chairmen of the commissions must be councillors. In addition to the standing commissions, the councils may set up ad hoc commissions and control groups to examine concrete issues (within its parameters) involving individual branches of the economy or the administration.

The local administration carries out both the self-government tasks of the people's councils (its decentralized powers) and the tasks of the uniform system of state administration (its centralized powers). With respect to centralized powers, the local administration is directed by the central administrative bodies. Insofar as decentralized powers are concerned, it is in fact subordinated to the people's council, whereas the central bodies' control over this administration is limited to checking the conformity of its actions with the law.

The leader and coordinator for the network of administrative organs and units subordinated to a given people's council is the chief of the local administration: the *voivod*, the president of a town, or town district. The *voivod*, who at the same time is the representative of the government in the voivodship, is appointed by the chairman of the Council of Ministers upon obtaining the approval of the voivodship people's council. The candidates are proposed by the minister in charge of local administration after consulting the presidium of the voivodship people's council. In this way, the voivodship people's council has the opportunity to express its view on the filling of the post of *voivod* on two occasions.

In *gminas*, towns or city districts the influence of the council is even stronger. The council elects its head from among the candidates proposed by the presidium of the council upon consulting the *voivod*. Here—unless the council rules otherwise—the head is the only "organ" of local administration able to exercise his powers with the help of a bureaucratic staff completely subordinated to him.

At the voivodship level, in contrast, next to the *voivod* are the heads of departments of local authority organs that enjoy the status of administrative organs. Unlike the *voivod*, whom the law describes as an organ of the administration equipped with general powers, department heads are defined as administrative organs with specific powers. They are appointed and recalled by the *voivod* upon consulting an appropriate standing commission of the voivodship people's council. The changes introduced after 1980 in the pattern of local authority included increased influence of the council in naming the chief of the administration, stricter control exercised by the council over the work of all the administrative bodies subordinated to it, the awarding of the status of separate administrative organs, and—most important of all—the identification of decentralized powers within the scope of work of local administration.

Residents' self-government operates according to somewhat different principles in the countryside than in towns. In the countryside, the basic organ of self-government is the general meeting of the inhabitants of a village. This meeting decides on the most important matters for the inhabitants, within the range of powers defined for their self-government. The meeting elects the village administrator, who while being the executive organ of residents' self-government, also fulfills some auxiliary duties on behalf of the local administration. The village administrator presides over the village council, which represents self-government between general meetings, and chairs village meetings, unless the inhabitants elect another chairman for the meeting. Similarly, in towns the basic organ of residents' self-government in "housing estates"—i.e. housing developments—is the general meeting of the inhabitants, but in larger developments a conference of delegates can be held instead. The executive organs are "estate committees", whose organizational pattern and principles of operation are defined in appropriate statutes. In cooperative housing estates, the role of residents' self-government is executed by appropriate organs of cooperative self-government.

Prospects for the Future

In the evolution of Poland's state system witnessed at the beginning of the 1980s, one can notice both constancy in the most general properties of a socialist state (such as the hegemonic role of the Communist party, the multiple forms of society's participation in the work of state institutions, the hierarchy of state organs subordinating the administration to representative bodies, and so forth) and changes in concrete legal arrangements. It appears that the changes that have been introduced express three main tendencies: the trend toward a further socialization of state power (for example, through the system of various self-government bodies and especially local self-government), the tendency to improve further the guarantees of the rule of law in the operation of the state (the establishment of the Tribunal of State and the Constitutional Tribunal), and the tendency to rationalize state structures and procedures through adjusting them to perform better the tasks of a given organ of power (e.g., the changes in the inner organization of the Sejm or the beginning of changes in the organization of the government's work).

The extent and consequences of future changes will, in my view, depend on two factors. The first is the PZPR's conception of exercising power in a given political situation and in the context of a given state of public opinion. The second is progress in implementing economic reform. In a socialist state the political system depends in large measure on the model adopted for economic management. In other words, the model of state power is determined by the model adopted by the political and economic leadership.

At any rate, it is possible to anticipate the continuation of the work previously begun and the completion of the changes already announced. Before long, new regulations governing elections to the Sejm should be passed. They will take into account the experience obtained in the application of new voting regulations for the people's councils. One should also expect more acts settling the powers of individual central administration organs, especially those directly involved in central economic management. It is especially important to adjust the structures of central economic administration to the requirements of management dictated by the reform. In fact, this is a prerequisite of the reform's success. Other changes will be forthcoming in the courts and the legal system.

But the question arises whether these fragmentary changes will turn out to be sufficient for the system of state organs to accomplish the tasks now confronting the state as a whole, its individual institutions, and the emerging ideological pattern of state power—ones that require it to be strong but democratic, efficient but legalistic, stable but flexible. In other words, will it not be necessary to introduce deeper reforms and adopt a new constitution? It is possible to arrive at a new constitution by various ways.[53] First of all, it is possible to adopt new theoretical assumptions and devise a completely new act on this basis, completely disregarding existing institutions and methods of exercising power. But it is also possible to introduce changes gradually and test them in practice and then generalize the already introduced partial changes in the constitution. It appears that the latter method of arriving at a new constitution has been adopted in Poland, at least as of September 1984.

Notes

1. For more on the subject, see Zbyslaw Rykowski and Wojciech Sokolewicz, "Konstytucyjne podstawy systemy naczelnych organow panstwowych w Polskiej Rzeczypospolitej Ludowej" (The Constitutional Foundations of the System of Supreme State Organs in the Polish People's Republic), *Panstwo i Prawo* (hereafter referred to as *PiP*), 5 (1983), pp. 37-49.

2. It is worth noting that in the so-called Gdansk agreements the new trade unions (i.e., Solidarity) acknowledged the "leading" role of the PZPR in "the state" but did not reaffirm the constitutional formula about its "guiding" role in "society". Cf. point 2 of the protocol of the agreement signed by the government commission and the Inter-Factory Strike Committee on August 31, 1980, at the Gdansk Shipyard and the protocols of the Gdansk, Szczecin, and Jastrzebie agreements, Warszawa 1980.

3. For more on the theoretical assumptions of the leading role of the Party, see: Andrzej Werblan, "Polish United Workers Party: The Leading Force of the Polish Working Class and the Polish Nation," in *The Political Sciences in Poland* (Warszawa: Polish Scientific Publishers, 1979), pp. 9-33; Adolf Dobieszewski: "The Party and Socialism," ibid., pp. 34-56.

4. *Dziennik Ustaw* (hereafter referred to as *Dz. U.*) no. 8, item 32.

5. *Dz. U.*, no. 2, item 15.

6. The Sejm regulations, amended in 1980, were published in the full version incorporating these changes, in *Monitor Polski* (*M.P.*), no. 29/1980, item 164. More changes were introduced in 1981 (*M.P.*, 26, item 224), 1982 (*M.P.*, 17, item 134, and *M.P.*, 18, item 146), and 1984 (*M.P.*, 10, item 65).

7. Cf. in particular Article 6 of the law of July 31, 1981, on the control of publications and entertainment (*Dz.U.*, no. 20, item 199).

8. The so-called first reading of the bill was held at a Sejm meeting on July 14, 1983, when the main lines of the draft were introduced on behalf of the government by Vice-Premier M. F. Rakowski. The Sejm sent the draft to appropriate committees for consideration.

9. *Dz. U.*, no. 41, item 185; error corrected in *Dz. U.*, no. 62/1983, item 286; amended by *Dz. U.*, no. 21/1984, item 100.

10. These are presented in detail by Leszek Garlicki, *Charakter ustrojowy nowych trybunalow* (The New Tribunals in the Light of Poland's System), *PiP* 3, 1983, pp. 34-37; a different view was voiced by Sylwester Zawadzki in a panel discussion related in the same issue of *PiP*, p. 126.

11. The decree of December 12, 1981, on martial law (*Dz. U.*, no. 29, item 154).

12. The decree was endorsed by the Sejm by way of a *law* rather than a *resolution;* the latter is the form in which the Sejm usually confirms decrees. Cf. the law of January 25, 1982, on the special legal regulations for the period of martial law (*Dz. U.*, no. 3, item 18).

13. The law of July 20, 1983 (*Dz. U.*, no. 39, item 175) modified Article 33 of the constitution as appropriate.

14. This refers to the law of December 5, 1983, on the state of emergency (*Dz. U.*, no. 66, item, 297). It applies only to the state of emergency, whereas martial law is still regulated by the decree of the Council of State of December 12, 1981, mentioned in footnote 11 and confirmed by the law of January 25, 1982.

15. An important exception to this statement is the constitutional law of February 13, 1984 (*Dz. U.*, no. 9, item 33), which extended the four-year Sejm tenure that began on election day March 23, 1980. This law did not specify for how long a period this would be; it merely obliged the Sejm to define the expiration date of this term by way of a law that was to be adopted no later than the end of 1984. Subsequently a new electoral procedure was adopted in early 1985 and new parliamentary elections took place in October of the same year.

16. The new voting regulations are discussed in detail by Feliks Siemienski, "Nowa ordynacja wyborcza do rad narodowych" (New Electoral Regulations for the People's Councils), *PiP* 5 (1983), pp. 3-19. The adoption of the law was preceded by lengthy discussions, as can be seen in the discussion over a draft of the electoral regulations that was held in the Institute of the State and Law of the Polish Academy of Sciences and was reported in *PiP* 4 (1984), pp. 120-122. However, the Sejm took these discussions into account only to a very limited extent.

17. Cf. article 1, paragraph 3 of the electoral regulations for the people's councils.

18. According to unofficial calculations, there were over a dozen such cases across the country.

19. Through the State Electoral Commission, a total of fourteen protests were submitted to the Supreme Court. Not all of them were settled by the end of September. So far, in only one case the Court ruled the election of one councillor to be invalid, which means that repeat elections would have to be held. Cf., the reports in *Trybuna Ludu*, August 30, 1984, p. 4, and September 25, 1984, p. 5.

20. This assertion was justified at length by Sylwester Zawadzki: "Ewolucja knocepcji socjalistycznego parlamentu w Polsce Ludowej" (The Evolution of the Concept of a Socialist Parliament in People's Poland), *PiP* 7 (1984), pp. 17-36.

21. This demand was repeated at a meeting of the Sejm presidium with the presidia of Sejm committees on April 27, 1983. Cf. the relevant report in *Trybuna Ludu*, April 28, 1983, p. 2.

22. E.g., Zdzislaw Jarosz, "Konstytucyjna regulacja struktury i funkcjonowania Sejmu" (The Constitutional Regulation of the Structure and Functioning of the Sejm), *PiP* 4 (1983), pp. 3-4.

23. Through a Sejm resolution of July 21, 1982 (*M.P.*, no. 18, item 146).

24. This is in addition to fifteen committees corresponding to the ministries or branches of the economy, which deal respectively with (1) the administration, regional planning, and environmental protection; (2) construction and the building materials industry; (3) mining, energy, and the use of natural resources; (4) transport and communications; (5) culture; (6) national defense; (7) education, science, and technology; (8) economic planning, budget, and finance; (9) welfare policies, health, and physical culture; (10) industry; (11) agriculture, the food industry, and forestry; (12) the home market, small industry, and services; (13) internal affairs and justice; (14) foreign affairs; (15) economic cooperation with other countries and maritime economy.

25. This happened in March 1981. Jan Szczepanski wrote about the Sejm's activity in filling the role of an arbitrator in "Blaski i cienie Sejmu" (The Bright and the Dark Sides of Sejm Work), *Odrodzenie*, special edition of May 7, 1983, p. 2.

26. Their legal nature was explained by Andrzej Gwizdz, "Uchwaly Sejmu okreslajace podstawowe kierunki dzialalnosci panstwa" (Sejm Resolutions Defining the Basic Directions of State Activity), *PiP*, 11 (1976), p. 11 ff. Cf. also, Wojciech Sokolewicz, *Konstytucja PRL po zmianach z 1976* (The Polish Constitution after the 1976 Amendments), (Warszawa: n.p. 1978), pp. 100–102.

27. *M.P.*, no. 5, item 20.

28. The law of October 8, 1982, on trade unions (*Dz. U.*, no. 32, item 216). The experimental character of this law is emphasized in its text, namely, in article 53, paragraph 6, which puts the Council of State under the obligation to examine the course of implementation of the law after consulting trade unions, three years after the date the law comes into force, i.e., from October 11, 1982, and if necessary, to propose amendments to the law.

29. The internal regulations of the Council of State have never been published and are unknown to the public.

30. One example is the Council of State resolution of June 19, 1981, regarding the binding interpretation of article 45, paragraphs 1 and 2, of the law on the people's councils (*M.P.*, no. 16, item 125). The interpretation provided by Council of State explains many technical problems connected with the appointment of local administration chiefs.

31. For more on this subject, see Adam Lopatka, "Nouvelle Regulation du Controle des Publications et des Spectacles en Republique Populaire de Pologne," *Droit Polonais Contemporain*, 3-4: 51–52 (1981), pp. 5–13.

32. On the basis of the law of October 8, 1980, amending the law on trade unions (*Dz. U.*, no. 22, item 83), the Council of State defined in its resolution the principles and mode of registration of trade unions (*M.P.*, no. 22, item 104). It is interesting to note that this resolution of the Council of State is dated September 13, 1980; i.e., it preceded by almost a full month the coming into force of the law on the basis of which it was issued. The lack of attention to legal detail is easily explained by the political fervor of those days. With reference to the Council of State's action in 1982, see in particular article 35, paragraph 6, and article 53 of the law of October 8, 1982, on trade unions.

33. The social consultative commissions were set up on the basis of the resolution of the Council of State of October 12, 1982, concerning the principles and methods of setting up trade union organizations in factories and institutions (*Dz. U.*, no. 34, item 222), and dissolved on the basis of the Council of State resolution of February 16, 1984 (*Dz. U.*, no. 13, item 52). For a lawyer, it will be interesting to note both resolutions were promulgated in *Dziennik Ustaw* rather than in *Monitor Polski*, where Council of State resolutions are usually published. The reason why this happened is that these are examples resolutions of the Council of State that function as executive orders. The constitution does not provide for the possibility of executive orders being issued by the Council of State. Therefore, when it is necessary to issue an executive act to implement a law of a generally binding nature and affecting the area of civil rights and when for some reason it would not be appropriate for the government to issue such an act, passage is delegated to the Council of State by including in the law a resolution that is de facto a quasi-order.

34. Cf. the law of June 24, 1983, on social labor inspection, and in particular article 23 thereof (*Dz. U.*, no 35, item 163).

35. This is what some Western authors appear to suggest: e.g., George Sanford, "The Executive in a Communist Political System: The Polish Case" (manuscript), a report presented at a conference of the European Consortium for Political Research in March/April 1981 at Lancaster University, which dealt with "Patterns of Executive Arrangements Across the World."

36. E.g., at its meeting on September 17, 1984, the government presidium examined the "sociopolitical situation in higher schools," among other topics. Cf. the *Trybuna Ludu* report, September 18, 1984, p. 1.

37. The powers of the Council of Ministers with regard to planning are defined in detail by the law of February 26, 1982, on socioeconomic planning (*Dz.U.*, no. 7, item 51). The lack of a modern law on the structure and powers of the government planning commission, taking into consideration the requirements of the economic reform, is a certain shortcoming. Cf. Kazimierz Strzyczkowski, "Problem ustawowej regulacji organizacji i funkcjonowania Komisji Planowania przy Radzie Ministrow" (The Problem of a Legislative Settlement of the Organization and Functioning of the Government Planning Commission), *PiP*, 6 (1984), pp. 96 ff.

38. By a resolution of the Council of Ministers, no. 168 (December 2, 1983), concerning the establishment of the Committee of the Council of Ministers for the Observance of Law, Public Order, and Social Discipline (*M.P.*, no. 39, item 227). The resolution gives the name of the chairman of the committee, who happens to be the current minister of internal affairs (paragraph 5, point 1).

39. This problem is currently regulated by the law on the universal duty of defense of the Polish People's Republic, as published in the full text, taking into account the amendment of November 21, 1983, published as an annex to an announcement of the minister of national defense of February 3, 1984 (*Dz.U.*, no. 7, item 31).

40. As he introduced the draft law at a plenary meeting of the Sejm, deputy Zenon Wroblewski observed that it incorporated "among other things, the experience gained by the Military Council of National Salvation (WRON)," *Trybuna Ludu*, November 22, 1983, p. 5. It is worth noting that shortly after the proclamation of martial law and the establishment of the WRON, there were isolated suggestions that the WRON deserved to become a permanent element of the system of exercising power.

41. Announcement of the chairman of the Council of Ministers of July 22, 1984 (M.P., no. 20, item 135).

42. Cf. for instance, Marian Rybicki, "Pozycja ustrojowa rzadu w systemie politycznym PRL" (The Position of the Government in the Political System of the Polish People's Republic), *PiP*, 10 (1982), p. 42.

43. By the Council of Ministers Resolution No. 190, of September 1982, concerning the establishment of the government Committee for Youth Affairs (*M.P.*, no. 23, item 194).

44. The composition and activity of the Legislative Council is at present regulated by the Council of Ministers' Resolution No. 46 of March 30, 1984 (*M.P.*, no. 10, item 66). The Consultative Economic Council was set up on the basis of the Council of Ministers Resolution No. 65 of April 1, 1982 (*M.P.*, no. 11, item 77). It is interesting to note that the resolution defines the Consultative Economic Council as a consultative organ of the Council of Ministers, the Government presidium, and the chairman of the Council of Ministers that works "independently."

45. The Council of Ministers Resolution No. 195 of September 3, 1982, concerning the establishment of the Public Opinion Research Center (*Dz.U.*, no. 7, item 31).

46. The law of July 14, 1983, on the Office of Minister of Internal Affairs and the scope of powers of the organs subordinated to him (*Dz.U.*, no. 38, item 172).

47. The need for such a law was convincingly justified by Jerzy Ciemniewski, "Niektore zagadnienia struktury rzadu PRL" (Selected Aspects of the Structure of Poland's Government), *PiP*, 8 (1981), pp. 42–57.

48. Although the law on worker self-management had been adopted on September 25, 1981, the stimulus to its implementation was only provided by the Sejm resolution

of June 29, 1983, on the further development of employees' self-management in state-owned enterprises (*M.P.*, no. 23, item 126). Other laws are as follows: the law of October 8, 1982, on socioprofessional farmers' organizations (*Dz.U.*, no. 32, item 217); the law of May 4, 1982, on higher education (*Dz.U.*, no. 14, item 113); the law of May 26, 1982, on the bar (*Dz.U.*, no. 16, item 124); the law of July 6, 1982, on legal consultants (*Dz.U.*, no. 19, item 145).

49. The theoretical assumptions of the new law are discussed in detail by Wojciech Sokolewicz, "Samorzad terytorialny w panstwie socjalistycznym" (Local Self-Government in a Socialist State), *Nowe Drogi* 1, (1983), pp. 45-63; "Samorzad terytorialny—o jaki nam chodzi" (Local Self-Government—What Do We Want It to Be?), *Trybuna Ludu* of December 16, 1982, and December 17, 1982; *Wokol zalozen do nowej ustawy o radach narodowych* (Discussing the Proposed Shape of the New Law on the People's Councils), (Warszawa: n.p. 1981), "Ustawa lipcowa posrod innych zrodel prawa" (The July Law Among Other Sources of Law), *Rada Narodowa-Gospodarka-Administracja* of January 14, 1984, pp. 31-35.

50. As authorized by the law, they are enumerated in the Council of Ministers' executive order of April 13, 1984, defining the kinds of state-owned enterprises, plants, and other state-run units subordinated to people's councils in individual units (*Dz.U.*, no. 25, item 127).

51. A critical explanation of the new legislation in this respect can be found in Henryk Rot, "Prawo miejscowe" (Local law), *PiP* 2 (1984), pp. 3-17.

52. For more on the matter, see Barbara Zawadzka *Nowa pozycja prawna prezydium rady narodowej* (The New Legal Situation of the Presidium of a People's Council), *PiP* 6 (1984), pp. 38-51.

53. Interesting remarks on the possibility of constitutional reform were formulated by Leszek Garlicki, "Konstytucja i nauka prawa konstytucyjnego (W zwiazku z praca 'Konstytucja PRL po 30 latach jej obowiazywania')" (The Constitution and the Science of Constitutional Law [in connection with the work 'Poland's Constitution after 30 years in force']), *PiP* 8 (1984), pp. 93-94.

Editors' note: In those instances above where "n.p." has been inserted, it should be understood that publisher information was not available in the manuscript sent to the United States and could not easily be obtained.

PART TWO

Social Structures and Attitudes

The second essential ingredient in understanding contemporary Poland itself and the interaction between the Polish state and society is the structure of that society. Although there are obvious continuities between prewar and postwar Poland, both Wladyslaw Markiewicz and Wladyslaw Piwowarski stress that Poland has become a very different national society since World War II. The achievement of a homogenous nation-state is, for them, both an accomplishment that laid to rest tensions previously existing among social groups and the source of a major portion of the present dilemma.

Markiewicz sums up the changes that have taken place in terms of three patterns. First, Poland today is a culturally homogeneous nation with little in common with the ethnic diversity characteristic of historic Poland. No longer is there the problem of national minorities. Second, the shifting of frontiers westward and the subsequent resettlement of millions of people brought with them a radical reconstitution of the Polish nation in such a way that it has become a very different national community, one in which previous social differences and class divisions have little relevance to understanding present realities. Third, the majority status of the Roman Catholic faith, coupled with the disappearance of alternative religious traditions, has introduced a social bond among the Polish people transcending all other crosscutting ties and cleavages.

Although Markiewicz touches on the religious factor only in passing and moves on to discuss in more detail the primacy of the working class, the peasantry, and these professional groups that fall within the category of intelligentsia, Piwowarski fills in with precision the extent of popular commitment to the Roman Catholic faith as a basic social fact. Piwowarski points out that the church is one of the few, if not the only institution providing horizontal ties cutting across the nation; it is, in short, the primary force integrating and maintaining the cohesiveness of the national community. Furthermore, because political pluralism cannot be expressed openly, writes Piwowarski, different philosophies of life and competing value preferences take the form of a cultural pluralism that is tolerated within the institutional church. That tolerance for diversity in social values, in turn, has solidified the church's ties with the people independently of the state apparatus, which is maintained from above and from without.

When Piwowarski's interpretation of the statistics on religious practice is combined with Markiewicz's synthesis of Poland's present social structure, the dilemma faced by the authorities in social policy becomes much clearer. The leveling and reordering of Polish society in the interests of socialism was a major objective in consolidating a socialist state. But once accomplished, this has had the effect of increasing the dichotomy between state and society and strengthening the role of the church as an institution opposed to the monopoly of power exercised by the authorities in imposing their will over society.

3

Change in Social Structure and the Increased Significance of the Working Class

Władysław Markiewicz

In contemporary sociology, the term *social structure* is one of the most important analytical tools, indispensable both in theoretical deliberations and empirical studies. However, because the term is widely applied in most social sciences, its meaning is anything but uniform. In this chapter I shall be using a more or less standard definition of this notion. By social structure, I mean the patterns, the mutual relationships, and the functional subordination of the component parts of social communities of different kinds, as well as the system of interdependencies between people, distances, and hierarchy in nonorganizational and organizational institutional forms.

Given such a broad understanding of the term, it can be assumed that almost every student of either past or present social reality occupies himself with one of the elements or aspects of social structure. As a result, there is an enormous wealth of literature on the subject, one that is impossible to digest even if one wishes to limit oneself just to bibliographical items concerning a definite society at a given stage of its development—as I will do in this paper, focusing on Polish society during the past forty years of socialist rule in the country.

During this period, the works of Stanislaw Ossowski, Jan Szczepanski, Wlodzimierz Wesolowski, Jerzy Wiatr, Stanislaw Widerszpil, Michal Pohoski, and other authors have laid a solid theoretical and methodological foundation for studies of change in social structure. These rely largely on original assumptions, due especially to the fact that Marxist conceptions of structural change have been purified by removing their earlier dogmatic distortions. Such distortions can be seen in the previous perception of only the class and strata dimensions of these changes, as opposed to the later enrichment of these phenomena with rational inputs from other contemporary conceptions of social stratification. This applies in particular to Robert K. Merton's *Social Theory and Social Structure*, which appeared in a Polish translation only in 1982 but was known and highly considered in Poland shortly after it was first published.

At the same time, after sociology was revived in Poland in 1956, broad empirical studies were begun on the structure of postwar Polish society and its component parts, such as social classes and strata, selected professional, regional, and generational groups. The working class, the peasantry, and the intelligentsia received the most attention in these studies launched and directed by such social scientists as Josef Chalasinski, Julian Hochfeld, Jan Szczepanski, Stefan Nowalowski, Stefan Nowak, Adam Sarapata, Bohdan Galeski, Jolanta Kulpinska, Dyzma Galaj, and many others.

The initially uncoordinated empirical studies and fieldwork, not always involving coherent research methods and techniques, were coordinated some years ago under a special project entitled "The Structure of and the Changes in Contemporary Polish Society." At first this project was supervised by Wlodzimierz Wesolowski; at present, Kazimierz Doktor is in charge of it. This project is part of a broad comparative study involving sociologists from various socialist countries under a program of multilateral cooperation among the academies of sciences in the socialist countries and some capitalist ones, including Finland, the United States, Sweden, and Britain.

Despite the successful development of studies of the transformation of social structure in Poland and the involvement of a considerable number of people and amount of funds, we still do not have and will probably not have for many more years a complete picture of contemporary Polish society at our disposal. This became particularly conspicuous in the years 1980–1981.

The Change in Postwar Polish Society

On the basis of the current state of research, we can say relatively little about the way in which the Polish society has changed as a result of fundamental transformations in its ethnic structure over the past forty years. On the strength of the Yalta and Potsdam agreements regarding the new place of the Polish state on the postwar map of Europe and the subsequent voluntary and forced relocation of the population, Poland became basically a uniform nation in terms of nationality. So-called alien ethnic groups of minorities as a consequence account for a very small proportion of the population of Poland, totally insignificant from a statistical point of view. This change was quite a shock, in comparison to the prewar period. Before the war, all regions in Poland had an ethnically mixed population, while Poles (who considered themselves to be the main—or according to the right-wing nationalist political parties—the only rightful citizens and masters of the state) were quite often in the minority, especially in the eastern regions. During the Second Republic (1918–1939) the problem of coexistence with these ethnic minorities was at the center of attention all the time, preoccupying public opinion, being exploited on the political scene, and affecting internal and international relations. At present, this issue no longer plays any role whatsoever, especially in the consciousness of the younger generation.

Generally speaking, the multinational nature of Polish society was the source of its weakness and caused a great deal of trouble. The conflicts and antagonisms among individual nationalities, often deliberately stirred up and kept alive by various forces, diverted society's attention from constructive efforts serving the good of all or the shared interests of the largest social classes and strata within individual ethnic groups. The conflicts also contributed to the perpetuation of various negative stereotypes and national phobias, lending credibility to the theory propounded by German chauvinists regarding the emphemeral character of the Polish state decreed at Versailles.

The fact that the socialist Polish state has been freed of the burden of coexistence with members of other nationalities, which previously accounted for a third of the country's population, is satisfying, but only moderately so. Today we are aware that when there are many cultures present in one area, the individual nationalities may develop cultural traits and customs enriching their adaptability, develop sensitivity to the needs and aspirations of other people, learn from one another to live a better, worthier, and more attractive life. In other words, we are aware that both our national culture and the culture of those ethnic groups with whom we coexisted have suffered in a way that is difficult to measure from separation and that these losses should be offset. This compensation may assume the form of development and the intensification of contacts and cooperation with other nations in culture, science, and travel.

Another outcome of the new geopolitical position of the country, extremely important from the point of view of the transformation of the cultural personality of the Polish nation, were the changes in the regional structure of the country. Moving the frontiers westward resulted in the disappearance of unique regions where a kind of frontier life-style and customs had been cultivated for ages, along with different political thinking, which had exerted considerable influence on the attitudes and behavior of society at large.

At the same time, unprecedented regional communities evolved in the Western territories as a result of the clash and diffusion of the cultures of the groups of people who came there from various parts of Poland and Europe. The processes of sociocultural adaptation and integration and the formation of a new society have been the object of special attention by Polish sociologists from the very beginning and have largely remained so until today.

The regional communities of central Poland, left intact by the shifting of frontiers, were also significantly changed because they, too, had to absorb migrants from other areas during the period of mass population movements. To sum up, it can be said that the regional structure of postwar Poland is largely dissimilar from the historical patterns characteristic of Poland before the war.

Another consequence of the geopolitical changes caused by the war and the accompanying demographic process was a radical change in the structure of religious faiths in Poland. The supremacy of the Roman Catholic faith became overwhelming and it is even possible to speak of its monopolistic position in that part of society that professes any religion. To illustrate this supremacy, it suffices to say that the Roman Catholic Church has over 16,000 churches and other places of worship and 21,000 priests, while all the remaining registered confessions have among them a mere 1,388 places of worship and 1,628 clergy. Besides, in the case of non-Catholic faiths, these are mainly small scattered facilities with nonprofessional priests, whereas in the Catholic church these are powerful religious centers with a numerous and well disciplined staff of clergymen.

As with the ethnic question, the appearance of a kind of monopoly in the domain of religion has had positive as well as negative social, moral, and cultural effects. On the one hand, it is a good thing to have a society that is not threatened by fratricidal religious wars and clashes, but on the other, it is more difficult to instill the virtues of humility, modesty, and tolerance in such a society.

Changes in the Composition of Social Classes and Strata

The changes in social structure and international position caused directly by the different shape and geopolitical location of Poland were accompanied by equally profound changes in the structure of social classes and strata. These involved changes in occupational, educational, and cultural structures as a consequence of the people's democratic revolution and the process of building socialism. Both the external and the internal factors, responsible for the changes in the composition and structure of Polish society and the place of the Polish state in Europe and the world, were interrelated and affected each other.

The classes comprising great capitalists, aristocracy, and large landowners, which de facto decided the fate of the nation and state previously, have now disappeared from the Polish social landscape. The occupying German forces deprived these classes of their attributes of power and of course killed a large proportion of them; thus, the elimination of these classes in Poland proceeded relatively smoothly, compared to the case in other countries where this often occurred in a dramatic way bordering on civil war. The ease of this change means that both the intensity of the hatred of these classes by those who expropriated them really was not great and resistance to the expropriation and deprivation of privileges was not very fierce.

The place vacated by the propertied classes, toppled as a result of agrarian reform and the nationalization of industry, was taken by the formerly oppressed and exploited classes, that is, workers and the peasants allied with them.

Today, after forty years, the above statement still attests to the fact that the collective political promotion of the working class, recognized as the hegemonic power and actual ruler of the popular state, started revolutionary and irreversible transformations in the structure of authority and the system of government. Even though these changes were not always introduced aptly and were sometimes opposed, they promoted democratization. These actions, in turn, accelerated cultural, material, and spiritual growth within the working class, in accord with advances elsewhere in industrialization and urban growth. They also produced a fundamental rearrangement of relations among the individual classes, strata, and professional groups and by the same token, also in the psychology of the Polish nation. From this moment on, the nation became increasingly vigilant about not allowing hierarchy or a division of labor in society based on level of economic development to contradict the socialist principles of equality and social justice. In other words, irrespective of the role assigned to the working class in the actual running of the state on a daily basis, the very fact that this class was proclaimed as the leading social force responsible for the nation and its successful development was tantamount, according to the masses, to the state's assuming an obligation to respect the striving for equality and justice stemming from the historical mission of the revolutionary proletariat. This remained the case even when conditions were unfavorable for the realization of these ideals, as witnessed by the fate of self-government institutions and workers' councils and the bureaucratization and alienation of the trade unions. Whenever the authorities became too tolerant of marked deviations from the social rules recognized by the postwar society as inviolable, the working class demanded their restoration in its characteristically firm and violent manner.

The peasant class was much slower than the workers to realize the significance of the change in social relations. As the Polish sociologist Jozef Chalasinski would say, the new system made it possible for this class to become a full-fledged member of the nation. But errors and distortions in farming policy were responsible for the fact that during certain periods farmers were regarded not just as a passive force but even as one that allegedly slowed down the process of building socialism.

The economic and social promotion of the peasant class was manifested by the elimination of extreme poverty in the countryside, the existence of which before the war was attributed to a population surplus estimated at some eight million people. In the first postwar years the surplus was still in excess of three million people. However, as a result of an intensive development policy, so many new jobs were created that eventually not only was the whole surplus absorbed, but also a dramatic increase in the employment of women and an excessive drain of manpower from the countryside occurred, while the class of part-time workers/part-time peasants became quite numerous.

Despite unquestionably fundamental changes, it will certainly be a long time before the social and technical reconstruction of the countryside and agriculture is sufficiently advanced to guarantee implementation of the authorities' plans for ensuring self-sufficiency in food production. It must be realized that the expectations placed on the intensification of farming by those in society yearning for a better life will not be fulfilled unless farmers and their hard work receive greater appreciation and support from other sectors of society. The revival of genuine peasant self-government bodies, thoughtlessly disbanded some time time ago, is an indispensable requirement for raising the prestige of farmers' work and according to the farmers the position they deserve as the providers of the nation and the closest ally of the working class.

Poland's transition from an agricultural into an industrial-agricultural country resulted in an exceptionally fast growth in the number of white-collar workers, commonly referred to as the intelligentsia. The factor distinguishing the intelligentsia from other social strata is their educational status. As a result of the educational revolution, the number of university graduates rose from 80,000 right after the war to over 1 million in 1980. There are also 6 million holders of secondary-school diplomas. Among the people employed in the public sector of the economy, the proportion of those without university or secondary-school education dropped from 76.8 percent in 1958 to some 25 percent at present. This testifies to the mass educational and cultural advancement of workers and peasants, as it is from these classes that today's members of the Polish intelligentsia come. In recent years however, it is the offspring of the intelligentsia who have obtained higher or secondary education, and educational aspirations of youth from working-class and peasant backgrounds have declined.

The popular democratic revolution made possible a relatively unrestrained development of private trades and small-scale retailing and service activities in the period of postwar reconstruction. During this time the petite bourgeoisie demonstrated an unusual ability to survive during the plagues that affected them from time to time. They were treated by the doctrinaires of those times as an indispensable evil and a transitional formation, decadent in both the economic and the moral sense. Despite these vicissitudes they have remained miraculously as a lasting element in the social structure of Polish socialism.

The Factors Accelerating Changes in Social Structure

The chief elements in the social structure were shaped as a result of the territorial and political changes outlined above. They have retained this same basic form until now, although changes have been taking place both within the classes and strata I have mentioned and in relations among individual strata. The main factors accelerating such change have been the rapid rate of industrialization and the accompanying urban growth, although the latter has not always kept pace with the former. The needs expressed in industrialization and urbanization for a highly qualified work force were in turn the most important factors determining the scope of a unique cultural revolution.

Although the industrialization of the country had already begun in the 1947–1949 Three-Year Plan, it was not until the Six-Year Plan 1950–1955 that official recognition was given to basic industrialization as the means for laying the foundations of socialism in Poland. Continued in subsequent five-year plan periods, this led to fundamental changes in social structure. Above all, the policy of industrialization resulted in dramatic changes in the composition of society, with workers becoming the largest social class. Whereas before the war they accounted for 28.6 percent of the population, today manual workers and their families number some 20 million people altogether and they represent about 54 percent of the population of the country.

Initially, the rural population was the main source of manpower for industry, but youth who have learned a trade in vocational schools have begun to play a larger role in recent years. These schools have been training more than 250,000 workers every year. Young people under thirty years old still predominate among blue-collar workers; of these, some 50 percent come from non-working-class families—in other words, they are first generation workers. Growth in the workers' qualifications has proceeded along with advances in mechanization and automation of production processes, especially in power generation, the steel industry, the extractive industries, and the textile industry. Totally new industries, sometimes rather pompously referred to as "national industries," have developed in socialist Poland. These include, for example, shipbuilding, the motor industry, and the chemical industry. Although in 1958 only 10.5 percent of workers had more than a primary education, in 1968 the proportion had risen to 21 percent, and at present almost half of all workers have secondary-school diplomas.

Naturally, the creation of a huge industrial potential, which now is a major source of national income and crucial for the maintenance and development of the country, significantly strengthened the position of the working class in society. Its hegemonic role in social and political life is quite conspicuous as a result.

The slogan regarding the leading role of the working class has, however, in the long run become a cliche. Furthermore it has begun to function in an ambivalent manner in social perceptions, as is consistent with such products of the imagination. On the one hand, part of the public has begun to believe that workers and their families are, by virtue of their membership in that class, overprivileged, relative to their real merits. This is a mystification, hiding the truth that many groups of workers fall below the national average with regard to wages, housing, health service, educational level, and accessibility to culture. In other words, it is still the workers that carry on their shoulders the main burden of the sacrifices that the Polish nation has to make because of its inherited backwardness and present aspirations. On the other hand, there is the argument about the leading role of workers in a socialist society. The way it is often formulated, especially various holidays and celebrations, frequently gives it the form of most harmful flattery. It serves to conceal the truth that the working class is often the breeding ground of such social ills as alcoholism, prostitution, juvenile delinquency.

Also hidden by such statements are the problems presented by whole groups of workers who display a very low work ethic, as manifested in absenteeism, high labor turnover, criminal waste, theft of public property, and so on. Also the principle of full employment can work both ways— even though it is regarded as one of the greatest achievements of the Polish working people, by creating a sense of security. For some, guaranteed employment has become the source of the will to work and an inducement to plan a life of their own and for their families over the long term; for others it has become an excuse for disregarding others, carelessness, and the lack of respect for any discipline.

However one looks at it, the raising of a work ethic among the working class and the awakening of motivation to perform good work is decisive now for the country's future and it will be even more important in the future. The consumer aspirations of predominantly young workers are disproportionate to their skill potential and unmindful of the necessity of improved working conditions in the approaching age of microelectronics and robotization. Naturally, the quality of work does not solely depend on a worker's subjective attitude but rather on the improvement and modernization of the system of operations in the whole national economy and its individual sectors. Present Polish authorities are aware of this, and for this reason they have embarked on an extremely ambitious program of reforming the national economy and management methods in industry. This program includes the creation of conditions for freer activity in self-governing workers' organizations and trade unions, independent of centralist bureaucratic restraints.

Industrialization exerted a great influence on the Polish rural population, which as I mentioned before, has been the main source of the work force for industry. The structure of both the farming and the peasant class underwent profound changes in the four postwar decades. In the years 1944–1949, after the forced breakup of large landed estates, concepts about farming focused on family farms. State farms, then accounting for some 10 percent of the country's farmland, were meant to be centers of culture and progress in farming. Then in the years 1950–1955, farm collectivization was imposed by force. This policy was soon abandoned, but the doctrine of the collectivization of farming remained in force until 1980. Only in 1981 were family farms officially recognized as a lasting element in the Polish economy; a constitutional amendment was even introduced to this end.

Poland now has the most backward farm structure in Europe. There are some 2.5 million farms with an area exceeding 1 hectare, the average size being 5.5 hectares. There has been hardly any change in this respect over the past four decades. Peasants and their families number some 7 million, while another 8 million inhabitants of the countryside work outside agriculture, mainly as manual workers. Members of farming cooperatives constitute another 150,000, an insignificant proportion of the working population in the countryside. State-owned farms exert a much larger influence on the social and cultural situation of rural Poland. These farms employ a total of half a million people, or just under 8 percent of the total number of the people employed in agriculture. Altogether, the public sector of agriculture employs about 1 million people, or 18 percent of total agricultural employment, if employees of farming circles and of cooperatives are included in the calculation.

The excessive fragmentation of Polish agriculture is responsible for the fact that the amount of farming machinery is highly unsatisfactory and that productivity remains very low—despite the fact that production has doubled over the past forty years. Inadequate progress in the modernization of farming is responsible for Poland's not yet attaining self-sufficiency in food production, despite having every opportunity to do so. This is due as much to errors in farming policies as it is to an essentially antiagrarian strategy of industrial development—one that was never oriented toward the satisfaction of the needs of farming. Only over the past several years have some attempts have made to restructure industry and increase significantly the volume of investment in farming.

Townspeople, including those with relatives in the countryside, persistently maintain that while peasants may be working harder, they also live in prosperity and comfort. However, studies of family income show that despite a considerable recent improvement in the financial situation of the rural population, consumption in some groups of that population is lower than in towns. Furthermore, despite all the change for the better in recent years, the same can be said about standards in rural health service, housing, and culture. This should be viewed as the main reason for the migration of young people, especially girls, from the countryside to towns and the resulting process of the aging of farm owners, along with a growth in the number of farms without likely inheritors.

A characteristic of the development of the intelligentsia during the four decades in question, its numerical growth, is the permanent diversification of its internal structure. Sociologists refer to this as the process of professionalization, by which they mean that as various areas of collective life become more complicated because of technological and socioeconomic progress, professional specialization tends to become increasingly narrow, requiring clearly defined education. As a result of these tendencies, the intelligentsia, customarily treated as a fairly homogeneous social stratum possessing its own social ethos, has in fact become divided into different professional groups often quite isolated from one another. The social prestige of one group may differ considerably from that of another. The highest prestige is enjoyed by scientists, doctors, and engineers, whereas office workers and even teachers and people in managerial positions occupy relatively low rungs on the ladder of social recognition.

In this chapter I have been able to present only very superficially some fundamental elements of the changes in the structure of Polish society since the end of World War II. I have not dealt with other important and very interesting aspects of these structural transformations—such as changes in family life, relations among different generations, or leisure activities. However, the unquestionable fact transcending all others is that over the past forty years Poles have become a completely different nation from the one they used to be. For this reason this period can be recognized as a turning point in Poland's 1,000-year-old history.

4

Polish Catholicism as an Expression of National Identity

Władysław Piwowarski

One of the features of Polish Catholicism is its "mass" character. This means that it is professed and practiced by a majority of the people, in fact almost all members of the nation, regardless of social barriers or divisions. However, it seems that Polish Catholicism functions differently on a nationwide scale than on the level of everyday life.

At the national level, Catholicism manifests itself in so-called global professions of faith. This is especially clear in the high percentage of believing and practicing Catholics. This percentage basically did not change after World War II, and in some periods it actually increased. In this respect, Catholicism certainly has a specific character that finds its explanation in the historical and contemporary determinants of life in Polish society.

At another level, that of everyday life, Catholicism manifests itself in other parameters, especially in ideological ones where significant changes have occurred. What is more, these changes are similar to those that can be observed in Western societies; these changes lead to selective attitudes. In other words, with regard to universal trends, Polish Catholicism does not show any peculiar distinction except that perhaps such changes are slower in Poland because of the political situation—for instance, the absence of conditions contributing to the spread of materialism and consumption-oriented life styles.

Considering the above distinction between the two levels of Polish Catholicism, one should assume that the nation's religion is Catholicism, manifested at the level of the global society and global professions of faith. It is difficult to say to what degree religion should be understood as an expression of empirical reality, as a nonempirical phenomenon, or as something subordinated to the reality of the existing world.[1] Global professions of faith are deeply connected with national values, and this means that religion and patriotism are interdependent. Thus, what has to be dealt with here is the phenomenon of "civil religion"—one that comprises the values and patterns of behavior accepted by large numbers of people in society, regardless of the degree of their allegiance to religious institutions.[2]

The nation's religion constitutes a strong integrating factor as far as both consciousness and behavior are concerned. In the consciousness of Poles, religion and national values constitute an integral whole as an indivisible legacy of national culture that serves the common good. On the one hand, these values determine the content of "consensus" on a global scale, and on the other hand, they constitute a point of reference for religious and national identification. In the sphere of behavior, one should emphasize the mass dimensions of religious practices that unite participants regardless of their class, social environment, or professional status. Participation in these practices is often a manifestation of support for religious and patriotic values, as well as of religious and national identity. It needs to be stressed that the Poles' national identity is expressed through religious behavior rather than through religious beliefs.[1] That is why religious practices are important for research concerning the nation's religiosity.

As already mentioned, the nation's religiosity has not undergone fundamental change. Therefore, it is safe to speak about its relative continuity in spite of deep transformations in the sociocultural and political context. It is noteworthy that religious symbols established under definite historical conditions tend to survive even if the causes that ushered them in and the mechanisms that supported them have ceased to exist.

In light of the above remarks I shall discuss the historical and contemporary determinants of the nation's attitude toward religion that might otherwise be difficult to understand. Next, I shall present those global attitudes toward faith that influence the religious and national values, on which there is the most general "consensus." Finally, religious practices as a specifically Polish phenomenon will be examined.

The Historical and Contemporary Context of the Nation's Religion

In order to discuss the historical and contemporary context of Poland's religion, it is necessary to concentrate on institutional religion, that is, the Catholic church in Poland, both past and present. One need not prove that from time immemorial the church in Poland has remained in close union with the nation, its needs and problems. Besides the evangelical mission the church has always performed, its functions should be understood in a broader way. These, on account of the specific character of the nation's history, fall in the range of its pastoral duties. In other words, the church has fulfilled not only a religious mission but a patriotic one as well: It has united religion with the nation. "The Church becomes weak," wrote W. H. Riehl in the nineteenth century, "when it isolates itself from the Nation's life. . . . It becomes strong and gets younger when again it comes into contact with people and their practical needs."[3] These words may certainly be applied to the situation of the church in Poland today.

The church developed its activity, both of a religious and patriotic character, especially in times when the Polish nation was deprived of its own statehood (through partitions, occupation, war). Then the church not only opposed the policies of foreign governments (for which it suffered together with the whole nation), but it also defended religious and national values in times of menace. "These values," writes the Reverend J. Majka, "were so closely intermingled that disloyalty toward either of them was felt as disloyalty to both, which resulted in the deepened loyalty to national values and readiness to make sacrifices in their defense."[4] From this period comes that well-known saying "To be a Pole is to be Catholic" (*Polak-Katolik*). Foreign rulers of the nation were well aware of the fact that the church represented and expressed real aspirations of the nation; hence, these rulers combined anti-Polish activities with antichurch ones by interfering with the affairs of the church and limiting its rights and even its control over strictly religious matters. Nevertheless, the church continued to perform its religious and patriotic mission, in this way contributing to the integration of a divided or enslaved nation.

It should also be stressed that after World War II the church in Poland not only did not lose its former position, but actually strengthened it. In the new sociopolitical reality a separation between the church and the state was enforced. Moreover—in accordance with ideological assumptions—the so-called planned secularization campaign began. However, the Marxist-Leninist authorities needed legitimization in order to "develop roots" in the Polish nation. This was already expressed in an ambivalent attitude of the authorities to the church in the first few years after World War II. There was an attempt to find possibilities for cooperation, for example, the agreement between the state and the church concluded on April 14, 1950. The state needed the church's help in order to normalize social life in the regained territories incorporated into Poland after World War II. Without the church organization, neither complete normalization nor integration of these territories into the present area of Poland could have been possible.

Whether it was the state authorities' intention or not, the position and role of the church in Polish society grew stronger in the following period. Destruction of the so-called illegal and legal political opposition, liquidation of religious organizations, the breaking of the concordat with the Vatican, and so on and so forth, resulted in the creation, at least implicitly, of the church as the only opposition against the atheist state. The church was a force that the state could not ignore. J. Kondziela wrote that it was an opposition that put forth no political alternative ("cultural resistance, opposition without a name").[5]

This opposition existed throughout almost the whole postwar period until other forms appeared. Being aware of this, the Polish episcopate and especially the two primates—Stefan Cardinal Wyszynski and now Jozef Cardinal Glemp—spoke not only in the name of Catholics but also in the name of the whole nation. In spite of administrative pressures and struggle with the church, the state recognized and properly appreciated this role of the church in the Polish nation, and successive ruling teams turned to the church for help. During the time of unrest in the years 1956, 1968, 1970, and 1980, top representatives of the church issued appeals to the nation for realism, which were preceded by "summit talks" between representatives of the authorities and the church. Generally from the political point of view, the church in Poland—in spite of the clash between its own goals and aspirations and those of the authorities—found itself reckoned with by the authorities because of its respected social position and its capacity for influencing the whole nation.

The contemporary context in which the church exists is now defined not only by the political situation but also by hidden sociocultural pluralism. Although pluralism is a complex phenomenon, for the purpose of this analysis it will be treated separately and on two levels: social and cultural.

Pluralism is not ordinary multiplicity; it also involves competition. From the social point of view, it is difficult to speak of pluralism in a socialist state. The state seeks to subordinate all the signs and forms of social life to chief ruling centers serving a definite ideology. In this way, all social groups and institutions lose their autonomy, their activities attuned to the goals of socialist society. These structures become subordinated and perform tasks that are "assigned" to them by higher authorities. When there is a lack of autonomous social structures, a type of mass society with poor horizontal interaction exists. The church understood this situation from the beginning and that is why, like the state, it influenced the whole society through developing mass pastoral services. It was possible and necessary in Poland exactly because of the lack of social pluralism. What is more, the church performed not only a strictly religious mission, but it developed functions also on a broader scale as well, These functions had already ceased to exist in pluralistic societies—for instance, an integrative function, a protective one in relation to the nation, or a critical one in relation to the socialist system. Thanks to this wider role of the church, "planned secularization" has not succeeded in Poland; rather, the influence of atheistic institutions has been successfully neutralized by religious ones.

However, it should be emphasized that social pluralism—as an unavoidable result of change in developed societies—is weakly articulated in Poland, both in the church and in society. But cultural pluralism, understood as a variety of competing points of view or philosophies of life, is more visible. An example would be the popularization mentioned above of various attitudes toward religion. Contrary to the situation found in democratic societies, this pluralism has no institutional support. What this means is that cultural pluralism becomes individualized; it is isolated from the social context, and is reflected instead in the religious life of the nation.

These are the historical and contemporary factors explaining why Polish Catholicism has been the religion of the nation. These factors, on the one hand, help the church keep its high status and fulfill its broad functions, but on the other hand, they influence the retention of basic values cherished by the nation and legitimized by mass participation in religious services.

Table 4.1
Overall Attitudes Toward Faith Among the Adult
Population in Poland (percents)

Type of Response	1960 urban N=144	1960 rural N=1280	1978 urban N=2966	1978 rural N=1989
Deeply religious	19.4	26.1	11.9	25.9
Religious	56.2	57.7	63.7	68.3
Subtotal	75.6	83.8	75.6	94.2
Nonbelievers	3.1	1.1	12.8	1.9
Others (undecided, indifferent)	21.3	14.6	11.5	3.9
No answer	-	0.5	0.1	0.1
Total	100.0	100.0	100.0	100.0

Source: Center for Public Opinion Polls (OBOP).

General Attitudes Toward Religion

In Poland no denominational censuses are taken; therefore, it is not easy to establish the denominational structure of the whole population. Virtually the only source of this information is the investigations of the Center for Public Opinion Polls (OBOP), whose results are, however, rarely published. The information obtained is based on subjective statements—individual responses to survey questions. Nevertheless, this information has a certain value as it gives a general outlook of the structure of religious views on a nationwide scale. Let us direct our attention to two examples of this type of investigation, from the years 1960 and 1978, because no results for more recent years are available.[6] These polls seem to provide interesting information about the state of religion in Poland, if only because there is a prevailing opinion that recent years have brought about an increase in religious feelings.

As can be seen on the basis of both surveys in Table 4.1, the great majority of people in Poland declared themselves to be "deeply religious" or "religious." In 1960, this was true for some 75.6 percent of adult city inhabitants and 83.8 percent of inhabitants of rural areas, whereas in 1978, the respective indices were 75.6 percent and 94.2 percent. These figures clearly point to an increase of religious attitudes in rural areas.

The ratios of "deeply religious" persons remained on the same level, whereas those of "religious" ones increased by 10.4 percent in rural areas. Although in towns the percentage of "deeply religious" people dropped, that of "religious" ones increased. On the whole, the share of believers did not change. There are no data for 1960 for the percentage of "deeply religious" and "religious" people in Poland as a whole, without division into urban and rural areas. But in 1978 the total came to 86.3 percent.[7]

In spite of the increase in the percentage of believers in Poland, there was an increase, especially in urban areas, in the percentage of nonbelievers from 3.1 percent to 12.8 percent—with the 1978 average in Poland being 6.5 percent. At the same time, one can observe in both rural and urban settings a distinct drop in "undecided" and "religiously indifferent" attitudes. The drop has probably been even greater in recent years, given the revival of religious attitudes among intellectuals; this may also be the case with nonbelievers.

Research results from 1978 concerning religious attitudes of the respondents' parents are also of interest. Those investigated state that 89.8 percent of their fathers were "religious," among whom 26.8 percent were "deeply religious" persons, whereas there were 95.6 "believing" mothers, among whom 34.7 percent were "deeply religious." As for the percentage of nonbelievers, the numbers are 3.3 percent and 0.9 percent respectively.[8] It is difficult to speak of a distinction between "two generations" due to the varying age of the respondents. However, one may generally assume that the older generation of Poles is more religious than the younger one and that through the family atmosphere, the former has a positive influence upon the religious feelings of the younger generation. The author of these studies wrote, "In spite of the ideological differences between the younger generation and their parents, there exists a strong bond between religious traditions and national one on this level."[9]

For the purposes of comparison, it is worth citing the results of surveys carried out in 1978 of a representative sample of youth about to leave secondary school in Poland (see Table 4.2).[10]

Individual responses referring to the "past" reflect the situation when the investigated young people were under the influence of their family, whereas "present" means the period when they were under the influence of day school or boarding school. It turns out that in the "past" there were 89 percent of deeply religious and religious young people and only 2.8 percent of nonbelieving ones. As they came of age, however, a clear drop occurred in the percentage of believing young people in favor of nonbelief and religious indifference. Still, the percentage of the believing youth is high: 77.4 percent. As compared with the percentage for adults in the country (25–65 years old), it is lower by 8.9 percent. It should be noted that religious instruction has not affected the religiousness of the investigated youth even though the majority of them took advantage of optional religious instruction classes. Moreover, it seems that the decrease of the influence of the family upon the religious attitudes of youth is not properly offset by the influence of church-sponsored instruction classes.

A separate category of youth is made up of students as a whole. The Department of Sociology of Religion at the Catholic University of Lublin

Table 4.2
General Attitudes Toward Religion Among Youth in Final Year of Secondary Education in Poland (percents)

Type of Response N=8909	Past	Present
Deeply religious	12.4	12.8
Religious	76.6	64.6
Subtotal	89.0	77.4
Nonbelievers	2.8	8.4
Others (undecided, indifferent)	8.0	14.1
No answer	0.2	0.1
Total	100.0	100.0

Source: Center for Public Opinion Polls (OBOP).

has at its disposal three representative samples carried out in Gdansk (1972–1973), Katowice (1974–1975), and Bialystok (1978–1979). These data are contained in Table 4.3.

In the case of students it is difficult to speak of a decrease or increase in religious feelings because of the lack of research that could be repeated in the same environment. But according to data coming from different urban areas (see Table 4.3), it appears that the percentage of deeply religious and religious persons is relatively high: Gdansk, 73.2 percent; Katowice, 75.6 percent; and Bialystok, 78.6 percent. Atheistic attitudes are not very widespread among students. A relatively high percentage in Gdansk might have come as a result of different responses in the category of "nonbelievers": practicing nonbelievers, 1.2 percent; nonbelievers with certain doubts, 6 percent; nonbelievers of conviction, 9.4 percent; and those actively opposing religion, 0.4 percent. Perhaps if different criteria were applied, the first groups would be added to those indifferent to religion; in this case there would be 9.8 percent nonbelievers.

Comparing the percentage of deeply religious and religious persons in the above categories of those investigated in Poland, one can notice that the youth in their last year of secondary education show a higher level of faith than adults in the 25–65-years-old category in urban areas, whereas students remain almost at the same level as adults in this environment— although, generally, students exceed the education level of the latter. This points to the fact that global attitudes toward faith in Poland in the period after World War II were always characterized by high percentages. Moreover, in some periods these percentages were even growing. Their increase may

Table 4.3
General Attitudes Toward Religion Among Students
(percentages)

Type of Response	Gdansk N=564	Katowice N=624	Bialystok N=575
Deeply religious	7.5	6.7	17.6
Religious	65.7	68.9	61.0
Subtotal	73.2	75.6	78.6
Nonbelievers	17.0	8.3	7.8
Others (undecided, indifferent)	8.0	15.4	13.6
No answer	1.8	0.7	-
Total	100.0	100.0	100.0

Source: H. Klincewicz, "Postawy swiatopogladowe mlodziezy akademickiej na przykladzie Trojmiasta: Studium socjologiczne" (World Outlooks of Gdansk Students: A Sociological Study), (Lublin, 1975), manuscript in the Archives of the Catholic University of Lublin; P. Dronszczyk, "Dynamika postaw swiatopogladowych mlodziezy akademickiej a kierunek studiow na przykladzie studentow Katowic" (The Relationship Between Changes in World Outlooks of Katowice Students and Their Line of Study), (Lublin, 1976), manuscript in the Archives of the Catholic University of Lublin. Research in Bialystok was conducted by M. Wydra. These findings are being processed at present.

be noticed, especially in rural areas and lately perhaps also among the working class and in urban areas. A number of factors, processes, and facts have contributed to this situation: the election of a Pole as pope, the pope's visit to his fatherland, or the workers' revival movement associated with the church and supported by it.

There is no doubt that the foundations of this general profession of faith lie in national and family traditions that seek to unite faith with patriotism, religion with the nation, and to treat these values as the common good for all Poles. This means that faith so generally professed certainly functions better at the global level than at the level of everyday life. Individual declarations of faith are not the only indicator in this respect. A similar function is performed by religious practices that are also a phenomenon of a mass character.

Table 4.4
Frequency of Religious Practices Among Adults in Poland (percent)

Type of Response	1960 Urban Areas (N=1144)	1960 Rural Areas (N=1280)	1978 All Areas (N=4969)
Practicing regularly	35.6	46.7	48.3
Practicing irregularly	34.0	33.3	21.4
Carrying out some practice	17.9	12.8	15.2
Not practicing at all	12.3	6.3	14.1
No answer	0.2	0.9	1.0
Total	100.0	100.0	100.0

Source: A. Pawelcznska, "Postawy ludnosci wiejskiej wobec religii" (Attitudes of the Rural Population Toward Religion), in Roczniki Socjologii Wsi. Studia i Materialy, vol. 8 (1968), (Wroclaw, Warszawa, Krakow: 1970), p. 74. Data from 1978 were supplied by Dr. K. Darczewska.

General Attitudes Toward Religious Practice

Research conducted by OBOP indicates that ritualism constitutes a significant feature of Polish Catholicism. This is manifested in the growth of participation in religious practices along with a simultaneous reduction in ideology and in related aspects of religiousness. Table 4.4 gives some information about religious practices.

There is a discrepancy between the 1960 and 1978 data contained in Table 4.4. In the first case, the question was what was the individual's attitude toward religious practices in general and, in the second, it was what was the individual's attitude toward participation in Sunday Mass. Consequently, this means that the category "nonpracticing" in 1977 refers to those who did not attend mass during the whole preceding year, although they may well have participated in other religious ceremonies.

According to Table 4.4, the number of respondents who practice regularly is relatively high and, between 1960 and 1978 it increased. This gradual increase of participation in religious practices was noticed earlier, especially in rural areas. For example, A. Pawelczynska points out that in 1965 those practicing "systematically" amounted to 61.6 percent of the population of the countryside. In comparison to 1960, it increased by as much as 14.9

Table 4.5
Participation in Religious Practices Among Youth in Final Year of Secondary Education (percent)

Type of Response N=8909	Past	Present
Practicing regularly	77.9	57.2
Practicing irregularly	10.2	13.1
Executing some practices	7.5	16.0
Not practicing at all	3.3	12.8
No answer	1.1	0.9
Total	100.0	100.0

<u>Source</u>: Z. Kawecki, "Przemiany swiatopoglaewe mlodziezy," (Changes in World Outlooks of Youth), in T. M. Jaroszewsk: (ed.), Przemiany swiadomosci spoleczenstwa Polskiego (Warsaw, 1979), p. 205. The categories have been changed, but this has had no influence on the research results reported here (author).

percent. Unfortunately, there is no information for 1978 regarding the difference between urban and rural areas. Taking into consideration the increase in percentage of believers in rural areas, one can conclude that there is an increasing percentage of people in the "practicing regularly" category.

Joining these two categories of Catholics "practicing regularly" and "irregularly," which from another viewpoint overlaps with the category of "Sunday" Catholics, the following percentages can be obtained: in 1960—69.6 percent in urban areas and 80 percent in rural areas; in 1978—69.7 percent in urban areas and 80 percent in rural areas; in 1977—69.7 percent in the country as a whole. Such high percentages of religious practices are found in no other Catholic country. In order to obtain a full picture of the state of religious practice in Poland, one should also add here people who rarely practice, that is, practice only a few times a year. When these people are added, one obtains the following: 1960, 87.5 percent in urban areas and 92.8 percent in rural areas; and in 1978, 84.9 percent in the country as a whole.[11] But it should be mentioned once again that the latter percentages refer only to participation in Sunday Mass. It follows, therefore, that in Poland there are few people who do not practice at all.

Let us now proceed to the frequency of religious practices among youth about to leave secondary school. These data are found in Table 4.5.

Among young people in secondary education the proportion of those practicing regularly dropped as compared with the "past," whereas the percentage of people practicing irregularly increased, as did the number of people not practicing at all. Generally speaking, 95.6 percent of the youth engaged in religious practices more or less systematically in the "past," whereas immediately before examinations, 86.3 percent did so. This can be explained not only by the decrease of the influence of the family or the increase of the influence of atheism but also by the specific situation of this group. However, the percentage of practicing youth about to complete secondary education remains high.

The participation of students in religious practices is similarly high. In the cities mentioned in Table 4.3, 40-50 percent "regularly" participated in the Sunday Mass; 50-80 percent take communion at least once a year; 55-72 percent say prayers often if not every day; 75-80 percent take part in religious instruction at different levels.[12] The data point to the manifestation of "external" religiousness by students. The causes of this situation may be found in the cultural inheritance of religion and the family, in the influence of the church, in the specific Polish situation, which is favorable to the maintenance of religious tradition, and in the case of some, the influence of groups on religious experience and the choice of religion.

As was mentioned before, the high percentage of participation in religious practices does not always point to depth of experience and personal religiousness. A number of various motivations come into play here, from religious to socionational and political ones. Of particular significance is the participation in mass practices because this is connected with patriotic manifestations. Something like the identification of two spheres of life—religious and patriotic ones—occurs. This finds its expression especially in the cult of the Virgin Mary, which has become very widespread in Poland since World War II. Religious practices connected with the Icon of the Czestochowa Virgin Mary have become symbols of the identification between the nation and the church. These, above all, have sparked mass manifestations and religious experiences.

The foregoing descriptions and analyses are not complete because they show only a certain aspect of Polish Catholicism, namely to what extent it manifests itself in so-called general professions of faith. Nevertheless, these general professions of faith characterize Catholicism as the nation's religion in the best way. They find their justification both in the past and in the present, because the Polish nation has been living for over two hundred years in a similar situation. It is a nation with a peculiar faith and peculiar practices, but at the same time it is a nation defending its dignity, sovereignty, and freedom, a nation where religion and church play an outstanding role.

At present, the nation's religiosity is endangered not only by an atheistic ideology but also by an emerging pluralism, especially a cultural one. That is why the values constituting the bases of "consensus,"—religion and nation—are all the more felt. Moreover, participation in religious practices protects, legitimizes, and confirms these values.

Notes

1. Cf. R. Robertson, *The Sociological Interpretation of Religion* (Oxford, 1970), pp. 43–47.
2. Cf. R. N. Bellah, *Beyond Belief: Essays on Religion in a Post-Traditional World* (New York, 1970), esp. chapter 1 entitled "Civil Religion in America," pp. 168–189.
3. W. H. Riehl, *Land und Leute* (third ed.) (Stuttgart, 1856), p. 320.
4. J. Majka, "Historyczno-kulturowe uwarunkowania katolicyzmu polskiego" (Historical and Cultural Determinants of Polish Catholicism), *Chrzescijanin w Swiecie*, 12 (1980), p. 39.
5. J. Kondziela, "Sozialer und politischer Wandel in Polen und die gesellschaftliche Position der katholischen Kirche," in *Werte und Gesellschaft im Wandel*, Hrsg. K. Zapotoczky (Linz, 1978), pp. 105–106.
6. A. Pawelczynska, "Postawy ludnosci wiejskiej wobec religii" (Attitudes of the Rural Population toward Religion), in *Roczniki Socjologii Wsi. Studia i Materialy*, vol. 8 (1968) (Wroclaw-Warszawa-Krakow, 1970), p. 73.

K. Darczewska, "Religion et famille polonaise contemporaine," in *Religiousness in the Polish Society Life (Chosen Problems)*, ed. W. Zdaniewicz (Warsaw, 1981), pp. 151, 157.

7. Ibid., p. 157.
8. Ibid.
9. Ibid., p. 152.
10. Cf. Z. Kawecki, "Przemiany swiatopogladowe mlodziezy" (Changes in World Outlooks of Youth), in *Przemiany swiadomosci spoleczenstwa polskiego*, ed. T. M. Jaroszewski (Warsaw, 1979), p. 204.
11. Pawelczynska, "Postawy ludnosci," p. 76.
12. Cf. W. Piwowarski, "Idealy wspolczesnej mlodziezy polskiej," (The Ideals of Contemporary Polish Youth), *Collectanea Theologica* 51 (1981), fasc. II, p. 71.

PART THREE

Socioeconomic Change and Dislocations

Three crucial policy areas of importance to any development program are agriculture, industry, and urbanization. Since its beginnings, the building of a socialist state in Poland has been identified with the socioeconomic development of the country. The transformation of Poland from an underdeveloped to a developed state has centered on the promotion of heavy industry and balanced regional development, an increasingly urbanized population, and a commercialized agriculture attentive to supply and demand factors shaping the national economy.

The opening chapter in this section deals directly with the agricultural question. Manteuffel states straightforwardly the view that the basic problem in Polish agriculture is not the lack of productivity but the failure of the authorities to accept its vital private sector as a basic fact and to work constructively within the limits imposed by a de facto mixed rural economy. He then supports his position with ample statistics on Polish agriculture. The underlying theme in this chapter is the continuing productivity of the land, despite the constraints imposed, and the increase in yields that have been immediately forthcoming whenever the most minimal incentives have been given to private agriculture.

The chapter on regional differences examines the overall pattern of Poland's economic development in light of two basic dimensions: the marked regional contrasts with which the postwar state began (as a consequence of the movement of the borders westward and the integration of industrialized areas previously under German rule), as well as the policies that have been followed to create a more integrated national economy. The standard way of dealing with these contrasts in Poland is to differentiate among strong, medium, and weak regions. Despite the fact that the strongest regions, economically speaking, continue to be in the west and in the center (around Warsaw) and the weakest are in the east, the cumulative impact of postwar economic expansion and infrastructure integration has been to raise overall living levels. This pattern, however, came to an end in 1980 and what Kruczala emphasizes is the deterioration of the economy since then, as seen from the regions, and the fact that the impact of this deterioration has been the greatest on the most developed areas.

Although Kruczala touches on this point only in passing, others have emphasized that the crux of the crisis that came to a head in 1980 was not so much its short-term political ramifications as its long-term economic prospects: the inability to reverse sustained economic decline, approaching breakdown. This theme is explicitly stated in the final chapter of this book. However, in order to understand this internal debate it is important to capture first the evolution that has occurred in rural-urban relationships, the impact of bureaucratization on social policy, the social-psychological dimensions of the crisis, and the prevailing structures of power.

Stasiak's chapter on rural-urban linkages and changes in population distribution complements Kruczala's discussion of regional differences. The essential idea stated here is the continued vitality of settlements in the countryside, in the midst of the shift of the majority of the population to urban areas. In order to understand the transformations that have occurred since World War II, the author engages first in a review of historic patterns of town-country relationships in Poland. From this base, he moves on to assess the social and technical infrastructure that has been developed to service rural and urban areas alike. Working within the context of a committee on regional development in the Polish Academy of Sciences, he reports the conclusion that bottlenecks in service delivery have been as great in urban as rural areas and that what is required is far greater decentralization—something past authorities have been unwilling to accept. What is of particular interest in his discussion of rural-urban linkages and the shift of the population to urban areas are his figures on the outflow of rural population from the least developed regions in the northeast and the relatively limited population loss in rural areas adjacent to the major urban and industrial centers.

Combined, these three chapters communicate the image of significant economic and social change in postwar Poland, generally favorable growth trends until the mid-1970s, and sustained crisis without resolution since 1980. The theme that begins to emerge here and that is reinforced in subsequent chapters is that Poland has reached the limits of growth possible under a centrally planned and directed economy. The cumulative crisis highlights the need for a fundamental change in socioeconomic policies as well as the inability to extricate these policies from political realities and to move out of the current stalemate.

5

Agriculture in Modern Poland

Ryszard Manteuffel-Szoege

As a result of the Potsdam and Yalta conferences held after World War II certain territorial changes took place in Poland: Poland's 1938 area of 389,720 square kilometers (38,972,000 hectares) shrank by 77,037 square kilometers. Therefore, today it amounts to 312,683 square kilometers (31,268,000 hectares). Simultaneously, Poland's territory moved westward, and in effect some one-third of the country's land in the west and north are territories regained after the war.

The State of Polish Agriculture After World War II

World War II caused enormous damage to the country's agriculture. This was especially true of its final year, when the whole war machine—the retreating Nazi armies and the victorious Red Army, supported by two Polish armies, rolled over the entire territory of the country. The majority of crops had not been gathered; the majority of fields, especially in the west and the north of the country, had not been sown with grain. Thus there was a tremendous drop in crop production in 1945. That year the statistical office hardly functioned, so there are no data available for this period. The first fragmentary postwar data refer to 1946, and there are additional fragmentary data for the years 1947–1949.

Nevertheless, accounts passed by word of mouth say that shortly after the end of the war in May 1945, agricultural production began to recover quickly. This can be also testified to by the data quoted in Table 5.1. Per hectare yields of basic crops in prewar and postwar Poland are shown in Table 5.2. When these data are compared, they show that per hectare yields of grain within the initial postwar years were lower by only 2 trundles as compared to the interwar period. Despite the remarkable drop in the country's population per square kilometer after the war, the yield per inhabitant was nearly equal, amounting to 4.14 quintals before the war and 4.35 quintals after the war.

Table 5.1
Harvest of Basic Crops in Poland Within Present
Borders Before and After World War II
(in millions of tons)

Annual Average	Grains	Potatoes	Sugar Beets
1934-1938	over 13.0	38.0	6.1
1947-1949	over 10.0	29.0	4.2

Source: Author's compilation from offical Polish sources.

Table 5.2
Per Hectare Yield of Basic Crops in Poland Within
Present Borders Before and After World War II
(in quintals)

Annual Average	Grains (4 types)	Potatoes	Sugar Beets	Pulse [a]	Rape [b]
1934-1938	13.8	138	265	10.2	-
1946-1949	11.8	121	180	10.5	8.4

Notes: a. Pulse refers to such edible seeds as peas, beans, or lentils.
b. Rape is a type of turnip grown for fodder and seeds used as bird food.
Source: Author's compilation from official Polish sources.

The years that followed saw further rapid growth of yields per hectare. Crop yields grew two-and-a-half times; oil plants, two to two-and-a-quarter times. Potato yields increased by 50 percent; those of sugar beets, by 60 percent and more. The only yields not to increase remarkably were those of papilionaceous plants grown from seed, and this happened because farmers had little interest in them. This was unfortunate because protein shortage remains among the country's most acute problems, and these plants provide an alternative source of protein.

In the latter part of the 1970s, however, this growth in crop yields ceased. This was due to exceptionally bad weather within two successive years, a drop in the production of mineral fertilizers, and the sociopolitical situation in the country.

Animal production also suffered an acute blow because of the war; yet it too showed rapid recovery immediately afterwards. Thus, livestock population initially decreased dramatically and so did yields per animal. Even though the livestock population was decimated during the final year of

Table 5.3
The Growth of Livestock Population in Poland
Within Present Borders (in millions)

Years	Cattle	Cows	Pigs	Sheep
1938	9.9	6.3	9.7	1.9
1946	3.9	2.7	2.7	0.7
1950	7.2	4.8	9.3	2.2
1955	7.9	5.4	10.9	4.2
1960	8.7	5.9	12.6	3.7

Source: Author's compilation from official Polish sources.

Table 5.4
Livestock Population per 100 Hectares of Farmland

Years	Cattle	Cows	Pigs	Sheep
1938[a]	47.6	30.2	46.4	9.3
1946[a]	19.1	13.4	13.1	3.6

Note: a. Within present borders.
Source: Author's compilation from official Polish sources.

the war, it quickly recovered in the years that followed. Then this development came to halt because of the accelerated collectivization of private farms in the years 1949-1953. This is illustrated by Table 5.3. The wartime drop in livestock population can also be seen by examining the decline in the number of animals per unit of area, in Table 5.4.

Immediately after the war, milk production per cow was dismally low, amounting to 1,200 liters per year. Although production today is still not very high, it is two-and-a-half times greater than it was right after the war. Also, per capita milk production is fairly high at present, despite a considerable growth in the number of inhabitants. It rose from 138 liters in 1946 to 310 liters in 1950 and 448 liters 1980.

Fatstock production also has risen over the years. Beginning with the extremely low level of 18 kilograms (kgs.) per capita in 1946, it increased to 68 kgs. in 1950 and to 123 kgs. in 1980. Fatstock production thus has more than quadrupled in Poland over the years since the war.

With regard to a general appraisal of the pace of growth of agricultural production in the four postwar decades, the pace has been similar to the growth rate of production in highly developed Western countries, but the gap between Poland and those countries has not been reduced. It is generally maintained that in the interwar period this gap amounted to thirty years and has remained unchanged to this moment, despite considerable production growth.

The Evolution of Agrarian Policy in Poland After World War II

Before the war, farms in Poland were classified into large holdings and smallholdings. The dividing line between the two ran at fifty hectares. However, because forests were included along with farmland before the war and have been placed outside agriculture since, it is necessary to exclude forests in order to compare the structure of agriculture before and after the war. In the interwar period, private farms above fifty hectares of farmland accounted for 18.0 percent of the overall farmland area in Poland, while farms of this size owned by corporate bodies accounted for another 5.7 percent; thus farms above fifty hectares of farmland accounted for 23.7 percent of the overall farmland area. In 1938, as a result of breaking up huge estates, this proportion was even smaller.

Consequently, large private farms before the war embraced a slightly smaller area than public-sector farms do today. To some extent, the latter are an equivalent of the huge estates before the war. For comparison, in 1946 the public sector of farming accounted for 6.9 percent of the total area of farmland in Poland. Another statistic for the purpose of comparison is the fact that the average size of one of the large holdings amounted to 413 hectares in the interwar period (1931).

The number of smallholdings in the interwar period was also similar to the number of private farms after World War II: 3.2 million. (This meant farms over 0.5 hectares of land.) In the interwar period, two-thirds of these farms did not exceed 5.0 hectares in size. The share of farms above 10 hectares was 11 percent. The average size of the farms above 0.5 hectares was 7.47 hectares of land and 6.68 hectares of farmland.

On September 6, 1944, the Polish Committee for National Liberation (which played the role of a parliament not yet formed) proclaimed a manifesto that settled agrarian matters in Poland. This occurred at time when Poland's eastern voivodships (or provinces) up to the Vistula had been liberated, but it was still before the war was over. One passage in the manifesto reads as follows: "The agrarian system in Poland will be based on strong, healthy farms, capable of efficient production, and being the private property of their owners." The promised land reform put the upper limit of farm size in principle at 50 hectares of farmland. In the former Western voivodships (Poznan, Bydgoszca and Silesia), where there was no land shortage, it was set at 100 hectares of farmland. This meant a limit on all farms, making them somewhat smaller than "socialized" farms are today. No Sejm act since has changed these principles, and they were reaffirmed by the Sejm law of July 1982.

As a result of the reform and of the settlement of the regained territories in the west and the north, peasants received 6,070,100 hectares of land after 1944. There were 814,000 new farms, while 254,400 farms were increased in size by an average of 1.9 hectares. The average size of a new farm in the "old Polish lands" (those originally forming the core of the Polish state) was 5.4 hectares. In the regained territories it was 7.9 hectares. As much as 95 percent of the land from the estates divided up in the old lands was given to farm workers, landless peasants, and smallholders. The rest was distributed among the owners of farms of an average size. In the regained territories, the land was mainly given to resettlers from areas that were incorporated into the Soviet Union and to smallholders from central and southern Poland.

In the period immediately after the regaining of independence, the direction of agrarian policy announced by the decree on agrarian reform of the Polish Committee of National Liberation was followed only to a limited extent. The new farms in the old territories were of a smaller size than the average farm had been in the prewar period; therefore, they did not contribute to an improvement in the overall farm size structure. However, the farms set up in the regained territories did not adversely affect the outcome, as their average size exceeded the average size of private farms before the war. But they were not very numerous. The agrarian structure was also improved by the 200,000-plus farms that increased in size. However, at the same time as the process of dividing up existing farms was moving ahead, for all effective purposes farm structure as a whole deteriorated. In the period up to 1950 the number of the smallest farms (those below five hectares of land) and the largest farms decreased, while the number of medium-size farms (those between five and fifteen hectares) increased. What this meant in practice was a trend toward the medium-size farm in the private farming sector. This trend was in line with current agrarian policy.

In the mid-1950s, undoubtedly in connection with the change in agrarian policy after 1956 reducing the emphasis on accelerated collectivization, a certain shift occurred in the trend toward medium-sized farms. There was a slow but steady decline in the share of the larger farms owned by part-time farmers, in part-time workers (two to five hectares) and in the medium-sized farms (five to ten hectares). This pattern was combined with a very slow but steady increase in the number of farms in the largest size group. The consequence of these patterns was a very slow but systematic movement to polarizing the farm size structure: increasing the proportion of the smallest farms (whose owners held jobs outside agriculture) and the biggest farms. This was a positive development that is in accord with the suggestions and projections that I shall refer to in the last part of this chapter.

In 1982, the average size of a private farm was 5.28 hectares in overall area and 4.75 hectares in terms of arable land. If farms under two hectares are left out of consideration, the average farm size would be 7.00 and 6.24 hectares, respectively.

There are two main sectors in Polish agriculture today: the socialized and the private sector. In 1946, after agrarian reform, the public sector (mostly state-owned farms) accounted for 6.9 percent of farmland (excluding forests). As a result of the agrarian policy that sought the socialization of farming, by 1983 the state already had at its disposal 30 percent of all farmland and 23.8 percent of arable land. State farms supervised by the Ministry of Agriculture and Food accounted for 18.8 percent of the area; cooperative farm 3.8 percent, and farms run by farmers' "circles," 0.5 percent. After 1975, the rate of takeovers of private farmers' land by the state was accelerated. Thus, by 1980 it reached 30.7 percent of national farmlands. However, after the years 1980–1983, when socioeconomic changes occurred in farming, a part of the land incorporated into the state sector was returned to private hands.

In the first years after World War II, as a result of the September 6, 1944, manifesto and the decree on agrarian reform, agrarian policy in Poland was conducive to the development of private farms. However, a change occurred in the autumn of 1948: Collectivization of private farms accelerated until it became the dominant trend. As a consequence, the earlier policy was totally abandoned. The years 1949–1953 thus mark the worst period of all for the private sector, coming in the wake of the good years, 1944–1948. Speedy collectivization was enforced by using economic sanctions, especially against the bigger farms. Some of these could not withstand the pressure and were taken over by the state. In those years, some 10,000 cooperative farms were set up in Poland, encompassing over 10 percent of the nation's farmland.

After the political changes that occurred in Poland in October 1956 (when Wladyslaw Gomulka became PZPR first secretary), the policy pursued heretofore on private farms was deemed wrong. Of the cooperative farms established in the preceding period, 90 percent dissolved themselves of their own accord and their share of the country's farmland dropped to 1 percent. There followed another relatively good period for private farmers. Compulsory deliveries of produce to the state were abolished and replaced by contributions to the Agricultural Development Fund, while the procurement prices were raised considerably. Private farmers obtained increased supplies of the elementary meams of production. The income and prosperity of farmers went up.

This continued until 1974, when another policy change took place. Verbal support for the development of the private sector was accompanied by a fresh acceleration in the socialization of farming. Legal acts tied the improvement of a farmer's living condition to his ceding over of land to the state. This resulted in a considerable transfer of land from the private to the state sector. But state farms and the surviving cooperative farms were unable to manage all this land. As a consequence, the productivity and financial performance of these plots deteriorated. In order to take better care of the land ceded by private farmers, a new form of public-sector farm was set up and new farming cooperatives were introduced: Cooperatives of Farmers' Circles, which were formally tied to farmers' "circles"—professional organizations set up for farmers. However, both moves turned out to be ineffective and led to enormous losses. This policy stayed in force until the end of 1979.

The following year (1980), the Central Statistical Office officially confirmed the exceptionally low efficiency of this type of cooperative farm. Private farms again received a positive appraisal. The political parties recognized private farms as a durable element of the Polish socialist socioeconomic system and the equal rights of all sectors of Polish farming. This assertion was confirmed by the Sejm and written into the Polish constitution in 1982. These changes have come to play an important role in strengthening the motivation of private farmers.

The Causes of Food Supply Troubles After 1979

The late 1960s and the early years of the following decade were a period of relative prosperity in Poland. It was also a fairly positive period for farming. The materials and equipment needed in food production were more readily available than in the preceding period. The number of tractors in Polish farms rose from 131,000 in 1965 to 401,000 in 1975, while the consumption of fertilizer went up from 56.4 kgs. NPK (nitrogen/phosphorus/potassium) to 181.9 kgs.; grain yields rose from 19.2 quintals per hectare to 24.8 quintals; and the number of pigs per 100 hectares went up from 70.2 to 110.9. Foreign credits were cheap and easy to obtain. The productivity and the economic efficiency of state-run enterprises in farming continued to rise and approached the level of private farms.

Until this point, the size of state farms had been kept within sensible limits. The public sector also included the few surviving cooperative farms (about 1,000). Being really good farms and having been established out of their founders' free will, they had weathered the wave of massive dissolving of such cooperatives after 1956. This, in my view, produced a mood of euphoria both among the party leadership and within the government and a conviction that the fast growth trend in the national economy and agriculture would be permanent. An extremely optimistic long-range development plan for agriculture was endorsed by the tenth plenum of the PZPR Central Committee in 1974. It set exceptionally ambitious targets, including the heavily publicized target of quickly catching up with or even overtaking in food production the highly developed Western countries, an idea that subsequently had a disastrous effect on the public mood, especially with regard to per capita meat consumption.

The adoption of the 1974 development program coincided with a dismal string of oil price rises that had begun in 1973, setting off a profound economic crisis that hit most countries in the world, Poland included. During the boom period, Poland unwisely borrowed huge sums in hard currency in the West, only to spend a large proportion of these funds on misconceived projects, a situation that soon led to terrible difficulties in the balance of payments. In farming, these credits were used mainly for financing the development of gigantic industrialized animal-breeding farms, a highly ineffective step given the low level of technological capabilities in rural Poland. Moreover, in order to ensure a significant growth of meat consumption, the country signed contracts with the Western countries, especially the United States, for the delivery of huge quantities of fodder grain and other fodder, whose amount exceeded one-third of the domestic production.

Poles in general and townspeople in particular got accustomed to eating even greater quantities of meat, which meant that a sense of meat shortage was created in a period of reduced import of grain and fodder and the resulting lower fatstock production. This was a false impression, to which at least three factors contributed. In the years 1980–1981—a period of working-class protest directed against the country's socioeconomic system as well as against the centralization of not only the management of the economy but also intellectual, social, and cultural life—strongly individualistic and independent Poles resisted the moves of the authorities. The latter did not realize at first what was really going on and through their actions increased the dissatisfaction and provoked spontaneous protests of a majority of the people.

The second factor was the fear of food scarcity or rather of famine. The older generation still remembered the years of hunger during World War I, the first years of independence after 1918, World War II, the Nazi occupation of Poland, and the initial postwar years. People, especially in the urban areas, began to buy whatever food they could lay their hands on, and as the later rationing system was not yet in force, they queued up for anything and bought out all the food there was. Consequently, the fear of hunger led to an opposite phenomenon: excessive consumption or, better said, excessive purchase of food, much of which could not be consumed and simply spoiled. This explains the paradoxical fact that precisely in the same year that the sense of food insufficiency was the strongest (1980), the consumption—or use—of meat per inhabitant was the highest in Poland's history, amounting to 74.0 kgs. Let me add that in 1983 this figure was 58.2 kgs. of meat and 7.0 kgs of fish. The 1983 consumption was at the level of the early 1970s, when meat consumption was considered sufficient.

The third reason for the public mood of food scarcity was the disarray of food retailing. Some improvement in this respect occurred after the introduction of rationing. Another contributing factor was the fact that some private farmers withheld the delivery of produce to state-run procurement centers. This led to increased free market turnover in food. Finally, I must mention the surplus of ready cash on the market, resulting first of all from the reduced supplies of industrial products, which meant that the surplus cash ended up on the food market, while food supplies could only be maintained at levels similar to those attained before 1980.

In 1985, the amount of food per capita was expected to be lower than in 1980–1981, but the average Pole could still expect a caloric intake of 3,445 kcal. a day, which compares favorably with the FAO norm of 2,772 kcal. per day for a person at rest. Therefore it should be recognized that in the years 1980–1981 there was enough food in Poland to meet the demand, and the impression of food scarity was subjective—attributable to organizational and economic factors and to the disorganized commodity and money market—rather than being a fully objective phenomenon.

The Present State of Agriculture and Food Production in Poland

Poland's population in 1983 was 36,571,000 people, 12.4 percent more than in 1970. The rural population numbered 14,828,000, which signified a 5.8 percent drop in comparison to 1970. A significant growth in the proportion of urban population occurred during the same period of time. The nonfarming population already accounted for over half of the population. At the time of the last census, taken in 1978, this proportion amounted to 51.3 percent of the population and has continued to rise. However, the proportions differ vastly from one region (voivodship) to another, ranging from 23.0 percent in the predominantly agricultural voivodships to 83.2 percent in the most heavily industrialized voivodships.

The rural population is older than the urban population and has a higher proportion of men. In 1978, people in the over-60 age group accounted for 15.1 percent of the rural population. Whereas the national average is 105 women to 100 men, in the countryside there were 116 men per 100 women that year, again with huge regional variations ranging from 96 to 100 in heavily industrialized areas to 141 in the farming regions. This led to problems, especially in farming. In many regions young farmers have a great deal of trouble finding a wife for themselves. But private farms run by single men cannot maintain production at a suitably high level over a longer period of time. From this has come the idea of facilitating employment outside farming for those farmers' wives who do not wish to work in farming.

Farmland

In 1970 the total farmland area in Poland amounted to 19,543,000 hectares. By 1983, it had shrunk to 18,879,000 hectares, including 14,534,000 hectares of arable land. In that year, private farms had 14,384,000 hectares—76.2 percent of the whole acreage—while the public sector held the remaining 4,495,000 hectares.

In 1982 in the private sector there were 2,842,000 farms over 0.5 hectares and 1,995,000 farms over 2 hectares of land. This meant that a certain, albeit small, polarization of farms in terms of size had taken place between 1970 and 1982. While the proportion of the smallest holdings, up to 2 hectares, increased from 26.9 percent 29.8 percent, the share of medium-sized farms, between 2 and 10 hectares, dropped from 60.5 percent to 54.4 percent. At the same time, the number of full-sized farms of 10 hectares or more rose from 12.6 percent to 15.8 percent. As I have already said, I consider this to be a positive tendency.

The State Land Trust (PFZ) still has at its disposal a considerable amount of land that does not permanently belong to either sector. However, most of the land is leased under contract to private farmers. A fairly large proportion of this land is fit for forestation. During the last thirteen years, the overall acreage of the land administered by the trust has diminished from over 1,000,000 hectares to just over 800,000 hectares.

Employment in Agriculture

It is difficult to establish the number of people active professionally in Polish agriculture. In the periods between censuses, these figures are based on estimates using various methods producing widely divergent results. But even the more accurate figures obtained from a census leave much uncertainty in view of the very large group of part-time farmers, part-time workers, and the fact that whether a person is classified as being gainfully engaged in farming or not depends on his or her verbal declaration. For these reasons, the figures quoted from various sources differ greatly.

Poland's population grew from 24.6 million in 1950 to 36.6 million in 1984. In the same period the number of people gainfully engaged in farming dropped from 6.5 to 4.1 million, that is, by one third. Employment in the public section of farming amounted to some 680,000 in 1983, including some 500,000 people employed in state farms.

Crop Production

Grain crops play the largest role in the national economy and in feeding the country. Grains are increasingly becoming a fodder crop, as some 80 percent of the harvest ends up as fodder, chiefly for pigs. In the first half of the 1970s, grain yields exceeded 25 quintals per hectare in an average year. The highest grain yield was recorded in 1978, but this was followed by a collapse of this trend. This was a result of two crop failures in a row, in 1980 and 1981, due to exceptionally unfavorable weather, a drop in fertilizer consumption, and weaker motivation for producers, especially in the private sector. The past two years (1983 and 1984) were very good from the point of view of the weather and the yield matched the 1978 level and averaged 27.3 quintals per hectare. In contrast, the potato harvest has been on the low side. This is caused by fungal infections and the Colorado beetle, combined by the shortage of chemical agents for combating these pests. The 1980 potato harvest was especially disastrous. Sugar beet yields are satisfactory. With the exception of 1980, yields have exceeded 300 quintals per hectare, and this growth trend continues.

There has been a tendency to reduce the acreage of potato plantings without reducing output, by increasing yields per hectare. Poland is the second largest potato producer in the world after the Soviet Union, with this crop accounting for 15 percent of the overall crop acreage. Potatoes are grown chiefly for fodder in Poland, especially for pigs, and as a raw material for the production of alcohol, starch, and so forth. The harvesting of potatoes presents a problem, especially in soils with stones. There are also difficulties due to the inadequacy of storage facilities. The growing of sugar beets has been showing an upward tendency. Other important crops are rape and papilionaceous plants, both grown for food and fodder.

Poland has vast areas of natural meadows whose use for food production is however considered to be unsatisfactory, chiefly because of the insufficient degree of drainage and irrigation. It is expected that water shortages will soon appear, and it will become necessary to build retention reservoirs and increase irrigation.

Animal Breeding

The basic farm animals in Poland are cattle. Not only do they supply milk and meat, but also they are ruminants that can consume fresh and dry fodder as well as plants that cannot be assimilated directly by man. Cattle are also the source of the bulk of manure, without which high yields would not be possible in Poland because most of the soil is deficient in organic matter and two-thirds of the land consists of light sandy soils.

Cattle population in Poland was highest in 1978 when it exceeded 13.1 million head. It subsequently decreased somewhat and amounted to 11,270,000 head in 1983, of which 7,780,000 were dairy cows. The number of dairy cows has been rather stable (in 1978 they amounted to 6 million). Because the size of the herd has been stable, the emphasis has been on quality and more rational feeding. Milk yield per cow reached the highest level of 2,766 liters in 1978, then regressed for several years. But in 1983 it approached the previous high when the level of 2,733 liters was achieved.

The second most important group of farm animals are pigs. Unlike cattle and other ruminants, pigs are a rival of man in that the grain and potatoes they eat are also human food. As with cattle, the pig population was the largest in 1978, when it exceeded 21,700,000, including 2,200,000 sows. However, the size of the pig population began to shrink rapidly in subsequent years as the import of fodder grain and other feeding staples diminished. In 1983, the pig population was some 15,600,000, including over 1,600,000 sows. Although further growth in numbers is considered necessary, that will depend on the volume of grain production in Poland and on the possibility of importing feed.

The number of sheep has been rising over the last ten years, as the profitability of sheep breeding has improved. In 1983, the size of the sheep herd was estimated at 4.1 million. As a ruminant, sheep have advantages similar to those of cattle.

The number of basic farm animals per 100 hectares in 1983 was as follows: cattle: 59.7, including 30.6 cows; pigs: 82.6, including 8.5 sows; sheep: 21.7; and horses: 8.5. Workhorses are still kept for farmwork and transport; their use is virtually confined to private farms, especially the smaller ones that do not have tractors. They can also be viewed to a certain degree as a reserve that can be used in the event of a shortage of oil, which is almost wholly imported.

Battery breeding of poultry, especially chickens, has developed over the last two decades, both for meat and eggs. In the peak period the number of chickens exceeded 70 million. At the end of 1983, they amounted to 56 million.

Food Industry

Food processing plants operate within and outside of farming organizations. The following kinds of plants can be found in farming enterprises: potato processing plants such as alcohol distilleries, starch works, potato flaking plants and syrup plants (which supply the farms with valuable by-products, mainly potato extract and pulp), fruit and vegetable canning plants run mostly by farming cooperatives (which make it possible to employ surplus manpower), feed mixing plants, green forage drying plants, and plants producing fodder concentrates.

Outside of farming organizations there are the following food processing plants: sugar refineries, industrial alcohol distilleries, and starch works; mills, silos, and storage facilities; major fruit and vegetable industry plants; the fermentation industry; oil plants; dairy plants; meat factories; and others.

The Availability of Production Supplies

There is much more capital equipment per hectare in the huge state-run farms than in private farms. This may appear to contradict the principle that the bigger the farm, the smaller the amount of fixed assets per unit of area should be. However, this paradox is the result of the completely different character of the equipment, technological standard, and materials from which it is made. Unfortunately these differences also affects depreciation costs and the cost of maintenance of the equipment. In private farms these costs are much lower.

The value of fixed assets is given in current prices, which are adjusted prices and are totally disproportionate to the real proportions between market prices. As a result, they reflect only the proportions between individual sectors. [It should further be noted that the discrepancies in the averages for all farmland, for public-sector farmland, and for private-sector farmland are to be found in the original source material and, hence, must be considered approximate representations.—Ed.] The average value of fixed assets per hectare of farmland in Poland in 1983 was 88,800 zloty, of which 116,200 zloty were public-sector assets and 61,700 were private sector.

Assuming 100.0 to be the average value nationwide, the index for state farms is 131 percent and for private farms, 70 percent.

As to the degree of mechanization of farm work in Poland, the number of tractors appears to be the best yardstick. Over the last decade, the number of tractors in private hands has increased considerably. However, in comparison to the state sector, these are tractors of a much lower value: They have smaller engines and a majority of them are old machines bought from state farms that had written them off. In 1970, there were 225,000 tractors, most of them in the state sector. In 1980, the total rose to 619,000 and in 1983 to 759,000. Of these 759,000, private farmers owned 557,000, and farmers' circles owned another 80,000. This means that 637,000 tractors altogether were at the disposal of the private sector. In terms of the ratio between tractors and hectares, there were 22 hectares of land per tractor in the public sector, while in the private sector the respective figure was 26 hectares, or 23 hectares if the tractors of the farmers' circles are also taken into account. The national average was 25 hectares of land per tractor. It should be borne in mind that there have been acute shortages in spare parts, batteries, and tires for tractors.

The level of supply of means of production for farmers is usually appraised in Poland according to the consumption of mineral fertilizers and concentrated fodder per hectare of farmland. The highest level of consumption of mineral fertilizers per hectare was recorded in the 1977–1978 crop year. As can be seen from the figures given above, 1978 was the best year so far in every respect, based on intensity of production and recorded performance. Fertilizer consumption per hectare, in nutritive content in kilograms amounted to 123.6 kgs. NPK in 1969–1970; 190.3 kgs. in 1977–1978; and 169.7 kgs. in 1982–1983. So far, the level of fertilizer used in the private and the public sector has differed vastly. In 1984 this amounted to 274.7 kgs. per hectare in the state sector, while in the private sector it was only half as much, 137.8 kgs.

The sales of state-supplied fodder amounted to 4,007,000 tons in 1970, 9,087,000 tons in 1978 (which was due to huge imports), and 3,799,000 tons in 1983, when imports were sharply down again. As in the case of fertilizer, there were pronounced differences between the public and the private sectors. The average supplies were 2.0 quintals per hectare of farmland, but the public sector received 3.6 quintals per hectare while the private sector received not even half of that amount, 1.5 quintals per hectare. Private farms had to use a much larger proportion of their grain harvest and other fodder plants for fodder, which adversely affected their commercial production. Even so, their production of food was higher than that of the public sector.

Investments in Farming:
Land Improvement and Infrastructure

State statistics do not provide data about the volume of investment outlays for individual years, adjusted for the changes in the prices of materials and labor. Nonetheless, it clear that in recent years this value in real terms diminished considerably as a result of the economic crisis that hit the whole economy. In 1983, investment outlays in agriculture

Table 5.5
Land Improvement Projects

Item	1970	1980	1983
Improved farmland[a]	5,585	6,267	6,269
Arable land[a]	3,773	4,313	4.359
Irrigated land[a]	26	46	50
Pastures and meadows[a]	1,812	1,954	1,937
Improved land as a percentage of total farmland area	28.6	33.1	33.3
Improved land as a percentage of all farmland requiring improvement	57.1	64.1	64.4

Note: a. In thousand hectares.
Source: Author's compilation from official Polish sources.

Table 5.6
Overall Farm Production, Production Costs, and Net Production

	Farming Overall	Public Sector	Private Sector
Overall farm production	88.0	69.3	93.8
Material cost of farm production	54.4	58.9	53.1
Net farm production	33.5	10.4	40.7

Source: Author's compilation from official Polish sources.

totaled 197 billion zloty. The percentage of these outlays by individual groups of projects, in decreasing order, was as follows: construction, 44.9 percent; mechanization, 36.5 percent; land improvement, 11.8 percent; miscellaneous other projects, 5.3 percent; electricity supply installations, 1.2 percent; and veterinary facilities, 0.3 percent. The view is widespread among farmers that the share accorded to land improvement projects, and in particular the value of investment outlays for land improvement in absolute terms, is much too low. The scope of land improvement projects is illustrated in Table 5.5.

Table 5.7
Per Capita Consumption of Basic Food Products in Poland

	1950	1960	1970	1980	1983
Basic cereal products (kgs.)	166.0	145.0	131.0	127.0	122.0
Potatoes (kgs.)	270.0	223.0	190.0	158.0	154.0
Meat and giblets (kgs.)	36.5	42.5	53.0	74.0	58.2
Fish (kgs.)	1.7	4.5	6.3	8.1	7.0
Edible fats: pure fat (kgs.)	9.7	13.6	18.0	21.0	18.9
Cow's milk (liters)	206.0	227.0	262.0	262.0	277.0
Hen's eggs	116.0	143.0	186.0	223.0	198.0
Sugar (kgs.)	21.0	27.9	39.2	41.4	45.0

Source: Author's compilation from official Polish sources.

Production and welfare infrastructure in the countryside varies greatly from one part of Poland to another. It is best developed in the central-western and the southwestern macroregions. The greatest deficiencies in this respect are recorded in the northeastern and southeastern macroregions. The most painfully felt shortages are the lack of surfaced roads, service outlets for farmers, and welfare institutions for the population.

Economic Efficiency

Economic efficiency in farming is determined according to three indices calculated on a per hectare basis. Although the absolute figures do not say much, interesting comparisons can be made between the state and the private sector. The latest available figures are in Table 5.6.

As can be seen from examining this table, private farms recorded higher overall production, lower material costs, and much higher net production per hectare. Net production, which is an equivalent of national income, was four times as high in the private sector as in the state sector. The trends observed in 1982 have been around since at least 1960.

The Consumption of Basic Agricultural Products per Inhabitant in Poland

The level of consumption in a country is best illustrated by the amounts of products of agricultural origin calculated in per capita terms. These figures show that there has not been and there is no hunger in Poland (see Table 5.7).

With regard to most foods, the growth rate generally has been what was expected. Until 1983 the per capita consumption of grain and potatoes was declining steadily. However, there was a growth in consumption of fish, fats, milk, eggs, and sugar. Only with regard to meat was the growth trend reversed after 1980, when consumption decreased dramatically in the wake of severe cuts in the import of grain and fodder. But even so, meat consumption did not drop below biological nutritional norms.

The Place of Polish Agriculture in the National Economy

Farming accounts for a very small percentage of state revenues. It amounted to 1.04 percent in 1978, 1.13 percent in 1980, and a mere 0.96 percent in 1983. As for current state expenditures, farming's share is somewhat larger and amounted to 6.13 percent in 1978, 7.00 percent in 1980, but only 4.48 percent in 1983.

However, a different situation prevails with regard to the share of farming in the investment outlays of the state. In 1983, 18 percent of the overall investment outlays of the state were in farming alone rising to nearly 30 percent when the development of the food industry and the industries supplying farmers with production means were also taken into account. The significance of this fact is shown by comparison with the share of other branches of the national economy in state investment outlays. In 1983, industry accounted for 28.5 percent of all these outlays, housing and other nonmaterial municipal services for 26.6 percent, while such important branches of economy as transport and communications used only 6.1 percent of the total investment outlays. These figures testify to the significance the authorities attach to agriculture and food production.

In recent years, the share of farming in the national income produced has been rising as a result of the difficulties occurring in other branches of the economy.

Farming was the branch of national economy least affected by the economic crisis that hit Poland. A drop in production—and a small one at that—occurred only in the crop year 1980–1981, and even that was mainly due to the exceptionally bad weather in 1980. In fact, in 1983 production returned to the level of 1978, the best year on record, as a result of very good performance in farming in 1982 and 1983.

The figures given in Table 5.8 show that farming's share in the national income rose from 12.9 percent in 1980 to 16.6 percent in 1983, whereas in absolute figures the national income from agriculture increased by 12 percent from 1980 to 1983. At the same time overall national income dropped by 12 percent, in industry by 15 percent, and in construction by as much as 28 percent.

Farming is a part of the country's food complex, supplying the economy with unprocessed produce. Most of the indices describing the share of the food complex in the national economy are in the area of 30 percent. For a precise statement of these percentages, see Table 5.9.

Table 5.8
Structure of National Income Produced, 1980-1983
(in constant 1982 prices)

	1980	1981	1983	Change 1980-1983 where 1980=100
Overall	100.0	100.0	100.0	88
Industry	50.2	48.7	48.9	85
Construction	11.3	11.3	11.0	72
Agriculture	12.9	14.9	16.9	112

Source: Author's compilation from official Polish sources.

Table 5.9
The Share of the Food Complex in the National Economy (in percentages)

	1978	1980	1982
Overall production	29.2	29.2	34.5
Net production	22.1	20.2	27.6
Employment in production (annual average)	33.4	33.5	34.3
Outlays for productive investments	29.4	29.6	30.6
Gross value of fixed assets (productive) on December 31	29.1	29.5	30.6
Imports	18.4	20.0	22.1
Exports	12.3	10.4	9.1

Source: Author's compilation from official Polish sources.

The Influence of Farming on the Current Situation in Poland

Throughout history, Poland has been a predominantly agricultural country. In previous periods it did not develop the strong bourgeois class characteristic of most Western countries. At the time of the outbreak of World War II as many as 60 percent of Poles lived off agriculture.

After the war, the professional structure of the country started to change rapidly. With a view to developing industry and transforming the character of the country from agricultural to industrial-agricultural, a large part of the national income produced in farming was allocated in the years of the

Six-Year Plan (1950–1955) to the establishment and development of big industrial projects. This was done by fixing low prices paid to farmers for their produce and by introducing compulsory delivery quotas for several basic kinds of produce (grain, potatoes, livestock, and milk) as well as by limiting supplies of materials. These actions coincided with the decision to accelerate the collectivization of private-sector farming.

As the nascent industry and the development of other branches of the national economy required manpower, surplus labor moved to jobs outside agriculture. This surplus labor came from the private sector and from those who could not bear the financial and personal pressures of the accelerated collectivization of private farms. Before long, ex-farmers accounted for over half of the people working in the nonfarming sectors. After a period of adapting to their new trades and new environment, this new nonagricultural population endeavored to obliterate the traces of their origin, and considering their work in towns as being more prestigious, developed a contemptuous attitude toward their former occupation and life-style. This went on for many years and led to more desertions from farming and even from the countryside. At present, less than half of the country's population lives in the countryside, while some 27 percent of the population lives off agriculture.

Because the people moving from the countryside to towns were first of all the most energetic ones, the authorities tried to stem the tide a little by expanding agricultural schools at the basic and medium level. There are more than 200 agricultural high schools operating in Poland, but a majority of the graduates take jobs outside agriculture upon graduation.

The contemptuous treatment of farming and the accelerated migration to other occupations slowed down during the traumatic years of 1980 to 1982, in the context of an irrational starvation panic. Looking hunger in the eye, townspeople began to appreciate the role of farming. Without much resistance, in fact with the moral support of the urban classes, the two largest parties passed resolutions on the durable character of the private sector of farming, on the principle of equal treatment of the public and the private sector of farming, and on earmarking 30 percent of all investment outlays in the next multiyear plan for the development of the food complex. These party resolutions were reaffirmed by the government, while the principle of the durable character of private farms was written into the constitution.

However, once the panic subsided, people outside agriculture began to envy farmers once again. For one thing, as the producers of food, farmers naturally had better access to it. Some very well-run farms, especially specialized ones, do produce handsome profits. This was an irritant for a certain proportion of the nonagricultural population; this led, in turn, to the emergence of antifarmer views and sentiments. Such people think that farmers are getting rich at the expense of wage earners. But this is a simplistic view. For in reality, the average income of a peasant family is considerably lower than the average income outside farming (amounting to 80–90 percent of the latter only), with the only exception being the year 1981, when procurement price rises were not accompanied by increases in the prices of materials needed in food production. Such envious people ignore the difficult conditions of the farmer's work, without regular working hours, without days off during the week and holidays during the year, as well as the enormous differences in social infrastructure between town and countryside, to the detriment of the latter. Thus, although many people may envy farmers, not many are prepared to work in farming or even in the countryside in general. From this situation stem the labor shortages in the countryside and periodical surpluses of people seeking jobs in various nonagricultural trades and professions in urban areas.

In the late 1960s and early 1970s, despite a much lower level of production and consumption of food products per inhabitant, the balance of foreign trade in farm produce grown in Poland's climatic zone was positive for Poland. This fact warrants consideration in the context of the problems at present with selling Polish industrial goods abroad because of their inferior quality. One of the ideas advanced in recent years has been to accelerate development of food production at the expense of other branches of the economy in order to export processed food products of a high quality. This has been considered more feasible under current Polish conditions than raising the quality of industrial products. This concept, however, did not receive widespread support, and I am mentioning it only in order to show the variety of the views on the topic circulating in Poland.

The Forecast for the Development of Farming in Poland

The forecast outlined below is not an official projection, nor is it the only long-range forecast for Polish agriculture. It was prepared by a large group of economists, biologists, and farming engineers under the auspices of the Polish Academy of Sciences and it has been approved and recognized by the academy so far. It spans more or less the period of one generation in farming and extends to the years 2010–2015.

Four variants of development of Polish farming were examined: a simple extrapolation of existing trends, a capital-saving pattern, a land-saving pattern, and a labor-saving pattern. It was recognized that capital was the most scarce factor (i.e., production means and energy). Therefore the capital-saving program was adopted. It is expected that Poland's agricultural land area will drop to 18,150,000 hectares and that the ratio of the public to the private sector will stay at 25/75 as it is now.

Agrarian Structure in the Private Sector

Vegetable plots—farming plots below 0.5 hectares—were recognized as a very positive element in the economy. It is estimated that their number will increase by some 50 percent, to reach about 1.5 million. As the number of small farms owned by worker-peasants (0.5–2.0 hectares) has remained virtually unchanged for the past two decades, as their yields per hectare have been very high, and as they were certain to play a positive social role in the future, it was decided to project their number as remaining at the present level of 800,000. The projection for the number of worker-peasant farms between 2 and 5 hectares of farmland, however, calls for a reduction by up to 60 percent of larger farms in the mixed category since they are much less productive and their owners often have trouble managing them properly. The number of farms in the 5-7 hectare range is to be reduced to a minimum, with their owners maintaining only vegetable plots and selling the rest of their land to neighboring farms over 7 hectares. This is because a farm of 5-7 hectares is too large to be properly run by a worker-peasant and too small to ensure a sufficient income for a farm family. The number of farms in the 7-10 hectares class is to decrease by 50 percent because in some regions with a lower productivity such farms are too small to ensure a decent living for a farm family (notably in the north and in the east). Also the number of farms in the 10-15 hectares category is to be decreased by 20 percent, whereas the number of farms with over 15 hectares of land is expected to increase by 150 percent.

In effect, this projection envisages a polarization of farms in terms of size: a growth of the number of vegetable plots, of smaller worker-peasant farms, and of the biggest farms—those that can ensure full employment to a farm family and allow it to earn a decent income.

The realization of this forecast would result in a drop in the overall number of farms (above 0.5 ha.) from 2.8 million in 1980 to 1.7 million in 2010. The number of people gainfully employed in the private sector of farming would drop from 3.9 million in 1980 to 2.0 million.

After 2010, the size of the average farm would rise to 7.3 hectares, if all farms above 0.5 hectares are taken into account, and to 11.6 hectares of farmland if only farms above 2 hectares are included. As a result, during the time period of the forecast, the size of the average farm would more or less double.

This forecast is very cautious, but it takes into account the record of a very slow growth in the size of the average farm in the decades since the end of World War II. The number of hectares for each gainfully employed person in the private sector of farming would be 6.5.

It is also estimated that the size of the rural population will stay at the present level of 15 million people. In addition, the forecast envisages the creation of nonfarming jobs for the rural population.

Crop Production

The structure of crop production should be similar to what it is now: grains, 55 percent; pulse, 2 percent; potatoes, 13 percent (down 2 percent); sugar beets, 4 percent (up from 3.2 percent); fodder plants, 17 percent (down 2.1 percent). The use of mineral fertilizers is to rise to 360 kgs. NPK per hectare and that of lime to 255 kgs. of calcium oxide. Grain yields are to reach 40 quintals per hectare.

Animal Products

Cattle should stay at the present level of 12 million, including 5.7 million dairy cows, whereas milk output per cow is to rise to 3,500 liters a year. The number of pigs is to rise to 27 million, compared to the highest level of 22 million recorded so far. The number of sheep is to increase from the record high level of 4 million to 5 million.

The Self-Sufficiency of Polish Agriculture

The envisaged level of crop and animal production should give Poland full self-sufficiency in food production, save for the import of a limited quantity of protein-rich fodder, to be offset by 1990 by the export of food products, assuming a level of meat consumption of seventy kilograms per inhabitant.

The outline of the forecast given above is not a plan, let alone a prophecy. It only presents the possibility that Polish agriculture has at its disposal the capacity to meet virtually all its food needs, provided the socioeconomic conditions assumed in the forecast are maintained.

Notes

All figures quoted in this chapter come from prewar Polish censuses and readily available standard statistical data published since the war, to which Manteuffel has had access as a leading authority in Poland on the country's agriculture (Ed.).

6

Economic Development in Light of Regional Differences

Jerzy Kruczała

Scientific studies of regions have demonstrated the wide scope and depth of problems related to the regional aspects of a country's development. The limited size of this chapter forces me to present just a sample of the regional aspects of Poland's development and to resort to a simplified method of presenting them. Although the choice has been mine, the scope of information also has depended on the availability of data pertaining to the problems discussed herein. The main sources of this information are the publications of the Central Statistical Office and the Polish Academy of Sciences' Committee for Regional Economics and Planning,[1] as well as materials yielded by a research project supervised by the Institute of Geography of the Polish Academy of Sciences. While they are quite ample, these materials do not contain much data for recent years that would be useful from the point of view of this chapter. These objective limitations have had a serious impact on the contents of what follows.

I shall focus on the contemporary evolution of regional differences in the development of the country, especially in recent years. However, space must also be devoted to an outline of the historic heritage regarding the country's territorial development. This heritage explains certain material and cultural differences among the parts of the country whose pasts varied considerably. The historic shape of many earlier geographical entities can still be seen today. Other elements in the country's development involve the continuation of systems whose origins go back to the distant past. Nine out of the eleven largest urban centers in Poland, exerting great influence on the regions surrounding them, have served as such centers for between 400 and 1,000 years.

The Historic Heritage

The beginnings of some of the contemporary entities that exert an influence on regional differences can be traced back to the period of the existence of the Kingdom of Poland—the period prior to 1795, when the kingdom was dismembered by neighboring states.

The aforementioned nine of the eleven most important towns at present were major urban centers already at that time. The origins of present industry in those towns go back to the concentrations of crafts and manufacturing that were shaped already before the end of the eighteenth century. Also some of the cultural differences, customs, and traditions of individual regions, connected with the country's division into districts prior to its partitioning in 1795, have survived to this day.

Some elements of the territorial division of the country, especially in its pre-1975 shape, as well as the very name of the basic unit of this division—the voivodship, which has remained in use to this day—also date back to the period near the end of the eighteenth century. This long existence of district boundaries has exerted an influence on the extent of regional differences.

Other regional differences emerged between 1795 and 1918, when Poland was partitioned into three parts and incorporated into Russia, Prussia (Germany after 1871), and Austria. In particular, there are differences in the development of technical and industrial infrastructure among the three parts of Poland (the nineteenth century was the period of the fastest development of railroads in Europe), as well as differences in the location of industry and the structure of farm ownership. These differences reflect the particular development paths of the three partitioning powers.

The parts incorporated into Prussia (or Germany) still have a denser network of railroads, a relatively even distribution of small to medium industrial centers, and a more advantageous structure of farm ownership than that found in other parts of Poland. In the nineteenth century, these lands saw the development of industrial districts that to this day form the core of Poland's industry (e.g., Upper Silesia).

The areas that were formerly part of Austria have a relatively less-developed transportation infrastructure, especially the railroad network. Few industrial centers had developed in those regions between 1795 and 1918. Austria did not support the industrialization of these regions because they might have started competing with the original Austrian lands. The few industrial centers that did emerge include the Bielsko-Biala textile industry concentration and the group of coal mines situated on the outskirts of that partition zone. The immense fragmentation of farmland, which developed as a result of Austrian legislation in force in those regions, has been a source of headaches until today.

The least developed part of Poland was that incorporated into Russia. In particular, the development of railways there lagged behind the other parts, and this legacy is still present. In the western part of that former partition zone, there are a few industrial centers whose growth began in the nineteenth century. In the vast eastern part of that zone, there was no industrial development at all in the nineteenth century, and even today the level of industrialization there is low. Here, too, farmland is fragmented as a result of Russian legislation.

The two decades of independent Poland between the world wars (1918-1939) also left behind some lasting regional differences. A number of new sections of railroad integrated the separate transport systems of the three partition zones, reducing distances and facilitating the removal of differences among regions. Only then did Cracow obtain a direct rail link with Warsaw; Upper Silesia was finally connected to the coast by a main line intended chiefly for the transport of coal via Gdynia, a huge new port serving all the regions of the reborn state.

The geographical distribution of industry changed somewhat as a result of the construction of the Central Industrial District (COP), which marked the beginning of the industrialization of the underdeveloped and overpopulated central part of the country and which was continued after 1945. At the same time, Warsaw was growing as the biggest population center, and its size and importance by far exceeded the remaining major cities.

The impact of the 1939-1945 war on regional structures consisted mainly of the near total destruction of some urban centers and regions, especially Warsaw, Gdansk, and Wroclaw. The effects of the damage took several decades to remove.

The Policy of Regional Development After 1945

Independent statehood was regained in 1944-1945. The introduction of a planned economy and a new regional development policy followed.[2] The country now included the regained territories—areas that until 1939 were recognized as a part of the German Reich but had earlier belonged to the Polish state.

The first national economic plan, which covered the years 1947-1949 was the plan of reconstruction. It reproduced the state of economy that existed before the damage, as well as the basic territorial and regional structures. The decision to rebuild Warsaw as the capital of the state was a dramatic one, considering the enormous extent of the damage. Already in that period some investment projects were launched, especially with regard to transport, that were aimed at bridging the differences between the regions belonging to Poland prior to 1939 and those forming the regained territories. The elimination of these differences proceeded along with the settling of the territories with Polish population. In some parts of these lands there was indigenous Polish population as well.

After 1950, the implementation of a succession of multiyear plans influenced the development of the regions. The following undertakings had great impact on the evolution of regional differences in Poland with regard to infrastructure:

1. the integration of the transportation network and its development in the areas that were less developed in this respect;
2. the intensive growth of seaports in the Gdansk region in the east and the Szczecin region in the west;

3. the modernization of the transportation network, e.g., electrification of the railways, improvements in the surface of roads, and development of the network of main routes.

These undertakings gradually facilitated the industrialization and development of the weaker regions (which could not easily be industrialized in the first postwar years precisely because of the lack of suitable infrastructure). They also spurred the growth of the coastal regions and helped level off the differences in the development of outlying areas.

The process of industrialization embarked upon in the 1950s and continued with varying intensity since has been the most important factor in regional development policies and the shaping of differences among individual regions. The scope of this process is illustrated by the growth of employment in industry (and private trades) from 1,463,000 in 1946 to 5,565,100 in 1975.[3]

Advances in industrialization measured by the growth of industrial employment differed from one region to another. The growth index measured in terms of industrial employment for 1975 compared to 1946 amounted to 380.4 for the country as a whole. For 37 voivodships that is, 69.3 percent of all regions, the index was higher than average, while in the remaining 13 voivodships it ranged from 200 to 380.[4] These figures confirm the tendency toward a dispersal of the industrialization process to include many regions.

Another trend in the process of industrialization has affected the development of regions is the priority given to the growth of heavy industry. There also has been a tendency to build or develop huge enterprises, not only in heavy industries but also in other industries. The latter tendency was one of the more prominent factors responsible for the concentration of the process of industrialization in some voivodships:[5] (1) In sixteen voivodships, industrial employment in 1975 exceeded 100,000 people; (2) in twelve out of these sixteen voivodships, the growth of industrial employment alone exceeded 100,000 people.

Urban development was also important after 1945. The large scope of this process is illustrated by the growth of urban population from some 8,969,400 in 1946 to 19,030,500 in 1975—from 37.5 percent to 55.7 percent of the population.[6] In addition to that, the character of some rural settlements changed as the size of their nonfarming population increased and municipal facilities were installed in them; these changes were not reflected in urban growth statistics.

Similarly, as was the case with industrialization, urban growth was characterized by considerable dispersion. Whereas the national urban population growth index between 1945 and 1975 amounted to 212.2, in thirty voivodships (i.e., 61.2 percent of the total number) it was higher or similar, while in seventeen voivodships the urban growth index ranged from 150 to 200.[7]

The goal of the urban growth was the emergence of conurbations. However, this process was periodically slowed down through various means,

Table 6.1
Regional Development, 1960-1978

	Regions					
	Strong		Medium		Weak	
	No.	Percent	No.	Percent	No.	Percent
1960	4	(8.2)	10	(20.4)	35	(71.4)
1978	10	(20.4)	20	(40.8)	19	(38.8)

Source: Author's compilation from official Polish sources.

both legislative ones (through the introduction of various regulations) and planning ones (through the policy of locating investment projects). As a result, the share of the population of big cities, those exceeding 200,000 inhabitants, rose from 24.5 percent in 1950 to only 34.7 percent of the total urban population, or 19.5 percent of the population of the country, in 1975.[8] Only the capital has over 1 million inhabitants. Compared to, say, the United States, the process of urban concentration in Poland can be regarded as slow.

The targets of regional policy formulated since 1945 spoke of a more balanced development in various parts of the country. A publication of the Polish Academy of Sciences reflects the changes in the relative "strength" of various regions from 1960 to 1978.[9] Although these studies did not cover the earlier periods, they did encompass the most important period for regional policies: 1961 marked the beginning of the period of intensification of regional planning. Drawing on the aforementioned publications, Table 6.1 records the changes in the "strength" of the regions that occurred in the period in question. These figures demonstrate the trend in the "activation" of the weaker regions. Nonetheless, a relatively large proportion of the regions was still regarded as weak.

The trends in policies and actual processes described above were accompanied by a degradation of the environment, that was not widely realized at first. In the period examined there was a relationship between the intensification of industrialization, urban development, and the general level of socioeconomic development of regions, on the one hand, and the rising threat to the environment in a given area, on the other. Environment-oriented efforts consequently have become increasingly important in regional policies.

Regional Differences

The present shape of the differences among the various regions of the country is examined here according to the administrative divisions of Poland. A region is identified with the voivodship, an administrative unit.

Economic Development　　　　　　　　　　　　　　　　　　　　　*121*

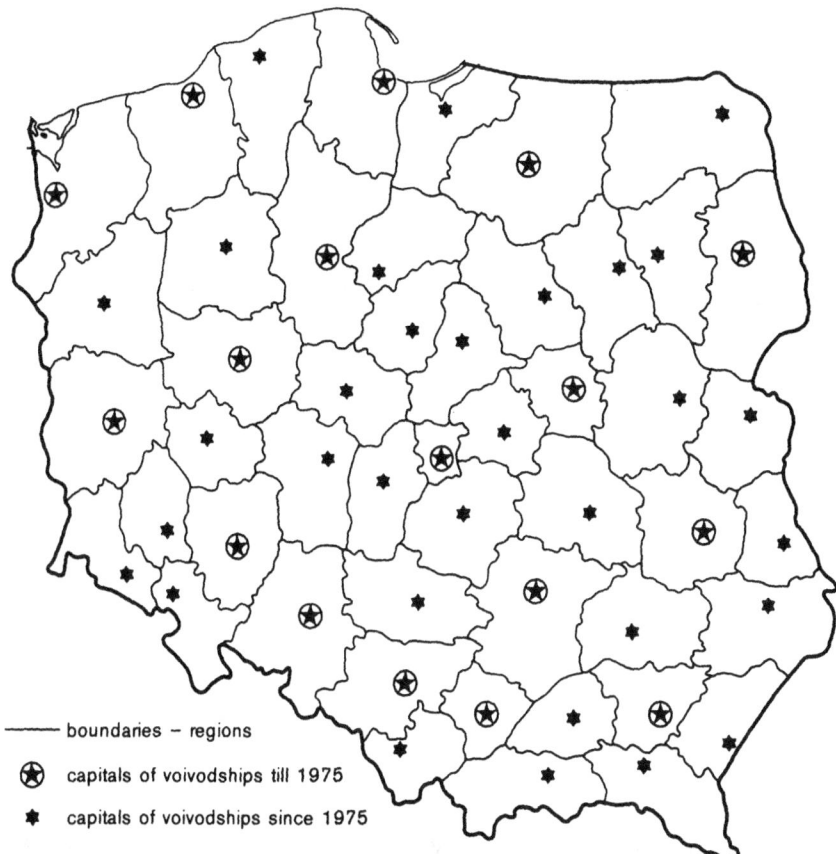

Map 6.1　Poland's territorial division into regions (voivodships).

This approach is justified by the state of regional statistics, the approach used in most scientific studies, and the planning system, which relies on central plans and territorial plans following the pattern of administrative divisions.

The present (1984) administrative division of the country was introduced in 1975. Poland is divided into forty-nine voivodships, or regions. (Until 1975, there were twenty-two units at this level, as can be seen in Map 6.1).

In terms of size, voivodships differ considerably. From this point of view, they can be divided into three groups, as can be seen in Table 6.2.[10]

The differences in the number of inhabitants are even greater. In this respect, as Table 6.3 demonstrates, the voivodships can be divided into four groups (according to 1982 population figures).[11]

The regional structure of Poland is quite diversified from the point of view of area and population in individual regions. Although medium-sized

Table 6.2
Voivodships by Size

Area (sq.km.)	Number of Voivodships	Class	Percent of Voivodships
1,500-5,000	15	small	30.6
5,000-10,000	29	medium	59.2
10,000-12,300	5	large	10.2

Source: Author's compilation from official Polish sources.

Table 6.3
Voivodships by Population

Population (thousands)	Number of Voivodships	Class	Percent of Voivodships
230-400	8	small	16.3
401-800	28	medium	57.1
801-1,260	11	big	22.5
2,360-3,860	2	very big	4.1

Source: Author's compilation from official Polish sources.

voivodships predominate, in terms of both area and number of inhabitants, the differences between the extremes are quite pronounced.

This presentation of contemporary differences among the country's regions covers the last few years, including certain aspects of the crisis as well as trends in changes that came with the initial period of economic reform. The vulnerability of the regions to the crisis, depending on their economic and social strength, is shown in various studies.

The state of industrialization of the country and its regions in 1982 can be illustrated by the index of 1,431 people employed in the public sector of industry per 100 square kilometers.[12] The respective indices for individual voivodships, shown in Map 6.2, demonstrate that seventeen regions, that is, 34.7 percent of the overall number of voivodships, have a higher index than the national average, and in six the degree of industrialization is at least twice as high as the average. A majority of the most industrialized regions are in the southern part of the country. In contrast, fifteen voivodships (30.6 percent of the total number), situated mainly in the east and the north, had an index of industrialization at least 50 percent below the national average. They form the least industrialized part of the country.

Map 6.2 Industrial development by voivodship.

In the years 1980–1982, the process of industrialization slowed down.[13] Employment in the public sector of industry, which is the main factor in industrialization, decreased by some 5 percent across the country. In forty-six out of the forty-nine voivodships, the index of industrial employment also decreased by several percent; the 12.9 percent decline noted in one area was an exceptional occurrence.

The drop in industrial employment was the most pronounced in the strong voivodships. These are the ten voivodships listed in Table 6.1 and classifed as "strong regions" in 1978. In seven out of the ten, the drop in industrial employment was higher than the national average. Among the weak voivodships, fourteen out of nineteen (listed in Table 6.1) recorded a smaller decline than the country on the average.

During 1983 the downward trend in industrial employment during the preceding years was arrested. The decline in employment that whole year was only 1 percent.[14]

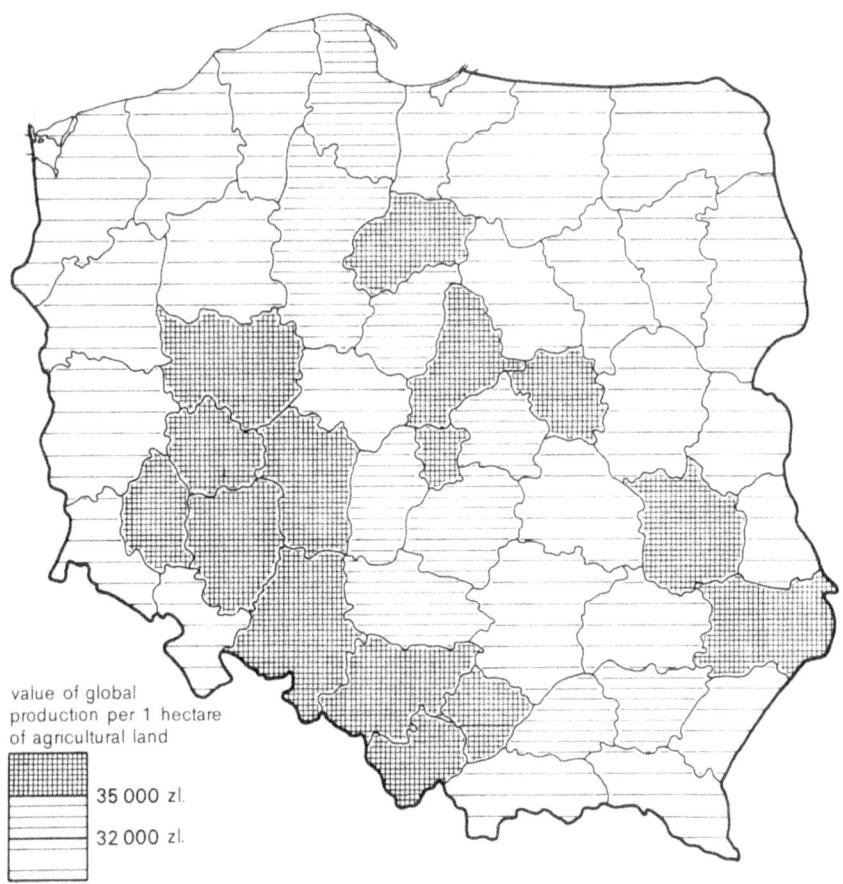

Map 6.3 Intensity of farming production by voivodship.

The regional differentiation in farming can be illustrated by figures relating to the value of total production. Farm production intensification measured in terms of the value of total production per hectare of farmland (in average 1976–1977 crop year prices) is confirmed by the growth of the value index from 33,900 zloty in 1978 to 35,400 in 1979. In 1981, this index dropped to 32,000 zloty.[15]

This index varied from one region to another. (In 1981, the difference between the lowest and the highest index was 1 to 2.05, as can be seen in Map 6.3.) In twenty-four voivodships, the index was higher than the national average. Most of them were situated in a central belt stretching from the north to the south.

Intense agricultural production occurred in recent years in the regions with a high degree of industrialization. Of the nineteen most heavily industrialized voivodships, thirteen (76 percent) were also among the leaders in terms of farm production. Of the twenty-four voivodships at the top in terms of total farm production, fifteen (63 percent) are also classified as the most heavily industrialized regions.

Besides the impact of the crisis, the situation in farming also depended on changing natural conditions. For this reason the 9.6 percent decline in farm production between 1979 and 1981 cannot be attributed to just one cause. This decline occurred in the majority of voivodships (89 percent, to be precise). The drop was the greatest in the weak regions: In fifteen out of nineteen (79 percent) the decline was greater than the national average. In contrast, in 60 percent of the strong voivodships, either the decline was lower than average or production actually increased.

Important insight into the contemporary evolution of regional differences can be seen by analyzing changes in employment in the public-sector share of the economy. These changes also illustrate indirectly changes in the public sector, which played a predominant role in most regions. (In 1982, it employed 66.6 percent of the total number of employed people, with private farms placing a distant second with 26.7 percent.) In addition, these changes reflect change in the number of jobs, which is a primary determinant of the standard of living of the inhabitants. Until 1979, employment in the public sector of the economy grew uninterruptedly. In 1980, that growth stopped, and in 1981 and 1982 this figure decreased by 1.7 and 2.2 percent respectively.[16]

Interesting results can also be obtained from a regional analysis of employment in the public sector of the economy. The division adopted—strong, medium, and weak voivodships—shows the following changes between 1975 and 1982:

1. employment increased in all the nineteen weak voivodships;
2. employment increased in a majority (thirteen out of twenty) of the medium voivodships; and
3. employment dropped in most (seven out of ten) of the strong voivodships.

The reduction of employment in the public sector of the economy in the weak and medium voivodships certainly had an impact on economic performance. However, it did not influence greatly the number of jobs in these voivodships.

As employment in the public sector has decreased, it has been rising outside this sector since 1975. In the years 1980-1982, employment outside agriculture in the private sector increased by 17.5 percent.[17] While this growth occurred in all the regions, it was the fastest in the strong voivodships and also in those at the medium level of industrialization in which there were conurbations.

The information about vacancies and jobseekers conforms to the above figures. The number of people registered as seeking employment amounted to 15,200 in 1975, 9,700 in 1980, and 9,000 in 1982. The number of vacancies was 94,600, 98,200 and 248,000 respectively.[18] The low number of job seekers, consequently, does not justify a breakdown of these figures among the forty-nine voivodships.

The growth in the number of vacancies is a result of the outflow of the work force from the public sector of the economy, especially in the strong voivodships. The growth of demand for manpower in 1982 in the same regions points to the public sector's efforts to rebuild the production and servicing potential of the areas.

Urban growth has continued uninterruptedly for the last few years, albeit with varying intensity.[19] In the years 1976-1979, the annual growth of the urban population exceeded 2 percent (with the exception of 1978). From 1980 to 1982 the growth was slower and slower, amounting to 1.8, 1.7, and 1.5 percent in the respective years. In 1983, there was a reversal of the trend: A 1.59 percent growth took place.

Urban population increased in all the voivodships in the years 1975-1982. However, this growth was relatively faster in the weak voivodships and slowest in the majority of strong voivodships. The crisis also had a stronger impact on urban growth in the strong voivodships. These phenomena were mainly related to the situation in housing construction.

The changes in urban demograghics point to a pattern of concentration that took place mainly as a result of the introduction of the new administrative division of the country in 1975. It turns out that the fastest growth in the number of inhabitants in the years 1975 to 1982 (28.2 percent) was recorded in the twenty-seven towns that were elevated to the status of voivodship capitals in 1975. At the same time, the population of the remaining twenty-two cities, which had already been voivodship capitals prior to that date, only increased by 13.5 percent. The latter group includes the capitals of all the strong voivodships. The location of voivodship capitals is shown in Map 6.1.

Urban growth under Polish conditions can be regarded as a factor in the general improvement of the material and cultural living conditions of the population—hence the tendency of people to move from countryside to towns. However, it should be noted that the problems with ensuring a balanced urban growth diminished the advantages of living in towns. The basic disparities were in housing construction and technical and social infrastructure. These disparities were more acutely felt in the regions that were urbanizing at a faster pace or that had conurbations. Especially in the former regions, the deterioration of the state of the environment had an adverse effect on living conditions.

The considerable drop in investment outlays in the years 1980-1982 hampered both attempts to level off the disparities described above (even though the growth rate of cities slowed down) and efforts to arrest the threat to the environment.

A summary of the results of studies of regional variations in the standard of living of the population was published for only 1974.[20] These are not, therefore, terribly fresh figures. The studies included thirty-one variables. Some of them concerned broadly conceived social infrastructure, such as

Table 6.4
Voivodships According to
Variations in Living Standards

Group	Value of 1974 Aggregate Index	Number of Voivodships	Percent
1	below 100	7	14.3
2	101-200	13	26.5
3	201-300	16	32.7
4	301-400	9	18.4
5	401-500	3	6.1
6	500 plus	1	2.0

Source: Author's compilation from official Polish sources.

the availability of health care services, schools, municipal facilities, while some concerned the "private" dimension of the standard of living, namely average incomes, the number of cars, TV sets, and so on. The author of the work ranked the voivodships according to the value of the thirty-one variables. In this respect, the voivodships can be divided into six groups: This division can be seen not only in Table 6.4 but also in Map 6.4.

After 1975, no more summary data on the standard of living of the population in individual regions were published. Therefore it is possible to present only general trends in these changes on the basis of selected data.

After 1975, there was a steady improvement in the indices regarding social infrastructure and "private" consumption in basically all the voivodships. But at the same time, internal disparities in the infrastructure were growing, especially in the strong voivodships.

In 1980, a number of indices began to deteriorate in the strong voivodships, while in the medium voivodships they have been improving at a very slow pace and in the weak voivodships, at a slow pace.

In the same period, elementary indices regarding the "private" dimension of the standard of living deteriorated in all the voivodships. Some indices, however, did not deteriorate but actually improved in the weak voivodships: These concerned the number of cars, television sets, or doctors per 10,000 inhabitants.

Changes in the state of the natural environment have taken an unfavorable course in recent years and ought to be recognized as a separate element of the crisis.[21] The crisis had multiple consequences (not only for the quality of life of the inhabitants of some regions), but it also meant pressure on investment outlays, limited availability of areas for construction, lower volume and quality of food, deterioration of the situation in forestry. In twenty-four voivodships there are areas designated as ones in which the environment is threatened. Out of that number, twenty-two rank among

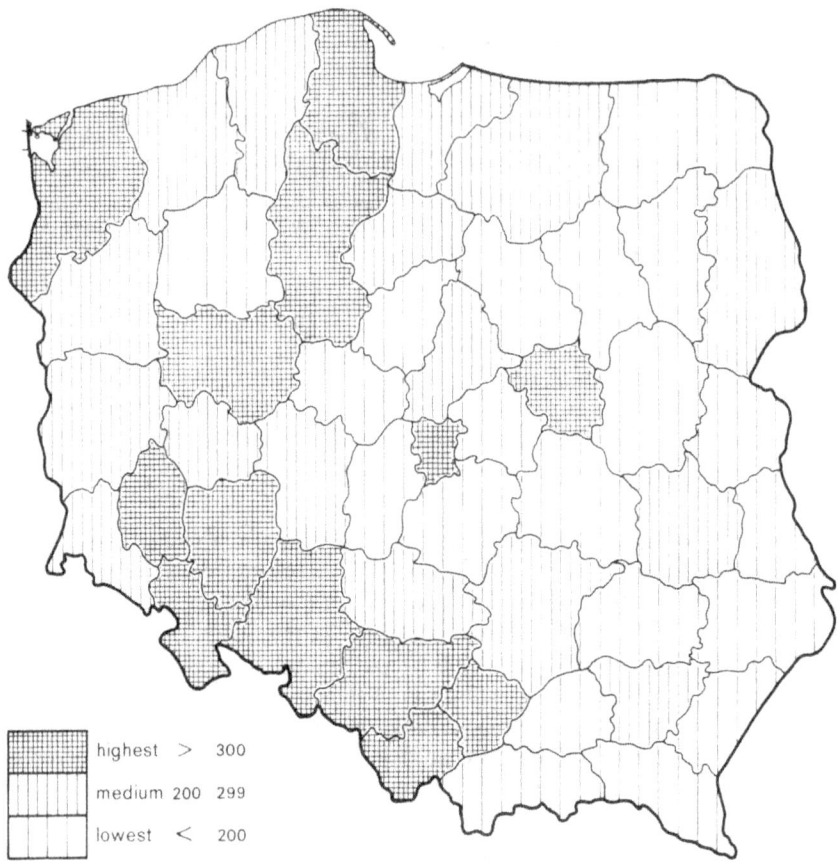

Map 6.4 Standard of living of the population by voivodship.

the most densely populated ones, with over 100 inhabitants per square kilometer; nineteen belong to the group of voivodships with the highest level of farming production, while fourteen have a forest area exceeding 20 percent of the overall area of the voivodship. The biggest threat to the environment is encountered in all the strong voivodships and in some of the medium ones.

The division of regions into strong, medium, and weak ones sums up in the most coherent way the differences among the regions.[22] The studies of the overall level of economic development of the regions, that is, the strength of voivodships, were made in 1978. The appraisal of the strength of voivodships was based on eighteen different indices regarding the level of production and other features of development. From some points of view, using the results of these studies is objectionable, but it is justified by the lack of more recent findings. Moreover, the considerable decline in investment from 1979 onward suggests that there have been no major changes in regional differences in subsequent years.

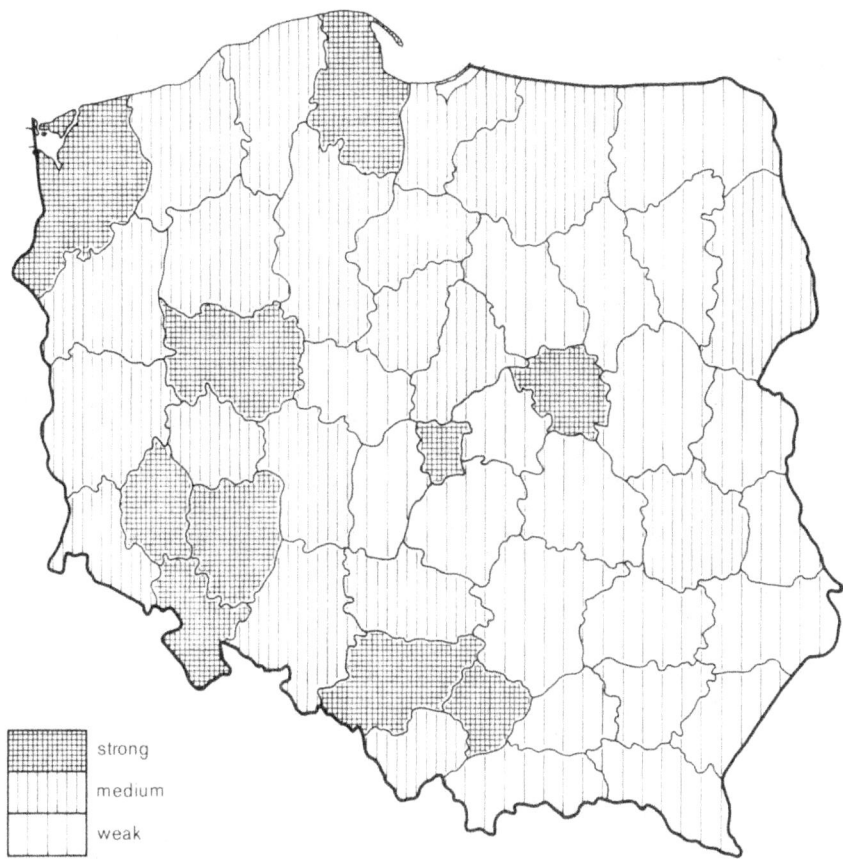

Map 6.5 Strong, medium, and weak regions.

These studies led to the division of voivodships into strong, medium, and weak ones. This division is shown in Map 6.5. It demonstrates that out of the ten strongest voivodships, most are situated in the southwestern part of the country, and that most of the twenty medium voivodships are in the western part of the country, and that a majority of the nineteen weak voivodships are in the eastern and central part of Poland.

Summing up the comparisons made previously of various kinds of differences among regions and their strength, it can be said that the crisis had its greatest impact on the strong regions and relatively its least impact on the weak ones. For the time being, there are no grounds for a similar appraisal of the effects of the reform.

The process of economic development was accompanied by great biological vitality in the country's population. Natural population increase in Poland in recent years has been among the highest in Europe.[23] The natural increase index stayed above the 1 percent level from 1975 and only dropped to 0.97 percent in 1981. Then, unexpectedly, it rose again to 1.02 percent, putting Poland at the top of European statistics in this respect.

The latest figures illustrate the biological resistance of the country's population to the crisis in most regions. This appears to be an important premise for examining the prospects for Poland's socioeconomic development.

Notes

1. Literally translated, the correct title is Spatial Economy and Regional Planning; in this context "spatial" refers to the analysis of economic patterns and relationships in their spatial dimensions (Ed.)
2. The data regarding the development of regions in the years 1945-1975 contained in this part of the chapter are given in such a way as to make them comparable with data on contemporary regional differences.
3. S. Misztal and W. Kaczorowski, *Regionalne zroznicowanie procesu uprzemyslowienia Polski 1945-1975* (Regional Differences in the Process of Poland's Industrialization, 1945-1975)(Warszawa: KPZK PAN, PWN, 1983).
4. Ibid., pp. 77, 78.
5. Ibid.
6. Ibid. and the author's own calculations.
7. Ibid. and the author's own calculations.
8. *Rocznik Statystyczny 1955* (Warszawa: GUS, 1956), pp. 47-48; *Rocznik Statystyczny 1976* (Warszawa: GUS, 1977), p. 34.
9. M. Najgrakowski, "Regiony silne i slabe w Polsce" (Strong and Weak Regions in Poland), *Biuletyn KPZK PAN*, vol. 116 (1981), pp. 69-80.
10. *Rocznik Statystyczny 1983*, (Warszawa: GUS), p. 111.
11. Ibid. pp. 32-33.
12. *Rocznik Statystyczny Wojewodztw 1983*, (Warszawa: GUS), p. 121.
13. *Rocznik Statystyczny 1981, 1982, 1983* (Warszawa: GUS).
14. GUS communique on Poland's economic performance in 1983, p. 7.
15. *Rocznik Statystyczny Wojewodztw, 1981, 1982, 1983*, (Warszawa: GUS).
16. *Rocznik Statystyczny 1980, 1981, 1982* (Warszawa: GUS).
17. *Roczniki Statystyczne 1976-1983* (Warszawa: GUS).
18. Ibid.
19. *Roczniki Statystyczne Wojewodztw 1981, 1982, 1983*.
20. G. Gorzelak, "Przestrzenne zroznicowanie poziomu zycia ludnosci," in *Problemy Gospodarki Przestrzennej, Ksiazka i Wiedza* (Warszawa, 1980), pp. 223-248.
21. *Obszary ekologicznego zagrozenia w Polsce*, (Warszawa: GUS, 1984).
22. *Rocznik Statystyczny 1983*, pp. 69-80.
23. *Roczniki Statystyczne, 1976-1983*.

7

Rural-Urban Linkages and Change

Andrzej Stasiak

The problem of urban-rural linkages in Poland has a long history and as a consequence has undergone a number of essential changes.

In 1946, Polish towns were inhabited by some 8 million people—about one-third of the total population. By 1983, the number had increased to some 22 million, or 60 percent of the total population. In the meantime the population of the rural areas remained fairly stable. Throughout the postwar period it has been in the neighborhood of 15-16 million, while its share of the total population has been steadily diminishing, from about two-thirds of the country's population in 1946 to about 40 percent now. The social and vocational structure of Poland's population has also been changing rapidly. In 1950, people employed in agriculture accounted for over half of the total work force, while by 1982 this share had dropped to about 30 percent. The proportion of people living in the countryside and earning their living outside agriculture had increased from about 22 percent in 1950 to about 51 percent in 1978. At the same time regional variations have been and remain very strong: In 1978 this proportion ranged from 23 percent of people in nonfarming occupations in the predominantly agricultural Lomza voivodship to over 80 percent in the heavily industrialized and urbanized Katowice voivodship. The share of agriculture in the national income has also dropped, from about 60 percent in 1950 to about 17 percent in 1983. These crude estimates indicate that the pace of change in rural-urban linkages in Poland in the postwar period was indeed fast.

There are many economic, cultural, and social determinants of the town-countryside relationship that I shall not be able to present in full in this chapter. Instead, I shall merely sketch out the picture rather than draw the full panorama that the situation certainly deserves. Some topics (such as demographic change, migration processes, social-occupational structures) will be discussed in some detail; others will merely be mentioned in passing, while many others, perhaps no less important, will be left out of consideration altogether. I shall also be referring only fragmentarily to the literature dealing with this subject, relying chiefly on source materials and supplying my own interpretation thereof. It must be said clearly that the problem deserves a serious systematic study which has been missing so far.

The Notions of Town and Countryside and Their Application to Polish Reality

Social science and historical studies have traditionally utilized the division of human settlements into town and countryside. This was originally justified by the development of those forms of settlement, and to some extent, it is still justified now, even though many of the ingredients that define the criteria for this division have lost their validity.[1]

In Poland, this division is largely of a formal nature, owing to the long development of the urban network. There are relatively many small towns. In 1983, out of a total of 806 towns, 449 had fewer than 10,000 inhabitants. Altogether, 2 million people lived in them. They are very strongly connected with rural settlement, frequently acting as local administrative and servicing centers for the surrounding rural areas. For this reason, this group of towns should be examined together with rural settlement. There is, in addition, a distinct group of 42 medium-sized towns (50,000–100,000 inhabitants) that usually act as regional centers, and 38 large towns of more than 100,000 people, including 5 with over half a million inhabitants (Warsaw, 1,600,000; Lodz, 800,000; Cracow, 700,000; Wroclaw, 600,000; Poznan, 600,000) that perform macroregional functions. On the whole, 90 percent of the urban population is nonfarming population, while in the larger towns this proportion reaches 95 percent. Towns occupy 3 percent of the country's area and have a relatively high population density of 1,030 people per square kilometer, compared to the national average of 112 persons per square kilometer.

Rural areas occupy some 94 percent of the country's territory, with farmland accounting for some 60 percent and forests and other wooded areas, 28 percent. These figures indicate that the traditional farming use of the countryside still dominates in rural areas in Poland. The roughly 15 million people living in the countryside are concentrated in 43,000 villages. The average population density in rural areas in 1978 was 51 people per square kilometer, and the average number of people per village was 350, which means that the typical Polish village is quite small.

These figures demonstrate that in principle the traditional settlement shape of the Polish village has been preserved: Over 40 percent of the villages had fewer than 200 inhabitants, and another 40 percent had between 200 and 500 inhabitants. Basically, in central and northeastern Poland small villages clearly predominate, whereas relatively big villages can be found only in southern Poland.[2] The differences are illustrated in Map 7.1. Despite profound changes in the occupational and social structure of the rural population, the scattered character of rural settlement is responsible for the continuation of distinct differences between urban and the rural

Rural-Urban Linkages

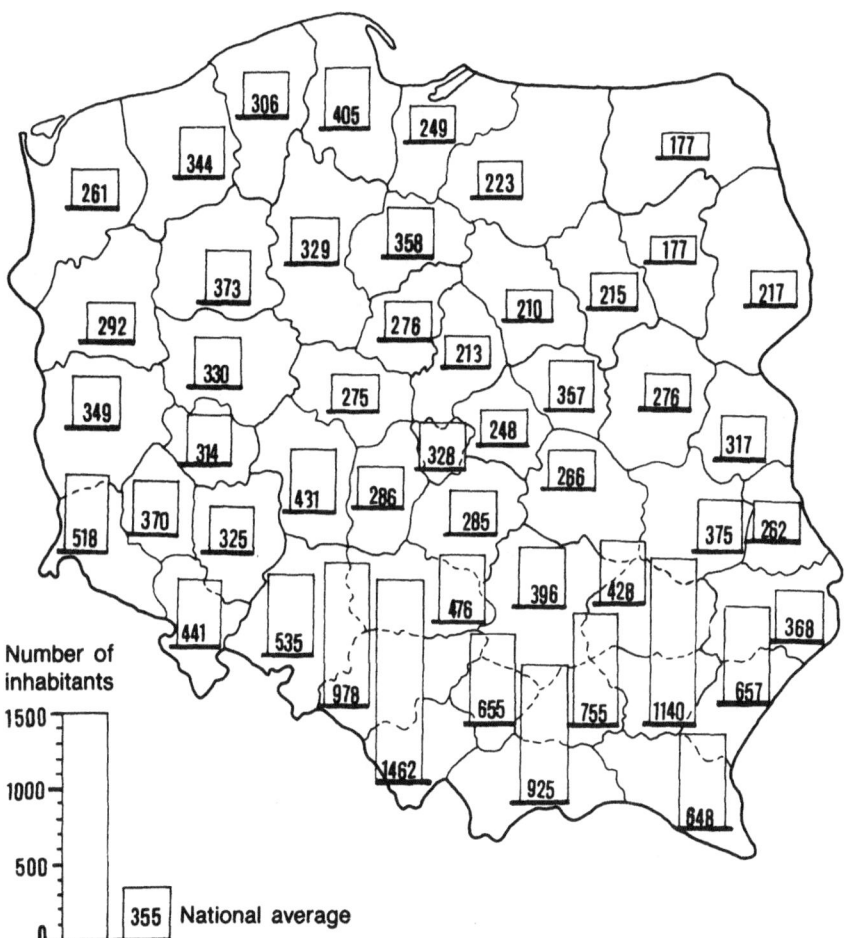

Map 7.1 The average size of a village according to voivodships, 1978.

areas. This settlement pattern determines the shape of daily life and the access to such elementary institutions of public life as schools, health service facilities, cultural institutions (cinema, library), and opportunities for entertainment. Naturally, technological advances facilitate contacts with the rest of the world for the villagers, especially radio, television, books, and the press—the media that can be taken advantage of without leaving home. Indeed, the rural population nowadays tends to match the urban standard of living by building good houses equipped with all creature comforts (running water, indoor plumbing, central heating, baths) as well as attempting to integrate popular culture with the more general, egalitarian national culture.[3] However, despite an extensive bus service (PKS) network, access to these elementary institutions is limited owing to the dispersed settlement pattern; this is one of the reasons for the mass migration of the younger population from the countryside to towns.[4]

Because of these developments, in the studies conducted for the Polish Academy of Sciences project, "The Multifunctional Development of Rural Areas up to the Year 2000," the academy's Committee on the Spatial Development of the Country (KPZK PAN) has attached a great deal of significance to the problem of furnishing the Polish countryside with social and technical infrastructure and the access of the rural population to these facilities, especially with regard to education and health service.[5]

Because the location of many institutions and infrastructure facilities of this kind is related to the administrative division of the country, I am of the opinion that it is wrong to centralize services excessively in administrative centers. Instead we should bring the authorities and institutions closer to the people. From this point of view, the establishment of some 2,000 rural and rural-urban *gminas* in 1973 was justified for servicing the inhabitants of the countryside. The abolition of *powiats* and the establishment of 49 voivodships in 1975 (instead of 22 voivodships before) also brought the regional centers closer to the population, especially in northeastern and eastern Poland, where there are few big towns. For this reason, in the Polish Academy of Sciences' publication entitled "An Evaluation of the Present Administrative Division of Poland and the Conclusions Arising from It" (also prepared by the KPZK PAN), I voiced the view that the present division into *gminas* should form the backbone of the administrative division of the country. I think there is no need to reintroduce an intermediate link such as the *powiat* and that the present division into voivodships should only be altered to a small extent.[6]

At present, the Polish village is a multifunctional area in which farming and forestry predominate. It also plays an important part in the ecological equilibrium of the natural environment, especially with regard to water resources. Rural areas play an important role in settlement, not only for villages and small towns but also for huge conurbations in that they act as recreation areas for townspeople and places where extractive industries can be located. All of this should be remembered when examining the relations between town and countryside. It is also worth recalling that a large part of Poland's population is of rural origin in the first generation. In 1978, out of the 33 million people born within Poland's present frontiers, those born in towns accounted for about 42 percent and those born in the countryside, for about 58 percent. Among the urban population, around 30 percent in that year were people born in the countryside, whereas among the rural population, 95 percent of the people were born in the countryside, which shows that the trend to return for permanent residence in the countryside from towns has not yet reached Poland.[7]

A Historical Outline of Changes in Town-Country Relations

The evolution of urbanization processes in Poland led to a relatively high level of urbanization at the end of the sixteenth and the beginning of the seventeenth century. This is shown in Table 7.1.

Table 7.1
The Change in the Number of Towns in Poland, 15th to 17th centuries

	Mid-15th Century	2nd Half of 16th C.	1st Half of 17th C.
Ethnically Polish lands of the Jagellon dynasty state	400	650	700
Poland within present-day frontiers	640	950	1000-plus

Source: S. Herbst, "Dzieje miast polskich od konca XV w do poczatkow XVIII w." (The History of Polish Towns from the End of the 15th Century to the Beginning of the 18th Century), in *Miasta Polskie w Tysiacleciu*, vol. 1, (Wroclaw, Warszawa, Krakow: 1965), pp. 37ff.

It is perhaps worth noting that at present, within comparable borders, there are some 800 towns in Poland. A comparison of this figure with the number of towns in the first half of the seventeenth century (1,000) demonstrates that the level of urban development was historically quite high. According to estimates, around 1578, the Polish lands of the Kingdom of Poland and Lithuania were inhabited by some 3 million people, out of whom about 700,000 lived in towns (i.e., about 23 percent of the total population). The lands corresponding to Poland's present territory were inhabited by 6.2 million people, including 1.5 million people living in towns (i.e., about one-fourth of the total).

This share of the urban population corresponded more or less to the share of the urban population in Poland in 1921. This should be borne in mind, because the Swedish invasion of Poland in the middle of the seventeenth century, the Northern War (1700–1721), and then the economic and political collapse of the Polish state in the eighteenth century resulted in an almost complete economic disaster for Polish towns. They began to rise again from the ensuing stagnation only at the end of the nineteenth and beginning of the twentieth century, in the era of capitalist industrialization.

The Change from the Mid-Nineteenth Century to 1939

The changes taking place in Europe at large in this period also reached Polish lands, but their intensity was very uneven. In the years from 1860–1870 to 1914 the rural population was in the majority. It can be

Table 7.2
The Share of the Population of Towns of 10,000-plus Inhabitants (percent)

	Ca. 1870	Ca. 1900	Ca. 1910
Poznan area	8.1	12.2	16.6
West Prussia	12.5	20.6	24.6
Upper Silesia	8.9	26.2	36.2
Cieszyn area	4.7	18.7	19.4
Kingdom of Poland	8.6	17.5	18.3
Galicia	5.6	9.6	13.1

Note: Total population = 100.0; these totals are partial.
Source: S. Kieniewicz, *Historia Polski 1795-1918*, p. 280.

estimated that 70 to 80 percent of all people earned their living by working in agriculture. In this period the disappearance of the feudal classes and the formation of a class society of the capitalist type began. The first distinct industrial districts emerged, absorbing relatively high numbers of migrants from the countryside. These districts included: (1) Warsaw with its surrounding industrial settlements (in 1864, Warsaw had 224,000 inhabitants; in 1914 that number rose to 885,000, or if the surrounding urbanized areas are taken into consideration, to about 1 million); (2) Lodz, a major textile industry center, which together with the neighboring localities, had almost 700,000 inhabitants around 1914; (3) the Silesia-Dabrowa basin with its huge concentration of heavy industry (mining of coal, zinc, lead, and iron ore and the steel industry) and a population of over 1 million people in 1914.[8] Although the region was divided by the border separating the Russian from the Prussian partition zones, it nevertheless constituted a certain geographical and economic unity, where the bulk of the modern Polish working class had its origins, chiefly those working in huge collieries and steel plants.[9]

However, it should be clearly realized that despite the existence of these few enclaves of faster urbanization and industrialization, generally speaking up to World War I the Polish lands had a low level of urban development and the majority of the people dwelt in the countryside where they were engaged in farming. This is illustrated by the share of the inhabitants of towns of 10,000 inhabitants or more in the total population of a given region. This can be seen in Table 7.2.

The Kingdom of Poland (the Russian partition zone), which was inhabited by over 40 percent of the Polish population, had a very low level of urbanization. Only in Upper Silesia—which contained a major concentration of industry and of the working class—was the level of urban growth relatively high, even though it was also considerably lower than that in the German state. At the same time in the rural areas, especially in Galicia and the Kingdom of Poland, a huge population surplus emerged as a result of a relatively high natural increase rate; it was far too great for the growing towns and industry to absorb.[10] As a result, the surplus population began looking for jobs elsewhere in Europe or the Americas. Economic migration from the rural areas in the Prussian partition zone was largely directed to the Ruhr basin, whose rapid development started after 1870, as well as to Berlin and other major urban centers in Germany. From Galicia and the kingdom, the migrants went chiefly to the Americas, especially the United States, Brazil, and Canada.

The estimated population losses through migration (mainly in the rural areas) in the years 1871 to 1913 were put at some 3.5 million people, or over 10 percent of the total population of Polish lands in 1914. Out of this number, some 2.3 million went overseas, including 1.9 million who went to the United States. Between 1896 and 1910 alone, Polish lands lost some 2.0 million people through migration; this amounted to almost 30 percent of the migration loss for the whole of Europe. Only Italy lost slightly more population through migration in that period (2.1 million). In relative terms, the losses to migration in Polish lands amounted to 29 percent of the natural increase.[11] The migration of the Polish rural population to the Americas before World War I and its assimilation to the new conditions have been described at length by W. J. Thomas and Florian Znaniecki in their monumental work *The Polish Peasant in Europe and America* in 1918–1920.[12]

It should also be remembered that the rural population's access to learning at the end of the nineteenth century was limited both for economic reasons (children were used in farmwork, lacked suitable clothing and shoes) and because of the lack of schools and teachers in villages. The worst situation in this respect prevailed in the Kingdom of Poland, where according to S. Kieniewicz, only about 30 percent of the population of towns and villages could read and write at the end of the nineteenth century. The best situation prevailed in the Prussian partition zone, but there the school served as a tool of Germanization. In Galicia, both elementary and secondary education and after 1870, also university courses were of a Polish character and constituted an important—if narrow—channel of social mobility for male rural youth. It took a great deal of effort and sacrifice, yet it was possible. This is confirmed by the reminiscences of Stanislaw Pigon, a professor of Polish studies. At the beginning of the twentieth century, peasants' sons accounted for some 16 percent of all students of Cracow's Jagiellonian University.[13]

World War I brought immense material damage to the Polish lands as well as huge population losses. The Polish state, reborn in 1918, faced many problems. It is worth remembering that hostilities had taken place on some 85 percent of Polish territory and that particularly damaging positional combat took place on 22 percent of the area. The overall losses to industry were estimated at 10 billion French francs in gold (in pre-1914 value). In the crop year 1918–1919, some 4.6 million hectares of land were left untilled, and in the following year this area still amounted to 3.5 million hectares, or nearly 20 percent of the country's area.[14]

In 1921, Poland had some 27 million inhabitants, three-fourths of them living in the countryside, which meant a generally low level of urbanization and industrialization. Peasants were the largest class, accounting for 53 percent of the total population; if the working population is taken into account, the percentage is higher, for two-thirds were farm workers. There had not been much change in the occupational structure in Poland by 1939 according to the estimates made by an authority on that period, Janusz Zarnowski. Peasants still accounted for over half of the total population at the end of that period and for over 60 percent if farm workers are taken into account as well. At the same time, the structure of land ownership was disadvantageous to the peasant population. In the 1920s, less than 1 percent of landowners had some 48 percent of all land. In contrast, of the 3.5 million peasant farms, only 0.4 million had more than ten hectares of land while over 2 million farms had less than five hectares of land.

There was a hunger for land and a surplus of labor in the Polish countryside. Before World War I part of the surplus was absorbed by other countries, either on a seasonal or a permanent basis. After 1920, these options were largely limited. Agrarian reform became necessary, as did the development of industry and the development of towns related to it. For political reasons, only a limited land reform was carried out; meanwhile, the development of industry and other branches of the national economy was hampered by the shortage of capital in a country destroyed by the war and later hit by the world crisis. This crisis took an especially acute form in Poland, affecting farming as well as industry. For this reason, the social and occupational structure of Poland's population in the years 1918 to 1939 was rather stable (see Table 7.3).

The lack of a developed industry and other nonagricultural branches of the economy limited the advantages of migrating to towns, in which the number of jobless was estimated at 1 million in the mid-1930s. Basically, the number of workers employed in large and medium industry did not grow.[15] As a result, there was hidden unemployment in the countryside that was estimated at some 5 million people.

The availability of housing and social and municipal infrastructure facilities (with the exception of education) was below the minimum acceptable level for a majority of the population. In the towns, the 1930s saw large-scale development of makeshift housing, while in the countryside there was a terrible overcrowding of substandard housing premises.[16]

One positive achievement of that period was the progressive development of education. In 1921 it was estimated that more or less one-third of the population above the age of ten could neither read nor write; in the countryside the proportion was even higher, 38.1 percent. By 1931 these

Table 7.3
Changes in Poland's Class and Strata Structure in 1921, 1931, and 1938

	Relative figures			Index of change until 1938, where 1921=100
	1921 %	1931 %	1938 %	
1. Working class[a]	27.5	29.3	30.3	190
2. Peasants	53.2	52.0	50.0	94
3. Petite bourgeoisie	21.0	10.6	11.8	107
4. Intelligentsia & clerical workers	5.1	5.6	5.7	112
5. Bourgeoisie	1.1	0.9	0.9	82
6. Landowners	0.3	0.3	0.3	100
7. Outcasts & demoralized elements	1.8	1.3	1.1	61
Total	100	100	100	

Note: a. Includes farmworkers, who in 1938 accounted for about 30 percent of the working class.
Source: J. Zarnowski, Spoleczenstwo Drugiej Rzeczypospolitej (The Society of the Second Polish Republic) (Warszawa: PWN, 1973), p. 32.

figures dropped to 23 percent overall and 27.6 percent in the countryside. By 1939, that share probably dropped to around 15 percent of the population. Secondary education was growing. In the school year 1937-1938, there were some 220,000 grammar school students, nearly half of them girls, while supplementary vocational schools had some 110,000 students. In the academic year 1938-1939, there were already twenty-eight higher schools with some 50,000 students. In that period, the enrollment of freshmen averaged 15,000 a year, including some 5,000 women (with rural youth accounting for about one-fourth of all students in that period). In the 1930s, the average number of university graduates year was 6,000.[17]

Naturally, the development of education, science, culture, administration, health service, transport (especially rail), and communications—the broadly conceived social and economic infrastructure—resulted in a growth of demand for highly qualified specialists and white collar workers. The educational status attained facilitated the mobility of youth with peasant backgrounds in nonagricultural trades, the civil service, and the army, which was also a path of professional career for a part of the younger generation.

However, the generally low level of economic development of the countryside and towns was an impediment to migration. It limited the growth of commodity exchange between them and the role of towns, simply because the Polish countryside was too poor to afford industrial products.

The Transformations in Poland Under Socialist Rule

Poland emerged from World War II with huge human losses (estimated at six million people) as well as enormous material and cultural losses. The takeover of power by working class and peasant parties made it possible to carry out a broad program of socioeconomic reforms, which released a great amount of public energy. The principles of socialist democracy, adopted as the foundation of activity, were supposed to lead to: (1) broadly conceived social egalitarianism, (2) accelerated industrialization and urbanization of the country, (3) elimination of differences between towns and countryside, and (4) a fairly balanced development of individual regions. On the basis of pacts concluded with the Soviet Union, Poland's territory was moved considerably to the west. This called for the social, economic, and geographical integration of the regained territories with the old lands and the reconstruction of a number of large towns, notably Warsaw, Wroclaw, Gdansk, and Szczecin, as well as some half a million farmsteads.

In general, it can be said that conditions were created for the elimination of the sharp class differences that had persisted until 1939. These conditions were the result of agrarian reform (over 1.5 million hectares of farmland were turned over to peasants, farm workers on large landed estates, and landless people); the nationalization of large and medium-sized industrial enterprises, banks, and commerce; the limitations on private property in trade and services; the control over housing resources in towns. Of course, differences among strata have persisted until today because the policy of intensive development of industry led to a clear acceleration of urban growth and a rapid increase in the size of the urban population (see Table 7.4) and of the population employed outside agriculture, especially in the public sector of the economy. This represents a qualitative difference in town-countryside relations between past and present.

Change in Occupational Structure

In 1950, those employed in agriculture accounted for about 54 percent of the total work force. By 1960 it dropped to about 43 percent, by 1970 to 34 percent, and since 1975 it has stood at the level of 29–30 percent. According to GUS studies made in 1982, only 25 percent of the country's population lived in households connected with the ownership of a private farm.[18] In 1938, the share of peasant population was estimated at around 50 percent.

Table 7.4
Poland's Population: Overall, Urban, and Rural, 1946-1983

	Years[a]					
	1946	1950	1960	1970	1980	1983
Overall[b]	23.6	25.0	32.7	32.7	35.7	36.7
Percent	100	100	100	100	100	100
Towns[a]	8.0	9.2	14.4	17.1	21.0	21.9
Percent	34.0	36.9	48.3	52.3	58.7	59.7
Countryside[a]	15.6	15.8	15.4	15.6	14.7	14.8
Percent	66.0	63.1	51.7	47.3	41.3	40.3

Notes: a. In millions.
b. Figures for December 31.
Source: Central Statistical Office (GUS), Yearbooks (Warszawa: GUS, selected years).

The changes in employment structures in the long term are presented in Table 7.5. These figures show that at present the level of employment in industry and farming is very much the same. Compared to other countries, it can be said that Poland still has a surplus of employment in farming, a similar level of employment in industry, and too little employment in transport and communications, trade, and a wide range of services.

However, it appears that no major change can occur in this respect until the size of the average private farm increases. At present, this size stands at some 5.0 hectares and has remained fairly stable over a long period of time. There are great regional differences in this respect, but these do not affect the general conclusion. If in the future employment were limited to 1 person per farm, this would yield an average of 20 people per 100 hectares, not including those employed in services for farmers. This level is certainly too high, more than twice as high as it should be but it is a consequence of the very slow growth in the size of the average farm.

It should be remembered that in 1931 Poland had some ten million people employed in agriculture, while now the figure is lower by a half. This means that employment has been reduced by five million, that is, almost the whole "hidden unemployment" of the 1930s has been wiped out. Out of the five million people employed in farming, about one million work in state and cooperative farms and as many as four million people work in private farms. However, if changes in technology and mechanization of farm work are taken into account, it turns out that theoretically there are still too many people working in that sector of the economy. Moreover,

Table 7.5
Changes in the Structure of Employment in the Years 1950-1980 in Selected Areas of the National Economy

	Years				
	1950	1960	1970	1975	1980
Overall employment (millions)	10,186	12,401	15,175	16,572	17,324
Percent	100.0	100.0	100.0	100.0	100.0
% employed in					
Industry	20.7	25.5	29.3	31.1	30.3
Construction	5.0	6.5	7.1	8.5	7.7
Transport/communications	4.5	5.6	6.2	6.4	6.5
Trade	4.8	6.0	6.9	7.2	7.5
Farming	53.6	43.3	34.3	29.3	29.7
Total	88.6	86.9	83.8	82.5	81.7

Source: GUS, Yearbook 1983.

excessive migration to towns has distorted the age and sex structure of the rural population, in which there is now too high a proportion of old people and too few women of marriageable age, especially in the private sector of farming.

In addition to basic change in the numbers and proportion of urban and rural population in the postwar period, the occupational structure of the rural population changed under the influence of broadly conceived urbanization processes. It should be noted here that in 1964 the urban population accounted for 34 percent of the total population and by 1983 this share rose to 60 percent, while in absolute figures it rose from 8 million to 22 million—almost trebled—whereas the size of the rural population has stayed in the neighborhood of 15 million all the time. In 1950, only some 20 percent of the rural population earned their living outside agriculture, whereas by now this proportion amounts to 50 percent (see Maps 7.2 and 7.3). These are people who live in the country and for the most part, commute to work in towns and industry centers. As a rule, they also have some land and form the stratum known as worker-peasants.

Another group, which is at present smaller but likely to increase in the future, are people who are employed in the countryside in nonfarming trades. Most of them supply services to the rural population. This group embraces teachers (a fairly large group), health service workers (mostly auxiliary personnel and a few doctors), cultural workers (a small group), retail trade employees (a large group), state administration workers, political party staff, and economic administration workers, as well as people employed in industry, transport and communications, and construction. In 1978, some 3.3 million people employed outside agriculture lived in the coun-

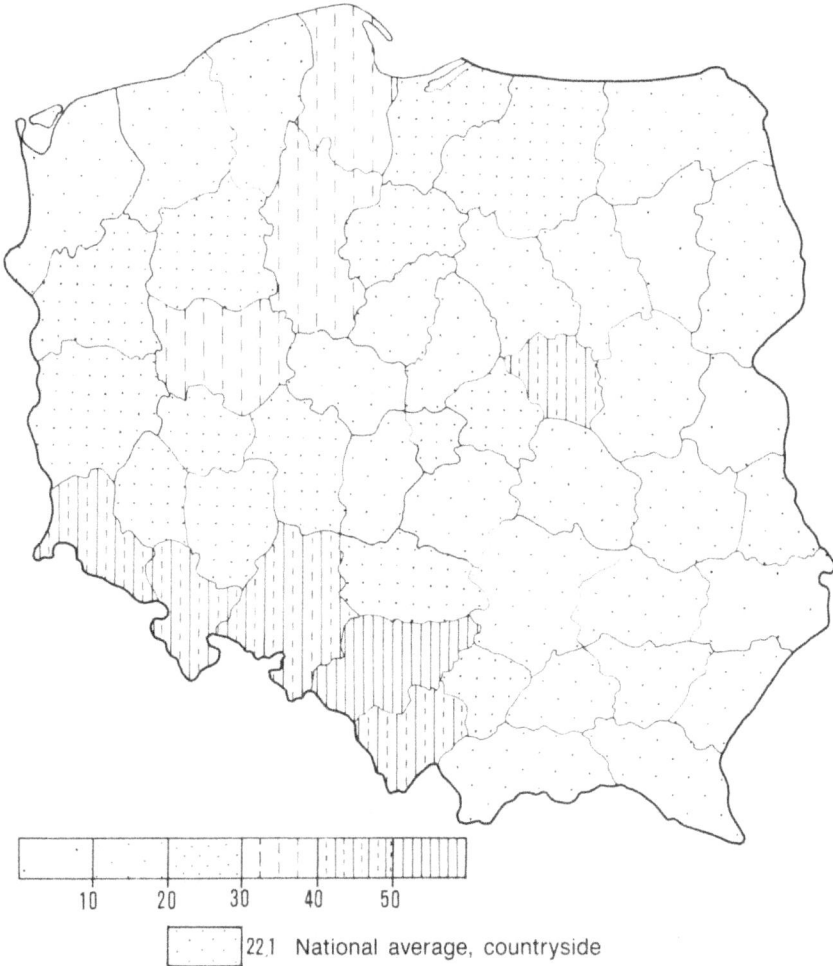

Map 7.2 The proportion of nonagricultural population of the countryside according to voivodships, 1950.

tryside. Some 800,000 people worked in the public sector of farming and some 4.0 million in the private sector. In 1978, the number of people employed in the public sector and resident in the countryside equaled for the first time the number of people working on private farms.[19] There are significant regional differences in this respect, to which I shall return later.

Changes in the Use of Rural Land

In these general considerations of rural-urban linkages I should not ignore the influence of several phenomena that appeared in Poland on a large scale after World War II.

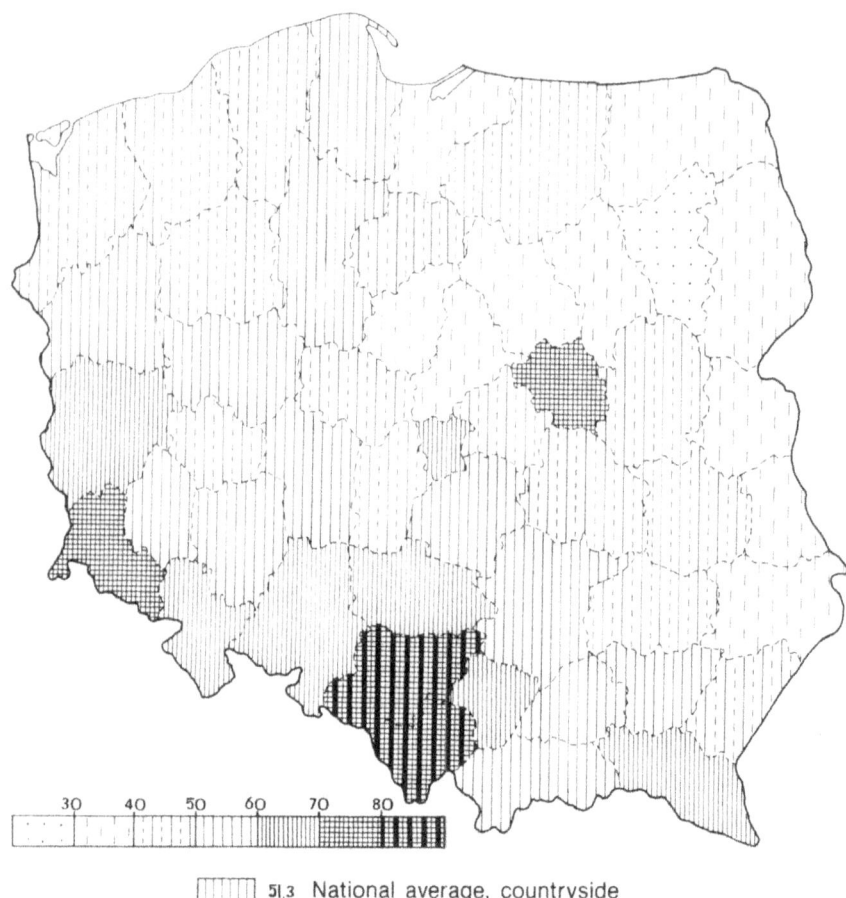

Map 7.3 The proportion of nonagricultural population of the countryside according to voivodships, 1978.

One is the emergence of suburban zones, usually connected with a major town, as population areas. This phenomenon could be occasionally observed before 1939, for example, in the Warsaw area or the Upper Silesian Industrial Basin (GOP), but the process was greatly accelerated after the war. At first it was connected with the development of electric commuter train networks (e.g., in Warsaw and the Gdansk-Sopot-Gdynia conurbation). Later on, beginning with the 1960s, came the development of public road transport (PKS commuter buses, urban transport buses extending far into the suburbs). This phenomenon is associated with the agglomerative phase of urban growth in Poland.[20] In large measure, apart from the ease of access by public transport, it is the outcome of technological development in industry (electric drive system for machines, new processes using far less materials).

Under Polish conditions, this process is also related to an "urban growth deficit," which means roughly that in medium and large towns the growth in the number of jobs was in excess of the number of new housing units. This led to large-scale commuting and the permanent settlement of nonagricultural population in rural areas within easy reach of the place of work. But in many cases commuting is not justifiable socially, when the one-way trip takes more than an hour. Another factor in this settlement pattern has been the growing affluence of society, especially the urban population, the shortening of working hours in nonagricultural jobs, as well as the considerable increase in the number of residents of medium-sized towns and big conurbations. For example, in 1983, about half of the urban population, or about 30 percent of the country's total population, lived in towns of more than 100,000 inhabitants.

In daily life, the urban population has little contact with the natural environment, for scenery or recreation. This fact has had a dual impact on settlement patterns. One manifestation is the mass holiday migrations of the urban population to the countryside, especially the seacoast, the mountains, and the lake districts. From this has followed the establishment of permanent and seasonal recreation centers, which provide jobs for a part of the local population. (On a mass scale this takes place in the Nowy Sacz voivodship.) In some parts of the country, villages have become transformed into so-called holiday villages catering to vacationers. This has been reflected in the shape and size of houses and buildings for pension accommodations. Classic examples of this trend are such places as Bukowina or Murzasichle near Zakopane or the region of Szczyrk and Wisla in the Silesian Beskid Mountains.

The other impact has been the emergence of dachas, or "country homes" in villages situated along the banks of rivers or lakes or other attractive locations, located at a distance of 60–150 kilometers from large conurbations and medium-sized towns. This trend intensified in the 1970s and was connected with the emergence of a rather large—by Polish standards—stratum of affluent people, who could afford a car, a dacha, and regular weekend trips to a country residence. The growing move to a five-day week also contributed to this trend.

The lowering of the average standard of living of the urban population in the years 1980–1983, the scarcity of gas, and rationing contributed to a reduction of recreational traffic. But it is expected that the trend will pick up again and will affect the development of rural areas as the level of affluence of the urban population begins to rise again toward the end of the 1980s. Areas suitable for recreation purposes occupy about 30 percent of the area of Poland.[21]

The Effects of Migration from Countryside to Towns

In the earlier periods, that is, in the first phase of industrialization (from the late nineteenth century to 1914) and in the years 1918 to 1939, Polish towns were not able to absorb the population surplus from the villages. In contrast, after World War II and especially in the 1970s, it seems that the towns took away too many people from the villages. To

Table 7.6
The Relationship Between Natural Increase in the Countryside and the Balance of Migration from the Countryside to Towns, 1950-1983

	Natural Increase (NI) (thousands)	Balance Migration (BM) (thousands)	Difference NI-BM
1951-1955	1,460	628	+832
1956-1960	1,418	420	+998
1961-1965	1,056	502	+554
1966-1970	837	697	+140
1971-1975	871	938	-67
1976-1980	815	1,067	-252
1981-1983	482	451	+31
1950-1983	6,939	4,703	+2,236

Source: Author's calculations on the basis of GUS Statistical Yearbooks.

some extent, this is confirmed by the relationship between the natural increase in the countryside and the balance of migration between the countryside and towns in the years 1950 to 1983 (see Table 7.6).

Natural increase in the countryside dropped from some 300,000 a year to 150,000–160,000 a year in the 1970s. This was the consequence of a large decline in the birthrate combined with a fairly stable rural population. In the 1970s the balance of migration from countryside to towns increased considerably, averaging some 200,000 people a year. In that decade, for the first time since the nineteenth century, the Polish countryside lost more population as a result of migration than it gained through natural increase. The crisis of 1981–1983 slowed this negative trend a little because the towns could not offer a sufficient number of jobs and accommodations (especially the latter). But the surplus of natural increase over migration was small (see Figure 7.1). However, huge migrations, involving as a rule the younger generation of villagers (20 to 34 years old), have distorted population age structures in the countryside. According to the 1978 census results, the proportion of people above the age of 59 in the countryside is much higher than in towns: 15 percent. The opposite situation obtains in the 20–34 age group, which accounts for 28 percent of the population in the towns and only 23 percent of the population in the countryside. Surprising phenomena have been observed with regard to the sex structure of the population of marriageable age, the 20–34 age group. The migration from countryside to towns included young rural women to a much greater extent than men. This left young men, and especially private farm owners, in a difficult situation when it came to finding a wife. This phenomenon

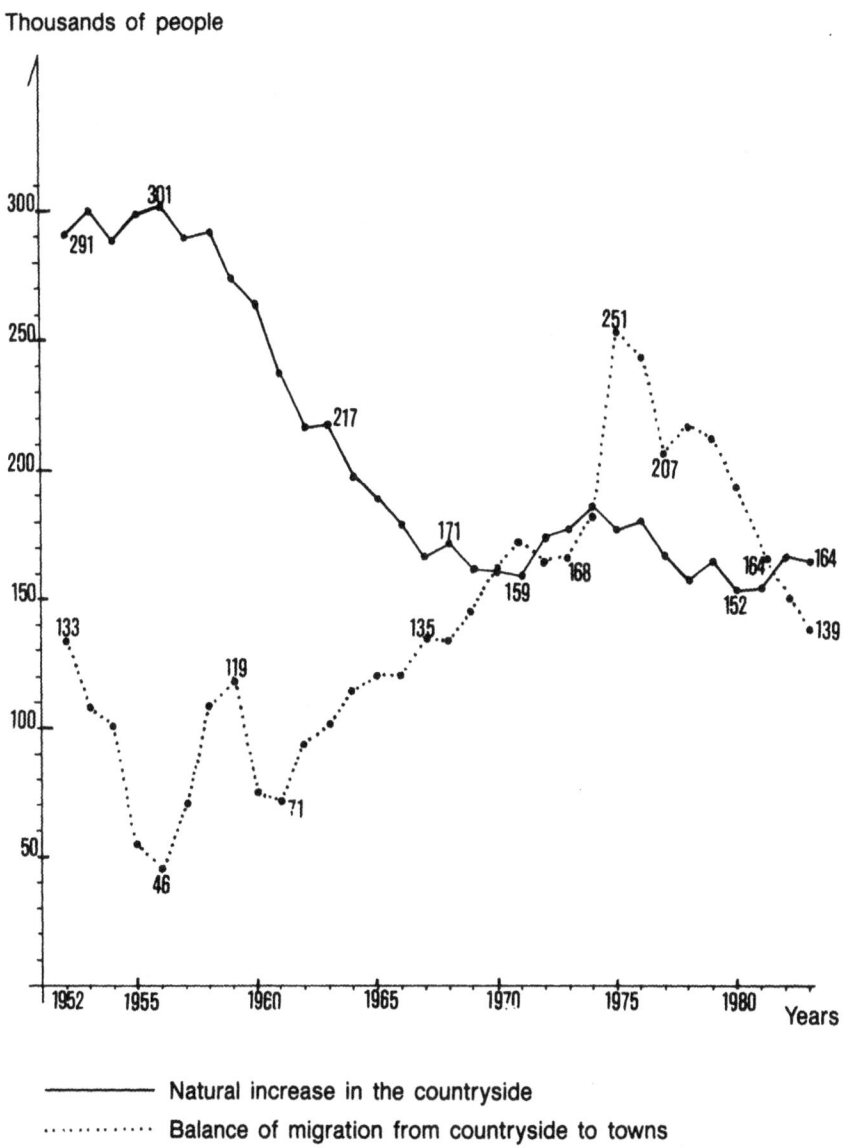

Figure 7.1 Natural increase in the countryside and the balance of migration between towns and countryside, 1952–1983.

threatens to undercut the intensive growth of farming production in private farms in the future, as the latter rely on the work of a whole family.

In the towns, there is a marked surplus of women of a marriageable age, while in the countryside there is an even more pronounced surplus of men. Naturally, there are sizable regional differences in either case. The share of old people (age 60 and above) is especially large in the eastern and central voivodships, which lost a great deal of population through migration. Bialystok voivodship tops the list, with about one-fifth of the whole population in that age group. The western and northern voivodships have the lowest share of people above 59 years of age, which can be explained by the settlement of young people there after World War II (see Map 7.4). The biggest migration of women in the 20-24 age group has occurred in the rural areas of the eastern voivodships. The number of men per 100 women there amounts to 144 in Bialystok voivodship, 141 in Lomza voivodship, 131 in Biala Podlaska voivodship, and 129 in the Suwalki and Ostroleka voivodships. In contrast, in the Warsaw conurbation, there are only 96 men in the 20-24 age group per 100 women; this is the result of the huge migration of young women to the Warsaw metropolitan voivodship (see Table 7.7 as well as Map 7.5).

Changes in the State of Rural Population in Individual Voivodships

Against this backdrop, it is interesting to compare the changes in the size of the rural population according to voivodships in the years 1950 to 1978. This is made possible by the Central Statistical Office's (GUS) analysis of the results of the 1978 national census. According to their figures, in the years in question, population growth for the Polish countryside amounted to 107.4 (1950=100). Out of forty-nine voivodships, rural population actually decreased in only eleven. These were mostly the northeastern and eastern voivodships together with the central part of the country, which were characterized by a low level of urban development. The highest losses were suffered by Bialystok and Lomza voivodships, which lost over 10 percent of the population compared to the 1950 level. The biggest gains were recorded by the Warsaw metropolitan voivodship—up 45 percent—and the Szczecin voivodship—up 33 percent (see Map 7.6).[22]

With 1970 taken as 100, the rural population of Poland in 1978 decreased to 97.7. In that period, population losses in the countryside were recorded in no fewer than thirty-seven voivodships, while in twelve voivodships the loss exceeded 5 percent. Again the biggest losses were recorded by the Bialystok and Lomza voivodships—90.3 and 91.8, respectively; Suwalki, with 91.8; and Olsztyn, with 92.1. All these voivodships are situated in the northeastern part of the country. Considerable losses also occur in the two Sudetes Mountain voivodships (Walbrzych and Jelenia Gora) as well as in some other voivodships (see Map 7.7).

Some growth occurred in voivodships that have ties with the cities of Poznan, Cracow, Warsaw, Katowice, and Gdansk (by 2-3 percent) and in

Map 7.4 The share of the population aged 60 and above in the countryside, according to voivodships, 1978.

the southern and southeastern voivodships that have a large proportion of farming population. In principle, it can be assumed that the traditionally agricultural voivodships—with a low level of urbanization and industrialization, a large dispersal of the settlement network, small villages, and a poor social infrastructure—are losing population.

The voivodships that offer village dwellers a chance of working outside agriculture are less susceptible to migration. The Sudetes voivodships are an exception: They combine improper use of farmland and a large share of obsolete industry with unfavorable natural conditions. The population is moving away from these areas. In general, however, it is moving out of agricultural regions. To some extent this is confirmed by sociological

Table 7.7
The Number of Men per 100 Women in the 20-34 Age Group, 1978

	Age Groups		
	20-24	25-29	30-34
Poland overall	104	102	101
towns	97	95	97
countryside	116	117	109

Source: A. Stasiak, "Wybrane problemy zagospodarowania przestrzennego wsi polskiej" (Selected Problems in the Spatial Development of the Polish Countryside), Miasto, no. 5 (1982).

studies made in the Suwalki voivodship, where the common view among the rural population is that those who have migrated to towns are living better.[23] A similar opinion was voiced by an expert in rural problems, Professor Dyzma Galaj, who has observed that "a farming family's work never ends," especially for the owner and his wife. This is work from which one can never take leave because a peasant farm can provide an infinite amount of work to do.[24]

In discussing rural living conditions, Dyzma Galaj goes on to relate a conversation he had with an elderly farmer. The man told him, "We peasants have it 400 percent better than before the war, yet we have it worse." What he meant by this statement was that, although old needs have been fully satisfied, new ones have emerged, and the failure to satisfy these needs makes life harder than before, when hunger was commonplace in the months preceding a new harvest:

> What kind of needs are these? They are the needs which allow man to live a better, more pleasant life during his leisure time. The peasants, who have to work without a break, cannot live a better life because they have no time to do so. . . . This applies to women in particular. At the age of forty, rural women are so fatigued that they feel and look old. It is therefore not surprising that they do not want to marry peasants if they do not have to.[25]

It appears that such remarks of a sociological and psychosociological nature indicate the importance of the influence of urban life-styles on the contemporary Polish village. Furthermore, it shows how difficult it is to predict the direction of further change in the countryside without taking into account many aspects of satisfying all the needs of the rural population, not only the essential ones concerning food, clothing, or housing.

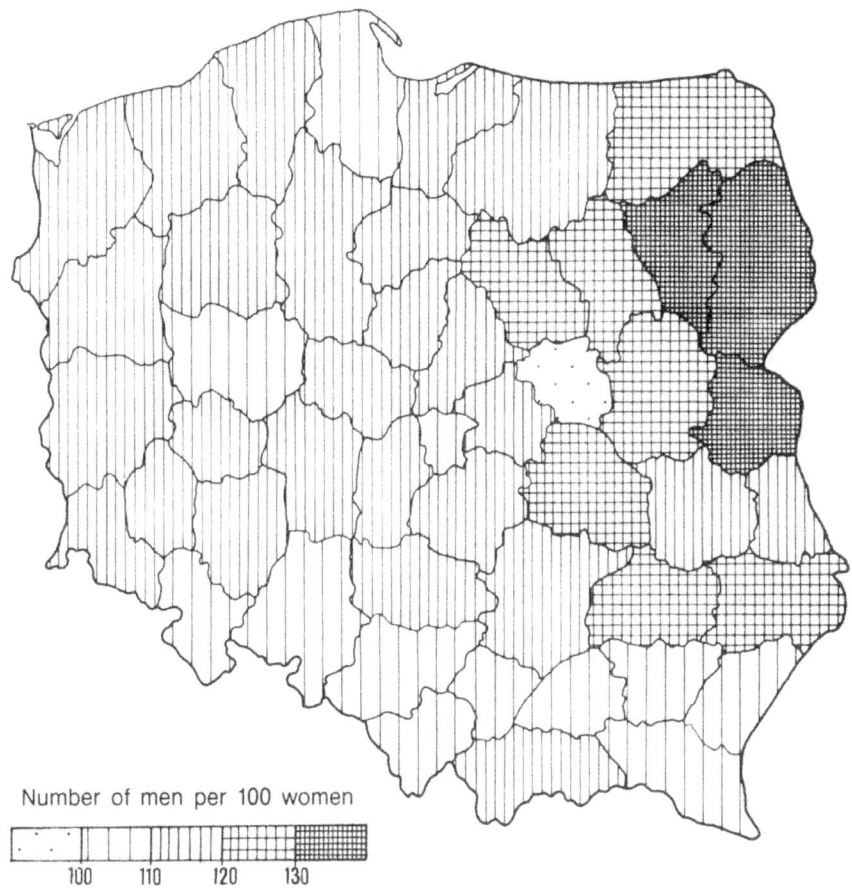

Map 7.5 Voivodship indicators of masculinization of the rural population in the age group 20-24, 1978.

Notes

1. Pawel Rybicki has discussed these developments in the larger European context and attempted a synthesis of these notions in *Spoleczenstwo miejskie* (Urban Society), (Warszawa: PWN, 1972), pp. 5-29.

2. A. Stasiak. "Wybrane problemy zagospodarowania przestrzennego wsi polskiej" (Selected Problems of the Spatial Development of the Polish Countryside), *Miasto*, no. 5 (1982).

3. Cf. the very interesting considerations of Professor J. Burszta in *Kultura Ludowa, Kultura Narodowa* (Folk Culture, National Culture), (Warszawa: Ludowa Spoldzielnia Wydawnicza, 1974), the chapter "Present-Day Reality," pp. 68-95.

4. R. Horodenski. *Warunki zycia ludnosci wiejskiej Polski Polnocno-Wschodniej* (Living Conditions of the Rural Population of Northeastern Poland), (Bialystok: Osrodek Badan Naukowyc, 1983), especially chapter 7, pp. 420-39.

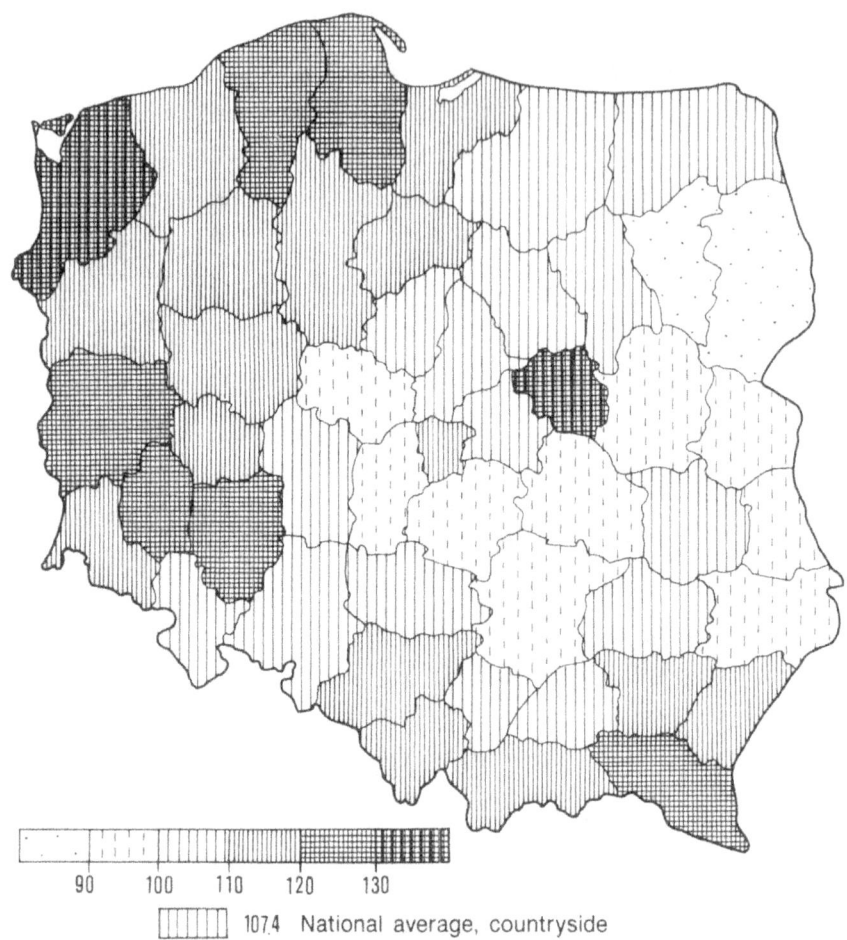

Map 7.6 Change in the rural population according to voivodships, 1950-1978 (1950 = 100).

5. "Wies Polska 2000" (The Polish Countryside 2000), *Biuletyn KPZK PAN* (Warszawa), vol. 122 (1983), A. Stasiak (ed). Cf. M. Mackiewicz, "Zroznicowanie przestrzenne mozliwosci korzystania z opieki zdrowotnej przez ludnosc wiejska" (Spatial Differences in the Accessibility of Health Service Facilities by the Rural Population), pp. 39-52; Z. Kwiecinski, "Przestrzenne zroznicowanie dostepnosci sieci szkolnej na obszarach wiejskich" (Spatial Differences in the Accessibility of the School Network in Rural Areas), pp. 121-138; and also D. Galaj, "System spoleczny w gminie" (The Social System in a *Gmina*), pp. 105-120.

6. "Podzial administracyjny kraju: Poglady i opinie" (Views and Comments on the Administrative Division of the Country), *Biuletyn KPZK PAN* (Warszawa), vol. 126 (1984), A. Stasiak (ed). Cf. "Moje poglady na temat podzialu administracyjnego kraju" (My Views on the Administrative Division of the Country), pp. 39-40.

7. All the above figures are based on "Migracje ludnosci: Badanie metoda reprezentacyjna NSP z dnia 7.XII.1978 (Population Migrations: A Study of a

Map 7.7 Change in the rural population according to voivodships, 1970-1978 (1970 = 100).

Representative Sample from the National Census of December 7, 1978)," *Statystyka Polska* (Warszawa), No. 140 (1981), Table 1, pp. 2, 20, 38.

8. S. Kieniewicz, *Historia Polski 1795-1918* (Warszawa: PWN, 1970).

9. A. Stasiak, *Miasto Krolewska Huta /Chorzow/. Zarys rozwoju spoleczno-gospodarczego i przestrzennego w latach 1869-1914* (The Town of Krolewska Huta /Chorzow/. An Outline of Socioeconomic and Spatial Development in the Years 1869-1914) (Warszawa: Arkady, 1962); A. Stasiak, *Przemiany stosunkow mieszkaniowych w Zaglebiu Slasko-Dabrowskim* (Changes in Housing Relations in the Upper Silesian—Dabrowa Basin) (Warszawa: IBM, 1966).

10. S. Inglot (ed.), *Historia chlopow polskich* (The History of Polish Peasants), vol. 1, 2, 3 (Warszawa: Ludowa Spoldzielnia Wydawnicza, 1970-1980).

11. E. Kolodziej, *Wychodzstwo zarobkowe z Polski 1918-1939* (Economically Motivated Emigration from Poland 1918-1939), (Warszawa: Ksiazka i Wiedza, 1982), pp. 27-28.

12. W. I. Thomas and F. Znaniecki, *The Polish Peasant in Europe and America*, vol. 1 (New York: Octagon Books, 1971), see the introductory remarks by J.

Chalasinski. In this introduction by sociologists Josef Chalasinski and Jan Szczepanski, Chalasinski remarks that "at the beginning, this was mostly a bachelor community. Men went on their own to reconnoiter. . . . Among the emigrants aged twenty-one and above men by far outnumbered women. . . ." (Since the 1970s, many more women than men have been migrating from villages to towns in Poland, which is a special sign of the times in the change of social postures.) "Initially, their settlements were more reminiscent of Polish villages than American industrial settlements. . . ." (One of the first institutions in a new immigrant settlement was the inn. Next came religious associations and parishes. Characteristically, the parishes were closed to outsiders.)

13. S. Pigon. *Z Komborni w swiat* (From Kombornia Out into the World), (n.p./ n.d.: Ludowa Spoldzielnia Wydawnicza, 5th ed.), especially chapter 3, "School Years," and chapter 4, "At the University, The Errant Years."

14. Cf. *Historia Polski*, Vol. 4 (1918–1939), Part 1 (1918–1921) (Warszawa: PWN, 1984, 2nd ed.), pp. 131–132, and *Historia Polski*, Vol. 4, Part 2 (1921–1926) (Warszawa: PWN, 1984, 1st ed.), pp. 20–21.

15. Z. Landau, J. Tomaszewski, *Druga Rzeczpospolita. Gospodarka. Spoleczenstwo. Miejsce w swiecie* (The Second Republic. Economy. Society. Their Place in the World), (Warszawa: Ksiazka i Wiedza, 1977). See the chapters on smallholdings and the number of workers.

16. A. Andrzejewski, *Polityka mieszkaniowa* (Housing Policy) (Warszawa: Arkady, 1959).

17. All the data concerning education and science are based on the *Small Statistical Yearbook 1939* (Warszawa: GUS, 1939), pp. 28–29, 327, 331, 333–35.

18. "Ludnosc wiejska zwiazana z rolnictwem indywidualnym. Badanie metoda reprezentacyjna. Stan w dniu 8.XII.1982" (Rural Population Connected with Private Farming. A Study of a Representative Sample), *Statystyka Polska: Materialy statystyczne*, 16 (Warszawa 1982).

19. A. Stasiak, "Struktury spoleczno-demograficzne wsi polskiej i jej przemiany" (The Socio-Demographic Structures of the Polish Countryside and Their Changes), in *Wies Polska 2000* 2

20. S. Leszczycki, P. Eberhardt, and S. Herman, "Aglomeracje miejskoprzemyslowe w Polsce" (Urban Industrial Agglomerations in Poland), *Biuletyn KPZK PAN* (Warszawa), vol. 67 (1971), A. Stasiak, "Procesy kształtowania i przeobrazenia aglomeracji miejskich" (The Processes of Shaping and Transforming Urban Agglomerations), *Gornoslaskie Studia Socjologiczne* (Katowice), vol. 7 (1969).

21. S. Wawrzyniak, "Ekspansja ludnosci na tereny wiejskie" (Population Expansion into Rural Areas); W. Kosinski, "Stan i perspektywy odnowy krajobrazu wsi polskiej" (The State and Prospects of Renewal of the Landscape of the Polish Countryside), in *Wies Polska 2000*, vol. 110 (1980).

22. Based on "Ludnosc: Gospodarstwa domowe i warunki mieszkaniowe" (Population: Households and Housing Conditions), National Census of December 7, 1978, *Statystyka Polska* (Warszawa: GUS, 1980), No. 128.

23. E. Stasiak, "Wyludnianie sie obszarow Suwalszczyzny" (The Depopulation of the Suwalki Region), *Wies Wspolczesna*, No. 6 (1980).

24. D. Galaj. "Sprzecznosc w przeobrazeniach spolecznosci chlopskiej" (Contradictions in the Transformations of the Peasant Community), *Wies i Rolnictwo*, No. 1 (1984).

25. Ibid.

PART FOUR

The Sources of Tension Within the System

Given the already extensive literature on Solidarity and Poland's political problems, what the authors in this section have to offer in the way of new insight is their placing the political events of 1980–1981 in their broader socioeconomic context. Their concern lies not with the specific crisis that came to a head in those years, but rather with the aftermath: the continuing tensions within the system that have produced a sustained and ongoing crisis without solution, one that continually skirts the edges of breakdown, yet contributes little to the resolution of the tensions that have produced conflict. The present reality entails living daily amid a systemic crisis permeating the entire fabric of Polish society.

In order to understand more fully the sources of social tension, Ciechocinska suggests that those interested in present-day realities look more closely at the "social infrastructure" of postwar Poland. By this term she means the entire system of social services provided by the state—everything that is done by the state in social policy to attend to the needs of individuals, families, and communities. Her assessment of these policy outcomes is, at least as I understand it, devastating: The egalitarian commitment in the socialist revolution imposed immediately after the war at such great price has been progressively undercut and destroyed as the administrative apparatus created to convert that commitment into specific programs has been rationalized and "improved upon" by the authorities. The tension resides in the conflict between bureaucratic norms emphasizing hierarchy, specialization, and rationality and social norms stressing equal access to the benefits derived from the socioeconomic progress experienced since World War II. Measured in terms of impact on people, hierarchy has meant dictating to recipients how social services will be organized regardless of the people's real needs or the conditions under which they live. Specialization has amounted to increased technical proficiency in the aggregate at the cost of reduction of basic services to ever wider sectors of society. Rationality has come to symbolize increased control and coordination of compartmentalized administrative operations, through the creation of a smaller number of more complex service centers, without dealing with the simultaneous decline in access to these services.

Against the technical discussion of this problem by Ciechocinska one should set Reykowski's broader, interpretative essay. Reykowski identifies two fundamental problems in the present social setting: the population's demand for social justice and the authorities' need for increased economic productivity to be able to respond to these demands in the form of new jobs, higher wages, and improved social services. He stresses the great extent of popular resentment against the state. He sees it as the result of a generalized consciousness of powerlessness, increased awareness of opportunities elsewhere (because Poles have always considered themselves to be a part of the West), and a strong sense of inequality in practice despite a continued rhetoric of equality.

As a consequence of these tensions, Reykowski identifies three dilemmas. First, there is the issue of how to achieve greater equality in the form of economic justice when decisionmakers must make choices about how the limited resources available will be used. The dilemma here, he writes, becomes one of determining what degree of destabilization Poland can tolerate without collapse. The second dilemma is derived from the first: how to have fundamental change occur without moving into open struggle against the state and ultimately revolution. The third entails confronting what Reykowski terms the Polish national mentality: how without sacrificing control to design programs that people will accept.

Each of the dilemmas outlined by Reykowski picks up on themes discussed in greater detail earlier in the book. The essence of these dilemmas lies in the juxtaposition of competing demands, each with its own rationale and indispensability, and in the impossibility of attending to any one basic demand without denying response to another equally important demand. In times past, this has been the source of social revolution, but that is precluded by the very structure of power, or what several contributors to this volume call "the system for exercising power." It is to the assessment of that system of power that the final two authors devote themselves, but before entering that terrain it is helpful first to consider the social context.

8

Problems in the Development of Social Infrastructure in Poland

Maria K. Ciechocińska

Problems in satisfying basic social needs were among the causes of the growing social discontent in the late 1970s that ultimately led to the events of the hot summer and August 1980. That state of affairs was a result of the administrative authorities' failure to appreciate the importance of the problem, as well as the limited financial means and relative ineffectiveness of the remedies that were undertaken. A significant role was also played by the mistakes made in the development of social infrastructure, compounded by numerous organizational changes, including the negative effects of the introduction in 1975 of a new administrative division for the country.

The state of the social infrastructure in 1980 was widely perceived as unsatisfactory, mainly because of a glaring discrepancy between the range of services promised in the authorities' program and their actual availability. That discontent demonstrated that the society was no longer willing to accept the ever longer waiting periods for a flat* in a housing cooperative, the queues outside a doctor's dispensary in a health center, the waiting lists for a given book in a library, the sick waiting for a vacant bed in a hospital or for surgery, the hopeless queuing outside shops, or the strain of commuting by overcrowded trains or buses.

In the end, the numerous shortcomings and scarcities added up to a political, social, and economic crisis. Production could no longer continue. In short, change and reform became a precondition for survival.

The society took a definitely negative view of the state of the social infrastructure. It pointed to the lack or improper location of basic facilities and their inadequate equipment and staffing problems and criticized the retention of deficient organizational structures and forms of work, which often clashed with the real needs of local communities.

---

*The British term "flat" is used here as the equivalent of *mieszkanie*. The word *apartment* refers in Polish to a much more commodious living unit in an apartment building (Eds.)

People considered the social infrastructure of 1980 to be actually worse than in earlier periods. This was confirmed by indices illustrating the diminishing availability of various services; the principle of general access, previously guaranteed by specialized state centers, was being abandoned in favor of limited-access solutions aimed at fulfilling the needs of, let us say, the work force of selected large enterprises or employees of some important state institutions. This favoritism led to a lower standard of services in the more generally accessible network, which had to cope with financial, material, and staffing problems.

The constrution of a network of large social service centers, restricted in access and isolated from the local communities where most people lived, represented a reaction to an earlier situation. These centers were designed to respond to the increasing difficulties people faced in obtaining access to the ordinary network, a network of smaller, specialized centers that lagged behind growing social needs because of insufficient investment and development of facilities.

But in practice these newer isolated centers meant a gradual segmentation of society and the emergence of discrimination in services, depending on the financial or political status of the employer. Tying the social infrastructure to employment resulted in further discrimination within a factory or institution. Very often this practice resulted in the denial of services to those who lived far away from their place of work and whose afterwork hours were limited because of transportation problems.

Not everyone in the social milieu was equally aware of the worsening social infrastructure, partly because along with this development came such spectacular ventures as the construction of a diagnostic center in Wroclaw, a children's health center (a memorial hospital built with the help of public contributions to honor the martyrdom of child-victims of World War II), an oncology center, and the like.

Public funds accumulated in the accounts of the National Health Fund were portrayed by the mass media as a proof of the development of social infrastructure. Some other actions, justified from the social point of view, were also taken, such as extending free medical care to more than six million private farmers and their dependents and compulsory kindergarten education for six-year olds. But at the same time, there were cuts in investment spending for social infrastructure projects.

The diversity of general-access social infrastructure centers is a yardstick of social and economic development. A failure to develop social infrastructure, cuts in the number of its centers, or abandonment of the principle of general access to them, despite a big demand for their services, leads to a return to basic services, covering only minimum needs, or to forgoing the satisfaction of many other social needs.

It is characteristic of Poland's social infrastructure that it is usually more difficult to meet everyday needs than exceptional ones. Such limitations can make people feel they are being denied the satisfaction of important needs. Individuals then stop seeing themselves as full-fledged members of society, and society as a whole becomes vulnerable to destructive activities; the sense of security disappears.

In this way the state and the functioning of the social infrastructure have become a source of many social tensions and local conflicts in Poland, and they contributed to the escalation of demands and strikes, even after the signing of the social accords in the summer of 1980.

Social Infrastructure as an Institutionalized System of Satisfying Social Needs

Definition of Social Infrastructure

In Polish studies, social infrastructure is defined differently than in the West. In centrally planned economies, the social infrastructure includes all the specialized centers and equipment serving to satisfy the needs of an individual and the family, as well as the needs of local and regional communities. The range covers the following sectors of the national economy: housing, education, health care and welfare, institutions for leisure, including cultural, recreation, tourist, and sports facilities, and finally retail and servicing centers.

This way of defining social infrastructure results from the division of the economy into productive and nonproductive sectors—a tenet of Marxist political economy and socialism. The productive sector is then subdivided into group A, which supplies capital goods, raw materials, and fuels and enjoys numerous privileges, and group B, which consists of enterprises that produce consumer goods.

Social infrastructure has been arbitrarily classified as part of the nonproductive sector, and this has multiple consequences. The abovementioned divisions are important for doctrinal reasons and are reflected in planning and management.

It is assumed that the proportions between the productive and nonproductive sectors in a centrally planned economy are related to production and consumption and to current and future needs of society and economy as envisaged in development programs. The state as owner of the basic means of production, must actively influence both production and distribution because it simultaneously performs economic and welfare functions, and cannot substitute economic for welfare functions anymore than it can do the reverse.

Defining the proportion and the relationship between production on the one hand and distribution on the other, as well as their regional impact, is an old dilemma in economy and politics. It is against this background that the mechanisms determining the regional allocation, the functioning, and the state of social infrastructure in Poland work.[1]

Social Infrastructure in a Welfare State

In Poland, the institutions that are in charge of social infrastructure equipment and facilities are owned by the state or by large cooperative organizations and enjoy a monopoly position. The private sector is of marginal importance in this field, except for housing where private ownership is permitted. The list of exceptions includes health protection, although the network of private medical care is very limited; some centers for handicapped children and elderly people, run by religious congregations of the "Caritas" type, as well as small private kindergartens. Also holiday accommodations can be rented from private persons. However, private travel agencies are rare.

There is a private sector in retailing, where shops under franchise to agents are quite numerous, and in crafts, where small-scale manufacturing is often combined with services. These are meant to supplement the socialized sector and are fully controlled by the state.

For ideological reasons the state has taken upon itself the duty of satisfying social needs free of charge. This is a generally binding rule.

The nationalization of social infrastructure thus creates a specific new situation in which socioadministrative organs become the administrators of goods and services that are distributed or rationed as required. This means that social infrastructure is excluded from the operation of market laws of supply demand; instead, there is administrative control over the satisfaction of social needs.

As a result of this system, nearly the whole social infrastructure system is composed of state-owned centers either entirely subsidized by the state budget or partially subsidized (e.g., the special care centers run by religious congregations, and the housing mentioned previously). Social infrastructure facilities are assumed to bring no profit; they supply their services free or for a nominal fee, or at cost at the most.

It should be emphasized that initially the profits that could have been made from the activity of social infrastructure centers were forgone for ideological reasons. This explains why social infrastructure in Poland is regarded as part of the nonproductive sector, despite its tremendous and unquestionable impact on the productive sector.

A welfare state has numerous advantages as well as disadvantages. The advantages include the implementation of egalitarian principles. In the name of equality a variety of centers and facilities rendering similar services were closed and replaced with a network of standard centers and institutions. To simplify matters it was assumed that the very existence of a center meant that the needs were satisfied in full. No one seemed to realize that needs are relative and changing and that the state might encounter difficulties while trying to implement obligations toward its citizens. It was not until the late 1970s that the question was asked in Poland whether it is the state alone that should be responsible for the satisfaction of the citizens' social needs, while the citizens need not care at all about their own fate.

Moreover, it happened that society's consumption needs and aspirations were growing faster than the possibilities of satisfying them. The state network of social infrastructure centers and facilities has produced a highly centralized model of services, the functioning of which requires the existence of an extensive administrative apparatus. At the same time, the latter did not guarantee effective action. As with the majority of large organizations, it is vulnerable to technocratic and bureaucratic solutions, and in case of temporary financial cuts, the reductions affect the range and standard of the services rendered while the structure itself remains largely unscathed.

This protective function of the state, presented here in a rather simplified way, is subject to major modifications brought about by the changing financial possibilities of the state's budget, the organizational forms applied in social infrastructure institutions, the pressure of consumers' needs and changing social aspirations.[2] It is worth noting at least two trends that are essential for the functioning of the social infrastructure: the tendency to develop a network of limited-access centers in factories and institutions catering to the needs of their employees and the tendency to introduce payment for an ever larger range of services.

The idea of fully free services was first abandoned in housing, when the state started to give up the distribution of flats free of charge and began favoring housing construction financed by the population itself and then housing cooperatives in the 1960s. In other fields, such as culture, education, welfare, recreation, and some forms of holiday resorts, the state started to depart from free services in the 1970s and authorized their provision based on commercial principles. The fees varied depending on an employee's income.

But in some other fields, for instance in public health care, administrative decisions were made to increase the number of persons entitled to free services. In 1973, such free services were extended to include private-farm owners.

Studies of social infrastructure demonstrate that the source of this weakness in a welfare state system is, among other things, part of the natural trend toward centralization in the social institutions although the most common and frequent needs require a decentralized network of centers and facilities. This meant that administrative decisions triggered a process of eliminating and weakening the lower-level servicing centers by higher-level centers.

It should be emphasized that replacement of smaller centers by bigger ones was not a result of public demand but of administrative measures taken to increase the centers' effectiveness and to benefit from economies of scale. The convenience and habits of the customers were taken into account to a lesser degree.[3] A state-owned network of social infrastructure centers and facilities usually entails the distribution of such services in self-contained districts. This means that the place of permanent residence automatically determines where a person will go for a respective service.

The Hierarchy of Servicing Centers in the Social Infrastructure System

The existing organizational structure of public infrastructure brings about a "hierarchization" of services. This does not usually occur in pure form but nevertheless proves to be a very useful model for analytical purposes.

The strong connection between levels of services and the administrative division of the country must be emphasized. This connection reflects the multitiered model of organization prevailing within social infrastructure: Forms of organization and areas of activity conform to the country's administrative divisions.[4]

There are five levels of services. The first consists of specialized centers situated as a rule in the capital and catering to the needs of all citizens of the country. The second level includes supraregional centers of national importance; the third level, regional centers, the fourth, supralocal centers, the fifth, local centers.

The level of services is determined by the area a given center covers, the extent of a center's organization, as well as its composition. Thus, for instance, the fifth level in health protection includes outpatient clinics providing internist, pediatric, orthopedic, and gynecological care. The fourth level includes these services, as well as other specialties and a local hospital, and at the third level they are all further expanded to suit the needs of the whole region. At the second level, there is also a clinic equipped with specialized analytical and diagnostic devices. The clinic is connected with a medical academy.

Such a hierarchy does not apply to all social infrastructure centers and facilities. Housing alone has always had the same character, although its forms may vary depending on the size of a settlement and the density of the population. Large-scale housing development, allowing for the construction of residential towers to house a thousand people or more, are unacceptable in small agricultural settlements where houses are dispersed.

There are also facilities whose existence is not determined by the level of service or degree of population concentration but rather by the number of potential customers, such as the number of preschool or school-age children. The level of services is determined by the frequency of use. The local centers are meant to satisfy elementary, everyday needs, while the needs for services of a higher order are satisfied in specialized supralocal, regional, and supraregional centers, as well as the national center in the capital.

The poor condition of the infrastructure in 1980 was largely due to a trend in the 1970s toward a formal monopolization of services by higher-rank centers that weakened the activity of lower-rank centers. This was not tantamount to better satisfaction of the needs because the higher-rank facilities were developed without paying due consideration to their accessibility either physically or socially.

Under such circumstances, the implementation of the democratic principle of equal social opportunities became questionable. This was further worsened by assumption of certain duties and financial resources by higher-rank centers that were being expanded at the cost of lower-rank centers. The reorganizations usually met central management requirements and not social needs, the target the centers were ostensibly meant to fulfill.

The levels of services described above are always reflected in the territorial organization of the country. The setting up of servicing centers equipped with proper facilities and apparatuses takes time, and all changes in the administrative division of a country mean promotion of certain areas and downgrading of the others.

Reasons for the Infrastructure's Low Efficiency

The Polish Paradox

The best point of reference for appraising infrastructure standards is the period of the late 1940s and early 1950s when the authorities put so much emphasis on social services that the achievements were really impressive. Social infrastructure became a tool of the political struggles and an element in the propaganda of the new social system. However, it must be admitted that in the war-ravaged country Poland was then, it was easy to obtain relatively good effects with modest means because the starting point was very low.

From the perspective of the end of 1970s, when everything ran into some kind of obstacle, it is hard to understand how, given the huge war disaster and the internal struggles, the authorities had managed to allocate so much money to social infrastructure, take care of its efficient functioning, and ensure a variety of services to embrace more and more social needs. Apart from that, the broad acceptance by society of the newly established facilities meant that society was united in endorsing the cultural patterns promoted and the new values brought by socialism. It all amounted to the democratization of society and the demolition of old class structures.

That was a phenomenon never to be repeated in Poland afterward, when in fact greater financial resources were available but were assigned mainly to further economic growth. Savings were always made at the expense of infrastructure facilities, despite a significant population growth as well as technological progress and cultural advancement.

In terms of general figures, the Polish paradox is that in the 1970s the country had a larger material base for social infrastructure facilities (with new centers being built and commissioned) while, at the same time, already existing facilities were permitted to fall into disrepair: This occurred because not enough care was given to their maintenance and because they were overused and overcrowded. This meant that the infrastruture largely failed to satisfy elementary social needs in many parts of the country.

The paradox was that the growing institutionalization of satisfying social needs became linked to a worsening of the quality of the infrastrature's functioning and services. Society felt that the personnel employed in the infrastructure, while possessing ever higher professional skills, were less and less involved in the work they did and had nothing to offer customers, patients, readers, or citizens but a formalistic attitude.

Thus it was often heard that in the 1950s similar facilities, although much poorer and inferior in equipment, were easily accessible to their users. The negative assessment of the infrastructure of the 1970s was justified by heightened aspirations and consumption attitudes, the latter a product of the propaganda favored by the ruling circles and the patterns of consumption, behavior, and style of life they promoted. Cuts in spending on infrastructure also affected the incomes of the staff, leading to dissatisfaction and generating a negative approach to work.

At the end of the 1970s, the myth of modern social facilities accessible to all collapsed. That proved to be quite a shock for a society that had had faith until then in a constant improvement of its living standards.

The End of the Myth of Prosperity

National propaganda, later termed the propaganda of success, instilled in society a myth about the unlimited possibilities of a socialist state with regard to the implementation of social goals, reflected, among other things, in its concerns for developing social infrastructure. The mass media did all they could to strengthen that conviction by reporting on new infrastructure projects being commissioned in various parts of the country. In general, the standard and the scale of those new facilities differed remarkably from the ones built earlier because they were intended to satisfy needs according to twenty-first-century standards.

The patterns and ideas were borrowed from the developed Western countries on the assumption that the socialist state would not refuse its citizens services according to world standards. In fact, there was quite serious talk about the possibilities of overtaking the richest countries.

It is worth noting that similar slogans had been launched as early as the 1950s, but at that time the rivalry between the socialist and the capitalist camps was limited exclusively to the production of material goods. The figures that had counted were tons of coal extracted, steel produced, kilowatt hours of electric power. At the beginning of the 1970s such programs were not formulated in so many words, but it is easy to find influences of such concepts as mass consumer society or the affluent state in the plans that were adopted.

It is hard to blame the authors of these visions, which were incorporated into various programs, for their line of thinking. One should remember that the opening of Poland toward the West (which started at the beginning of the 1970s after a period of ascetic consumption and programmatic rejection of, for instance, mass private car ownership) generated a psychologically vulnerable climate for a fascination with an abundance of material goods. The idea of possessing them quickly became a measure of individual success for the citizen living in a country with a socialized, centrally planned economy.

Finally, one should remember that then Poland could easily obtain foreign credits on convenient terms, a factor creating still more possibilities for changing the material shape of infrastructure facilities. Those ventures were made in the name of modernization and general progress under the motto of building a "Second Poland" of the twenty-first century, a slogan addressed to the hearts of Poles.

The changes that were being introduced did not take into consideration regional culture, tradition, habits, and the convenience of people, to say nothing of the real financial and social costs and the incommensurable moral costs of those ventures. Their architects and the reformers themselves usually had the best of intentions. Driven by their own technocratic visions of organizing everyday life for the millions of people living in various regions, in towns and countryside, the planners offered solutions that had not been carefully thought over, tested, and accepted by society—in the name of the well being of the people and of a country that was shortly to be elevated to the rank of an industrial power.

The fascination with Western prosperity was compelling and, at the same time, extremely superficial. No one thought then about the mechanisms that make society affluent; no one listened to the criticisms that signaled unsolved or unresolved conflicts and social tensions characteristic of postindustrial mass consumption societies.

By the beginning of the 1980s, these observations and studies of the majority of rich countries had already become passe. Worldwide economic recession and stagflation had given rise to new socioeconomic problems that had not yet been solved. With the shrinking resources of fuels and raw materials in the modern world, an end came to yet another myth, that of Utopia and affluence for everyone. After that came the time to revise existing living standards and life-styles.

As early as the first half of the 1970s the level of aspirations in the majority of the highly developed countries was adjusted to the reality that effectively limited consumption for the majority of society. High growth in consumption again became a strongly guarded privilege of the few. A sharp struggle for existence in the face of genuine unemployment put aside visions of a state guaranteeing prosperity to all its citizens.

But in Poland at the beginning of the 1970s, the creation of general prosperity based on foreign credits became an established idea. An underdeveloped social infrastructure, seen against the background of a relative economic expansion, inevitably led to the emergence of serious tensions. This was the first sign that the myth of attaining a high standard of life comparable to that of the richest societies of the West was collapsing. Figures 8.1 and 8.2 capture dramatically this overall expansion of the Polish economy and then its collapse, with all its implications for consumption, capital formation, investments, and working assets. Such is the background against which expectation regarding state-provided social services, frustrations in failure to obtain needed services, and bureaucratic errors in meeting these needs must be seen.

Changes in the Number of Servicing Centers and Their Model

Changes in the number and distribution of centers according to levels of service were a result of, among other things, differences in the levels of socioeconomic development and changes in the territorial organization

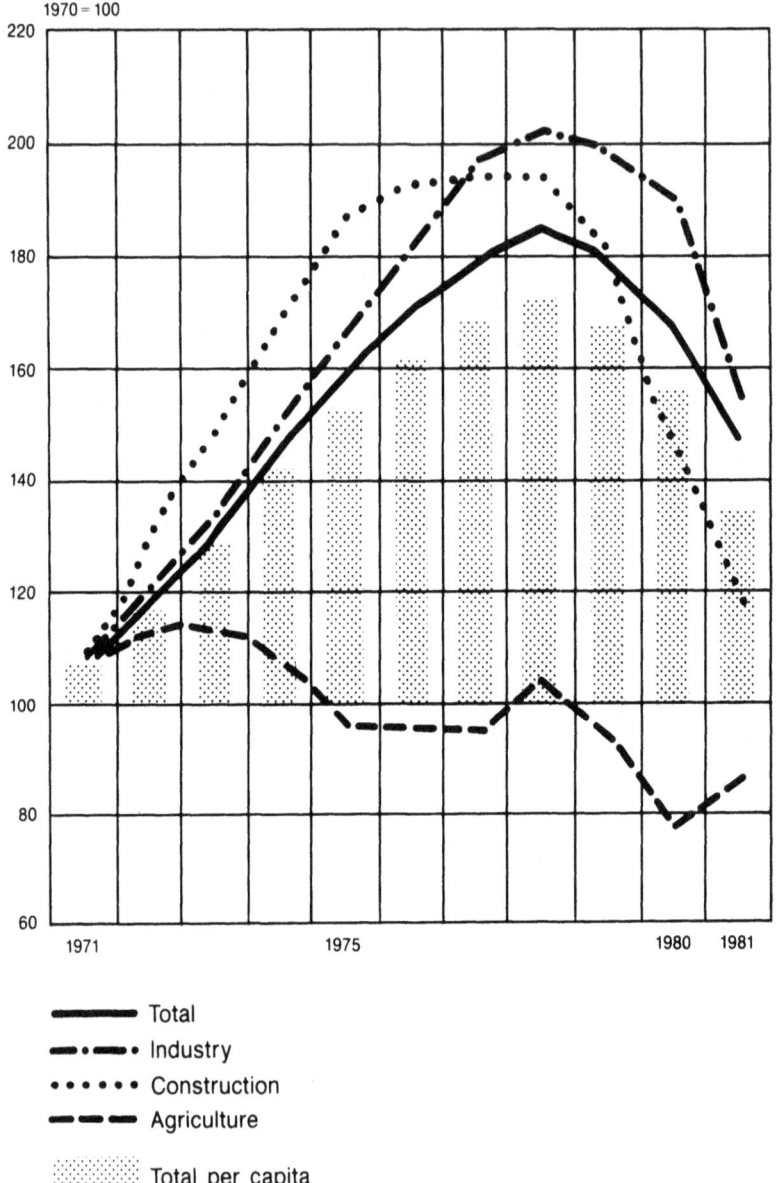

Figure 8.1 National income produced in 1970–1982 (constant prices) (1970 = 100). (Source: Maria K. Ciechocińska, "Trends in Changes of Living Standards in Poland (1960–81): An Attempt at Defining Regional Disparities," *Geographia Polonica*, vol. 51, forthcoming. Reprinted by permission.)

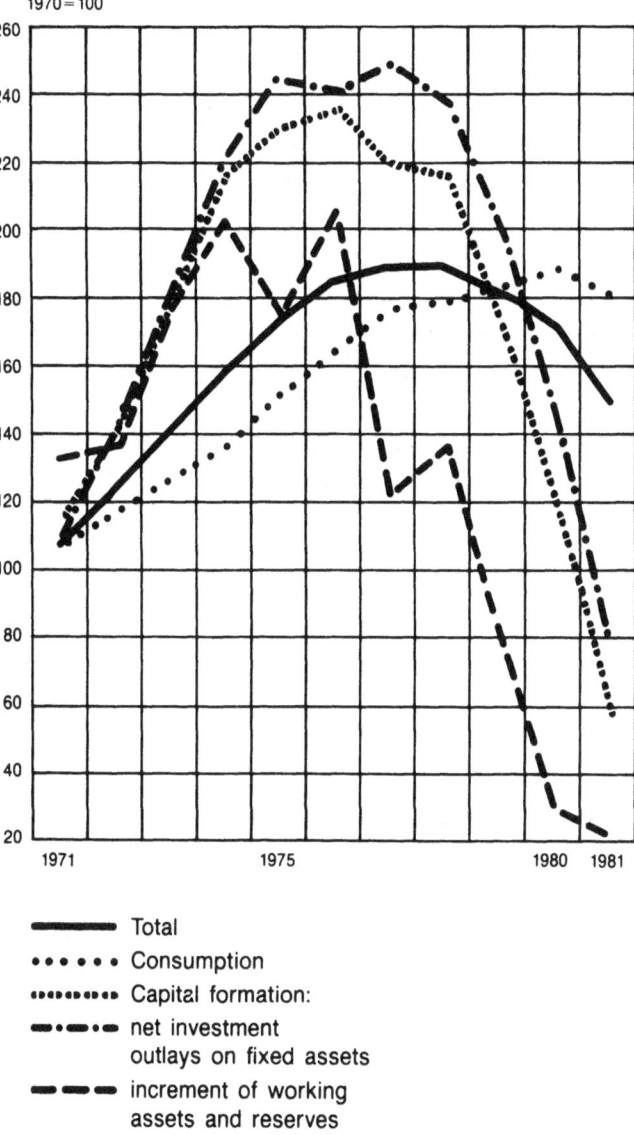

Figure 8.2 National income distributed in 1970–1982 (constant prices) (1970 = 100). (Source: Maria K. Ciechocińska, "Trends in Changes of Living Standards in Poland (1960–81): An Attempt at Defining Regional Disparities," *Geographia Polonica*, vol. 51, forthcoming. Reprinted by permission.)

Table 8.1
The Number of Units in the Territorial Organization of the Country, 1960-1980

Year	Level of Units		
	Basic (Community)	Middle-range (District)	Regional (Voivodships)
1960	6,331	396	22
1973	2,365	392	22
1975	2,327	-	49
1980	2,070	-	49

Source: Based on I. Kokotkiewicz's "Administrative Division of the Country Against the Background of the Old Division, Planning, and Resort Divisions," in A. Jaroszynski and S. M. Komorowski (eds.), Gospodarka przestrzenna Polski i organizacja terytorialna kraju (The Spatial Economy of Poland and the Territorial Organization of the Country), (Warszawa: Institute of the Organization of Management and Training of Cadres, Institute of Socioeconomic and Regional Geography at Warsaw University, 1982), p. 132.

of the country, introduced in two stages in the 1970s. Those changes are shown in Table 8.1.

In 1972 the terminology used for the community, the smallest territorial designation, was changed from *gmina* to *gromada* and their number was decreased. In 1975 the *powiat* (district) was eliminated; these had been middle-level administrative units, which had functioned as a natural base for supralocal service centers.

In that way, a three-tiered division was replaced with a two-tiered one. It was explained that by reducing management structures, authorities could be brought closer to the citizens and that the distribution of higher-rank authorities all over the country would be advantageous. It was assumed that the setting up of a larger number of smaller voivodships would make them more easily accessible.

As a result, the number of the nominal centers corresponding to the first, second, and third level of infrastructure increased from twenty-two to forty-nine. Many of them were promoted to a higher level by force of arbitrary decisions; formerly fourth-level centers, they were unable to perform the functions they were entrusted with. They needed time and money to get the necessary equipment and staff and to get out of the old rut.

The biggest changes, as shown in Table 8.1, occurred in the basic units, that is the fifth-level service centers, the number of which rapidly declined. Map 8.1 distinguishes 449 local centers, taking into consideration only

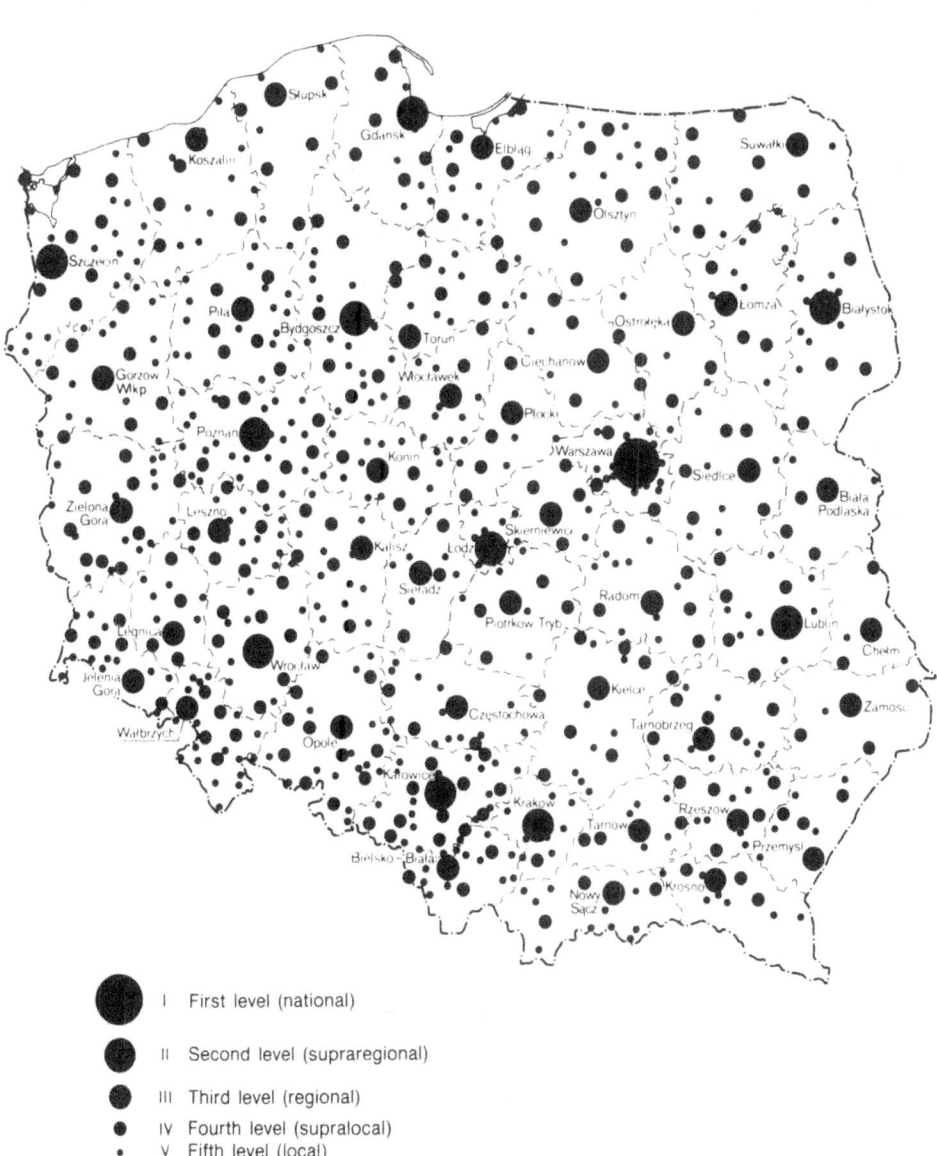

Map 8.1 Service center according to delivery level. (Map drawn by T. Lijewski for the author.)

urban centers, whose number was relatively small in many parts of the country where *gminas* performing the functions of local centers prevailed.

Changes introduced in the territorial organization of the country in 1975 caused the elimination of 392 middle-rank units (see Table 8.1). Only 32 of the former *powiat* capitals were promoted to the rank of third-level service centers. Among them were not only towns with a relatively good social infrastructure, such as Bielsko-Biala, Czestochowa, Jelenia Gora, Legbica, Radom, Tarnow, Torun, and Walbrzych, but also towns with a neglected infrastructure.

The second group included Biala Podlaska, Chelm, Ciechanow, Elblag, Gorzow Wielkopolski, Kalisz, Konin, Krosno, Leszno, Lomza, Nowy Sacz, Ostroleka, Pila, Piotrkow Trybunalski, Plock, Przemysl, Siedlce, Sieradz, Skierniewice, Slupsk, Suwalki, Tarnobrzeg, Wloclawek and Zamosc. On Map 8.1 they are marked as third-level service centers.

Some of the previous middle-rank units that were abolished took over the functions of fifth-level centers and were transformed into local centers.[5] This was due not only to changes in the territorial organization of the country but also to their inferiority in terms of available infrastructure facilities.

However, more than half of the units, 245 in fact, retained their status as a link between local and regional levels—despite the elimination of the *powiat*—and thereby set up a network of supralocal, fourth-level service centers. They owed their status to their infrastructure in addition to their convenient location along main roads or railway lines. The decisive criterion was frequency of connections by public transport.

Changes in the number of service centers in Poland led to changes in the organizational models of institutions, facilities, and equipment for social infrastructure.[6] Highly ineffective models of infrastructure development were selected, with organizational goals prevailing. In other words, the satisfaction of social needs was subordintaed to political and doctrinal goals.

Cardinal mistakes can be made even in the name of full social justice. A simplistic understanding of the egalitarian principle in this case led to the uniformity of social facilities. The organization of infrastructure facilities was determined by technocratic visions of their functioning, which produced models convenient for bureaucratized management. Among such models were *gmina* collective schools, *gmina* health centers in the rural areas and amalgamated health care facilities in towns, and *gmina* cultural centers. The organizational structures of housing cooperatives were also changed, and the latter were deprived of their self-governing character. The new models did not pay due respect to differences arising from regional diversification or settlement arrangements or differences in demographic and social structures and in regional patterns of culture.

Restructuring was governed by the drive to concentrate facilities. Small and weak centers were closed down and replaced by larger ones. This change was supported by arguments that big centers could be better equipped and staffed and that highly organized centers allegedly cost less to run.

In practice, this meant the loss of a substantial number of small and dispersed outlets, which were gradually replaced with large, collective units. Similar moves occurred in all areas of social infrastructure, both in town and countryside.

New community centers were planned with a larger territorial bases in mind, but they turned out to be less adaptable to local conditions. It should be emphasized that the centers set up in the 1970s were not provided with the necessary financial means, supplies, and properly trained staff. A relatively large administrative apparatus that was not at all interested in the rendering of services was established.

Rural population living in scattered settlements and earning its living from individual farming was the first to feel the negative effects of this action. The elimination of small but highly useful centers built by the local communities was carried out under the motto of progress and modernization. In the name of economy of scale, infrastructure facilities were built farther away from the place of residence of their prospective users. It was assumed that it would be very easy to reach the local service centers, such as *gmina* collective schools, *gmina* health centers or *gmina* centers of culture, by public transport and private vehicles.

In this respect, the implications of the worsening fuel and energy crisis were not perceived. It is worth observing at this point that many developed Western countries embarked on a reverse process at that time. Trends toward decentralization and deurbanization there came about as a reaction to growing fuel prices.

It soon turned out that the newly built Polish network was too costly to maintain and hardly accessible because of transportation difficulties. Moreover, local communities often refused to accept the closing down of their traditional facilities.

Due to hasty administrative decisions, many centers disappeared. The old network of infrastructure facilities was destroyed, and the new one did not take over the services rendered by the old.[7] And because of a specific nature of Poland's settlement structure, high-level centers were not always able to make up effectively for the shortcomings at the local level.

As a result of the reorganization campaign, the number of elementary schools decreased from 26,678 in 1970–1971 to 13,110 in 1980–1981.[8] This was due to the introduction of *gmina* collective schools, and it meant that the number of children per school and per class greatly increased.[9] Studies carried out by J. Niemiec showed that elementary schools were closed in 8,170 villages between 1970 and 1979.[10] In 1970, one out of two villages in Poland had a school, but in 1979 only one out of five had.[11] This translated into a loss of 17,671 classrooms in the years 1974–1977 alone.[12]

The target was to introduce ten grades of compulsory education as a replacement for schools that hitherto had only eight grades. As late as 1981 the Ministry of Education officially conceded that 43 percent of the villages in Poland were not populous enough to warrant the running of schools even with only the initial three grades. In 39 percent of the villages three-grade schools were appropriate, while eight-grade schools were viable in only 18 percent of all villages.

Thus the school model that was being implemented was not suited to rural conditions. It should be added that in 1975 the rural population amounted to 15 million, 44.3 percent of Poland's population.[13] The decrease in the number of basic territorial units, shown in Table 8.1, was followed by a similar drop in the number of social centers. Very often the introduction of organizational changes was not completed as the economic collapse approached in the late 1970s.

The new models of infrastructure centers automatically increased the demand for public transport, but the Polish Railway system (PKP) demonstrated a growing lack of interest in local passenger traffic, and the PKS bus and trucking enterprise systematically reduced the frequency of services. In this way changes in the territorial organization of the country deepened the regional differences in access to social infrastructure.

Regional Differences in Access to Social Infrastructure

The key problems in the studies of social infrastructure in Poland have been identified as the accessibility of servicing centers of various levels and the assessment of the efficiency of the new solutions. Programmatic assumptions speak of the necessity of observing the principle of an equal start in life, especially with regard to youth, and a trend toward the leveling out of differences between town and countryside as far as satisfaction of everyday needs goes.

Studies carried out in 1970 demonstrate substantial differences in meeting elementary needs. This was a result of the complex historical development of Poland, which from the end of the eighteenth century until 1918 had been partitioned by the neighboring powers and therefore had undergone different urbanization and industrialization processes from those of Western Europe.

Vast areas of the country, especially in the eastern and central parts, had low to middle ratios of social infrastructure development, while the network was well developed in the northern and western regions. This pattern emerged from studies of geographical differences in three indicators: the number of people per retail outlet, the number of hospital beds per 10,000 people, and the percentage of youth attending high schools.

That network overlapped with higher-level servicing centers, which were defined according to their location on a two-hour "isochron" of accessibility by public transport, as well as their inclusion of such selected infrastructure outlets as museums, universities, theaters, concert halls, or research centers. Higher-level centers were hard to reach by public transport in many regions of northern, eastern, and central Poland.

The changes in the territorial organization of the country introduced in 1975 offered no solution to the problem, which was exacerbated by lack of convenient rail or bus connections with the newly established voivodship capitals. Map 8.2 illustrates this problem on the basis of transport con-

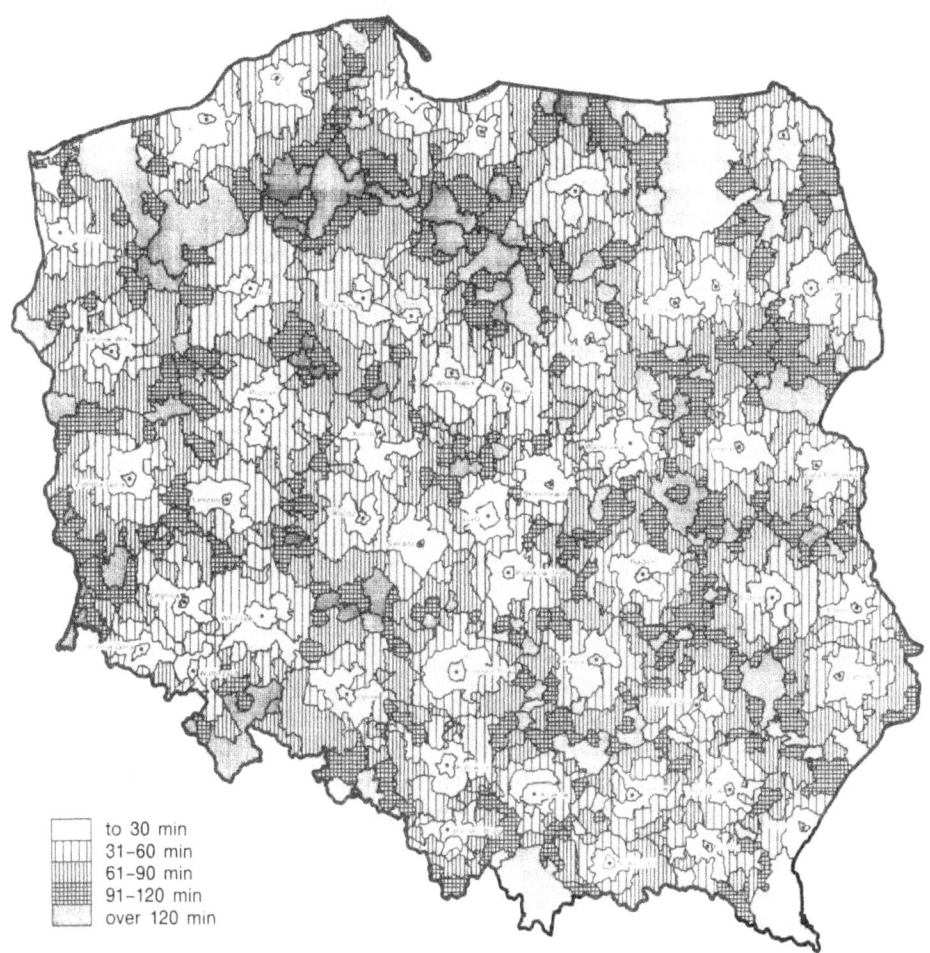

Map 8.2 Accessibility of regional centers (voivodships) from local centers in 1978-1979: Time required by the most convenient means of public transportation. (Map drawn by T. Lijewski for the author.)

nections in 1978-1979. The criterion used by T. Lijewski to select centers was that of the time it takes to reach a given center by the most convenient means of public transport in areas in which travel from the fifth-level local centers to the third-level centers in the new, smaller voivodships took more than two hours. Map 8.2 shows some of the difficulties that emerged in the wake of the new territorial organization of the country.[14] Many centers were not adequately prepared to render the new services because of their inadequate equipment and facilities and the failure of the transport and communications systems to cover the needs of areas assigned to them administratively.

Another factor of significance is a varying density of the network of the towns that constitute the fourth- and fifth-level centers (see Map 8.1). In the Poznan voivodship, for instance, there are thirty towns of that size; in Opole and Szczecin voivodships, twenty-eight each; in Bydgoszcz voivodship, twenty-five. But Chelm and Zamosc voivodships have only three such centers each. More examples can be found in Map 8.2. The accessibility of the local centers, that is the fifth-level rural facilities, is a separate problem. It has been a tradition in many parts of Poland that rural areas are more advanced in terms of civilization than towns.

It should be noted that in 1980 many infrastructure facilities were practically inaccessible when cancellations of the already rare bus connections became commonplace. The development of private motoring could only slightly facilitate access to the centers. Problems of accessibility remained unsolved as the mechanisms of social selection started to operate in local communities and that effectively eliminated some people from obtaining basic services.

An improvement in access to infrastructure could have been achieved by improving public transport, increasing the frequency of connections, as well as completing the development of the existing network, all of which would have reduced notably the pressure on higher-level centers. But in practice, an opposite solution was found. Fundamental changes were introduced instead in the way in which the social infrastructure functioned, territorially and organizationally, and these changes could not bring about the expected results.

Housing Problems

Housing was arbitrarily classified as part of the social infrastructure, even though a majority of residential buildings are one-family houses and therefore differ fundamentally from other kinds of institutions that serve collective consumption and render services to selected territorial communities. One argument in favor of the classification is that housing is part of the nonproductive sector.

An analysis limited only to social infrastructure centers seen in isolation from housing would not be logical. The activity of infrastructure outlets is meaningful only in relationship to territorial communities, or agglomerations of people. From this perspective one must consider housing as an important component. Besides, the situation in housing is usually the product of the same socioeconomic policy that in Poland shapes the living conditions of an individual, family, and society.

Housing construction in Poland requires large financial outlays. Because of the climate, this housing must be solid and expensive. Doctrinal assumptions precluded the development of a large-scale private housing sector. For the past forty years, housing has been a permanently unsolved problem despite some statistical improvement. There were many reasons for this problem. One was the war, which destroyed a substantial part of residential buildings. Then came mass migrations of rural population to towns due to socialist industrialization. In any given year, the number of newly built flats has always been lower than the number of marriages.

An exceptionally negative assessment of housing in the late 1970s and early 1980s stems from an increasingly small number of houses built in the face of the mounting pressure of the postwar baby boom, people who grew up and wanted to set up their own families. Another factor complicating the housing situation even further was the decay of older buildings and shortsighted modernization trends in towns, which most often meant demolition rather than repair of old buildings. Municipal housing construction in towns for the lowest-income families practically disappeared.

The symptoms of the crisis in housing appeared first in towns (1975) and then in the countryside (1976). The number of newly built rooms and flats began to decrease. These unfavorable phenomena were manifested earliest and most acutely in cooperative housing construction, and later they also appeared in the nonsocialized sector in the countryside (1978) and in towns (1979).[15]

It is estimated that there were 1.7 million people (or 6 million if dependents are included) on the housing waiting list in Poland in 1980. This leaves out people living in small towns where there are no housing cooperatives and people who wanted to improve their living conditions but had no chance of even being entered on a waiting list in a cooperative.

Out of those 1.7 million, nearly 4 percent (over 50,000) lived in premises unfit for habitation, and 24 percent lived in overcrowded flats with less than 5 square meters per person.[16] Nearly 13 percent rented flats and rooms, and some 3.5 percent lived in workers' hostels, student hostels, and boarding houses. Some 30 percent (half a million people) lived in flats without running water, and 44 percent (750,000) lived in flats without toilets.

It is enough to compare two figures, the 300,000 marriages and 250,000 newly built flats in a year, to realize the scale of the social effects of the fact that the housing construction program collapsed in the 1970s. It should be added that the highest number of new flats was 206,000 in 1978, while the number of marriages in the same year amounted to 330,000. Since then, the number of new flats has been decreasing yearly.

All this happened in the same decade in which as many as 175 prefabrication plants were built. The already bad housing situation was further worsened by the disastrous policy of the Housing Department, which favored industrialized building at the expense of older traditional building crafts, which were disappearing. This policy had the effect of slowing down the growth in the number of flats. The introduction of new technologies in housing was combined with a 30–50 percent drop in productivity. The consumption of cement grew by 30 percent; glass, 40 percent; and outfitting and finishing materials, 100 percent.

The state of housing in the late 1980s is a product of the clash between the economic needs of the country and the social needs of its citizens. In the 1970s, housing construction received close to 5 percent of the national income instead of what was projected in national plan: at least 7 percent. Given the backlog in housing construction and falling national income, this figure should amount to at least 9 percent. The same refers to investment outlays: Housing construction should amount for at least 30 percent if housing is to become a significant factor of development.

The reality, though, was quite the opposite of the slogans that promised each family a flat of its own in the near future. Housing construction, like car production or computer manufacturing, might have become a driving force for the whole economy. That never happened. Housing was put on the back burner; it had no lobby of its own to compete with those of, for example, the engineering or motor industries.

The potential of private housing construction was utilized to only a very small degree. It is worth noting that the share of private housing in the years 1955–1960 amounted to 54 percent of overall floor space, while in 1978 its share fell to 38.6 percent. Nevertheless, in spite of all the administrative limitations imposed, houses built by owners themselves with occasional hired help remained cheaper than one-family houses built by specialized enterprises.

The housing crisis hit in particular the younger generation entering adulthood and was most sharply felt in regions where young people were the most numerous. A profound shortage of flats nationwide meant that the arrival of children lowered the living area per person. A census taken in 1978 revealed that only 8.5 percent of all couples with children in towns had flats whose usable floor space per person exceeded 20 square meters, while among childless couples that index stood at 33.8 percent.[17]

It was very much the same in overcrowded flats with less than 10 square meters of usable floor space per person: One-third were inhabited by couples with children (31.2 percent), while only 15.7 percent of childless couples were in the same situation. In rural areas, overcrowded flats with less than 10 square meters per person were inhabited by 33.4 percent of the couples with children and 18.6 percent of couples without children.[18]

These figures testify to the fact that housing problems affect principally young people of marriageable age and young families with small children. Due to this, the housing crisis becomes a generation crisis. And in many regions, where a large percentage of immigrant workers gets flats from their employers, this is perceived as discrimination against the local population, and it becomes a factor contributing to the disintegration of local communities.

Closing Remarks

Social infrastructure institutions serve many kinds of needs and can help public life run in an organized, efficient, and smooth way. The institutional solutions that are applied to problems in social infrastructure are examples of interference in autonomous socioeconomic processes.

Each infrastructure sector has its own characteristics and serves different needs. The various parts of this chapter outline the problems related to the functioning and shortcomings of social infrastructure in Poland. I have tried to demonstrate this in a way comprehensible to an outsider who is not familiar with unique Polish organizational and structural solutions. For the sake of clarity, statistical data and illustrations were kept to a minimum. Instead of analyzing the situation in separate areas of infrastructure, I have given only the most characteristic examples and general trends. My aim has been to make it possible for foreigners to understand the role that the infrastructure has played in the unique socioeconomic crisis that afflicted Poland at the end of the 1970s.

The unsatisfactory state of the social infrastructure is now visible to both society and the authorities. The Politburo report presented at the PZPR National Delegate Conference held in March 1984 pointed out that Poland lags behind other CMEA countries (i.e., those belonging to the Eastern European Common Market) in terms of education facilities, health protection, culture, urban transport, tourism, and ports. According to statistics, Poland has, for instance, 20–80 percent fewer hospital beds per 10,000 people, several times fewer places in nurseries and kindergartens, half of the books in libraries, a dozen times fewer gyms, and so on.[19]

This is not only a problem of the figures themselves, which show Poland to be inferior in certain respects, but also of organizational structures and functions, as I have attempted to demonstrate in this chapter. This is also a problem of perceiving social demands and the social acceptability of the solutions introduced by the authorities.

The housing problem was selected for special analysis because of its gravity. In many parts of the country, the waiting time for a flat after making the necessary down payment averages fifteen years, but a twenty-year waiting period is not at all uncommon. Therefore, the aforementioned Politburo report speaks about the necessity of making up for a multiyear housing deficit and of solving as soon as possible the housing problems of those whose situation is particularly alarming. A number of steps have already been made to ease their plight. The authorities have stated that no more unrealistic promises will be made as this would be plainly dishonest. It is necessary to cut costs in housing construction, and the people interested in improving their housing standards should increase their share in the labor and financing.

This is an example of a way of thinking and of a search for solutions to existing problems that may be even more acute in the future, in view of the current demographic situation. It is expected that the shortage of infrastructure facilities will increase over the next few years in view of the new baby boom, which after putting a strain on nurseries and kindergartens, will move on to schools and other infrastructure facilities, magnifying the demand for services.

Notes

1. A. Kuklinski, *Gospodarka przestrzenna i studia regionalne* (Space Economy and Regional Studies), (Warszawa: PWN, 1980), chapter 3.
2. M. Ciechocinska, "Infrastruktura spoleczna" (Social Infrastructure), *Biuletyn komitetu Przestrzennego Zagospodarowania Kraju, Polska Akademia Nauk* (Bulletin of the Committee for Spatial Economics and Regional Planning, the Polish Academy of Sciences), No. 116 (1981), pp. 50–68.
3. M. Ciechocinska, "Ocena ogolnych tendencji zmian w stanie infrastruktury spolecznej" (Evaluation of the General Tendencies of Changes within Social Infrastructure), *Biuletyn KPZK PAN*, No. 123 (1983), pp. 84–99.
4. M. Ciechocinska, "Infrastruktura spoleczna w badaniach geograficznych" (Social Infrastructure in Geographic Research), in *Metody analiz geograficznych w planowaniu przestrzennym* (Methods of Geographical Analysis in Spatial Planning), ed. B. Malisz, (*Dokumentacja Geograficzna* [Geographical Documentation], 1979), vol. 3, pp. 71–83.
5. T. Lijewski, "Dostepnosc komunikacyjna placowek infrastruktury spolecznej roznych rzedow obslugi w swietle badan geografii transportu" (The Accessibility of Transportation to Social Infrastructure Facilities at Different Levels of Service in Light of Research on Transportation Geography) (Warszawa: unpublished report, KPZK PAN archives, 1981).
6. M. Ciechocinska, "Infrastruktura spoleczna a organizacja terytorialna kraju" (Social Infrastructure and the Territorial Organization of the Country), in *Gospodarka przestrzenna Polski i organizacja terytorialna kraju* (The Spatial Economy of Poland and Territorial Organization of the Country), ed. A. Jaroszynski, S. M. Komorowski (Warszawa: Instytut Organizacji Zarzadzania i Doskonalenia Kadr, Instytut Geografii Spoleczno-Ekonomicznej e Regionalnej, Uniwersytet Warszawski, 1982), pp. 156–80.
7. M. Ciechocinska, "Nowe i stare problemy infrastruktury spolecznej" (New and Old Problems of Social Infrastructure), in *Dylematy polskiej przestrzeni* (Dilemma of the Polish Space), ed. A. Kuklinski (Wroclaw-Warszawa: Ossolineum, Wszechnica PAN, forthcoming).
8. *Rocznik Statystyczny Wojewodztw, 1981* (Statistical Yearbook of the Provinces, 1981), (Warszawa: GUS, 1981), p. 515, table 1(709).
9. Ibid., p. 522, table 12(720).
10. J. Niemiec, "Praktyka realizacji zbiorczych szkol gminnych. Ocena stanu uzyskanego w 1980 r" (Experience in Elementary Community Collective Schools. An Evaluation of their Status in 1980), (Warszawa: unpublished report, KPZK PAN archives, 1981).
11. Ibid.
12. Ibid., p. 9.
13. *Rocznik Statystyczny 1983* (Statistical Yearbook 1983), (Warszawa: GUS, 1983), p. 38, table 11(68).

14. T. Lijewski, "Przestrzenne zroznicowania stopnia dostepnosci do urzadzen infrastruktury spolecznej" (Regional Differences in the Degree of Accessibility to Social Infrastructure Facilities), (Warszawa: unpublished report, KPZK PAN archives, 1982).
15. *Rocznik Statystyczny 1981* (Statistical Yearbook 1981) (Warszawa: GUS, 1981), p. 498 table 31(666).
16. H. Kulesza, "Geografia nie zaspokojonych potrzeb mieszkaniowych" (The Geography of Unsatisfied Housing Needs), *Biuletyn KPZK PAN*, No. 118 (1982), p. 120.
17. *Rocznik Statystyczny 1981*, p. 484, table 28(663).
18. Ibid.
19. *Trybuna Ludu*, March 17-18, 1984.

9
Sociopsychological Aspects of the Polish Crisis

Janusz Reykowski

The beginning of the 1980s will surely receive special treatment in Poland's history. What kind of treatment will it be? Will future historians decide that it was a dramatic, but temporary "mishap" resulting from a faulty implementation of a properly devised project for building a new society? Or—as some contemporary critics of socialism maintain—will history prove that this was a moment when it became evident that the whole project was totally wrong and the only thing left to be decided is the question whether the return "to the right path" should proceed faster or maybe not so fast? Or perhaps will it be necessary to admit that this moment finally showed the end of a certain epoch and that society now faces some entirely new tasks, and the way it will solve those tasks will determine its future?

I am one of those who subscribe to the last view of the contemporary situation described above. In other words, my view is that the principles on which the development of Polish socialism has been based so far have played their historical role and become outdated. As such, they no longer serve social development. Polish society has to find new principles, ones corresponding to the new social needs and the new circumstances under which a socialist state has to function.

Two Main Problems

During the dramatic post-August 1980 months there was a a great deal of talk about repairing or renewing virtually everything. A reform seemed to be actually at hand. "Had we not been impeded, we would have achieved extraordinary successes and very quickly so," ardent followers of the great reform seemed to believe. But if they had carefully thought about what needed to be reformed and what real, not illusory, means the society had at its disposal, their appraisal of the situation would not have been so optimistic.

In my opinion, August 1980 has laid bare the two main problems facing Polish society, the solving of which will be a time consuming and painful process. The first problem is the clash between the model for the management of the economy and the possibility of realizing the principles of efficiency and social justice as conceived by a considerable part of the society, perhaps by its majority. At the beginning of the 1980s, the economic model had already lost its former advantages. Production was too small (compared to existing potential); there was much more waste than common sense could accept; and the way goods were distributed caused feelings of hopelessness and a growing sense of injustice.

At this point I will leave aside the question of efficiency and will deal with the question of justice. Social justice has always been a tenet of socialism. It is not accidental that psychological studies on the value systems of people with various political orientations have shown that the price they put on the value called "equality" distinguishes those of left-wing orientations from all others. But how, in practice, can one ensure social justice with respect to the availability of goods?

Prewar Poland was a country characterized by deep social inequalities. Although the takeover of power by the Communist party brought about a drastic alleviation of former inequalities in Poland, it did not eliminate them altogether. Sociological studies of Polish society as well as everyday observations demonstrate clearly that Poland (like all other countries with some degree of economic development) did not manage to achieve equality. However, contrary to the claims of some critics, the degree of inequality in Poland is now much lower than it had been and lower than that in many other countries, mainly in the wealthiest ones. But how one can attain equality without implementing the principle of *uravnilovka* (wage leveling), generally considered as harmful?

In socialist Poland, the practical implementation of the slogan of social justice, which has been present on the banners of the working-class movement for more than a century, has entailed the social advancement of the masses.

Data collected by sociologists show that the process of pushing huge groups up the social ladder continued throughout the initial decades of socialistic rule in Poland. This climb included all the three main indicators of social status: material consumption, participation in culture, and access to power. The changes not only meant that the respective social classes and strata advanced as a whole, but they also meant that a large proportion of the members of groups previously at the lower levels of the social structure moved to groups higher up. This process, very pronounced in the 1950s, could still be perceived in the third decade of Poland's socialist development.

One could hypothesize (and this is the view voiced by Professor M. Pohoski, a Polish researcher on this phenomenon) that social advancement was one of the main forms of compensating for inequality in postwar Poland. To make social advancement possible, a basic condition had to be met, namely, a constant expansion of the number of places on the higher levels of the social ladder. Such expansion is made possible by economic development.

However, it is common knowledge that the conditions for economic growth have been worsening in Poland since the 1960s. This was connected with faults within the economy itself (namely, the aforementioned "inefficiency"), as well as with the worsening of the world economic situation and the almost worldwide recession of the mid-1970s. For the Polish economy this meant a loss of the ability to compensate for inequality. This inevitably generated a sense of injustice, which was spreading as more and more social groups felt the effects of the obstacles to social advancement. At the same time, various malpractices emerged in the distribution of goods, which added to people's sense of being shortchanged. In effect, society's attention became focused on cases of flagrant injustice in the availability of goods, obscuring the more important and graver processes affecting the increasingly larger communities.

It is obvious that not all social milieus and strata have suffered the effects of this process to the same degree. Thus, for instance, the situation of people entering employable age or young employees was exceptionally difficult: They found out that "all seats at the table have already been taken." The process of achieving family and professional independence was halted, and prospects for the future (such as getting a flat of one's own) looked more and more dim. All this occurred in a situation in which both the ideology and propaganda promoted visions and aspirations that remarkably exceeded those cherished several decades back.

The economy of the late 1970s stimulated consumption. It is not important here to decide whether it arose because of "natural" aspirations or intensified them beyond measure. What is important is that the expectations that emerged could not be satisfied, given the way the economy was run. Moreover, those who wanted to fulfill their own aspirations could not do so by increasing their productive efforts—whereas it was possible to get access to goods through economically dysfunctional steps (such as cronyism, waiting in long queues, corruption).

Thus it might be said that Poland entered the 1980s just as the previous economic order began to collapse, because it was ineffective and unable to implement the idea of social justice. This means that in the current decade Poland faces the necessity of working out a new order that would solve the two problems identified here.

The other big problem to have emerged in the wake of August 1980 was the lack of correspondence between the ways of governing, on the one hand, and the aspirations and the level of education achieved by a significant part of society, on the other hand.

The manner of exercising power resulted from the way power had been taken over by socialist forces and the circumstances in which it was exercised. Power in Poland was taken over by revolutionary means and it was assumed that it was legitimized by being used for the benefit of the working class.

The basic premise of this legitimacy was the obligation to pursue a policy of implementing the social goals of socialism, the main one, the advancement of the working class. The legitimacy of the authorities was derived from the premise that in the new European order established after World War II, they offered the best possible conditions for Poland's development.

The protection of the country's international and geopolitical interests, as well as belief that fulfillment of the "revolutionary promise" was being accomplished, were based on the assumption that power was concentrated in the hands of forces that could guarantee the implementation of both those objectives. Those forces were personified by the Polish United Workers' party (PZPR), and this assumption was embodied in the thesis concerning the leading role of the party in the period of socialist construction. The party felt authorized to consider that a policy pursuing such goals expressed the interests of the working class in Poland primarily, but also the broader interests of the popular masses.

The doctrine itself contained the thesis that the fulfillment of this leading role would be based on the principle of democratic centralism, which implies a democratic process of defining goals and programs, centralist rules of controlling their implementation, and a democratic assessment of the results. In practice, however, all decisionmaking rights became concentrated in the power centers. The more such rights were in the hands of the authorities, fewer were left to the broad circles of society. Such a situation had a significant sociopsychological impact.

The principal effect of this concentration is in the way citizens view responsibility for what is going on in society. They tend to lay responsibility on those who hold power and do not feel responsible for anything. Psychology describes this phenomenon in terms of "external attribution of responsibility." In extreme cases, the world becomes divided into those who are responsible for everything ("they") and those who bear no responsibility for anything ("we").

Such an understanding of social life also influenced the ideology proclaimed by Solidarnosc in the first months after its birth. According to that ideology, the union would monitor the authorities while bearing no responsibility for practical action whatsoever. This concept was based on the illusion that it is possible to devise an effectively functioning society in which a nonresponsible majority would control the responsible minority. That illusion was based on an earlier experience that contributed to the emergence of the "ideology of nonresponsibility," which is inevitable whenever individuals and groups feel they have no control over what is going on.

This way of apportioning responsibility influences social attitudes. Thus, for instance, many people tend to assume a demanding attitude expecting that all their "legitimate" needs and aspirations will be taken care of by those who are charged with responsibility. Needs and aspirations are treated as legitimate if they can be justified by ideological promises. The feasibility of the demands is not taken into account whatsoever because those in power are looked upon as omnipotent. People who are not treated as real partners by authorities cannot understand the authorities' situation or see the limitations the latter must take into account.

One could say that it is childish to make unrealistic claims: Children do not understand what their parents can and cannot afford. Is this to say that Polish society is immature and its demands are childishly unrealistic? It makes no sense to use the idea of immaturity in this context. What I mean is that individuals and groups that feel they have no influence on important decisions about their own fate but are convinced that others do ("those in power") address their demands to those "others." From the subjective point of view, such demands are quite legitimate, especially when one can quote ideological assumptions that sanction certain expectations (e.g., housing, health care, just distribution of goods.)

High demands are associated with hostility toward those in power and are a typical consequence of resentment that builds when an individual feels impotent and dependent on some power. The less justified an individual finds the limitation of his freedom, the stronger is his/her resentment and the greater his/her aspirations to participate in decisions about his own surroundings. The processes taking place in Poland could strengthen this resentment.

One such process has been mass-scale educational advancement. The higher the degree of education, the greater the desire is to participate actively in public life. The changes taking place during the forty years of socialist rule in Poland encouraged educational advancement, but that was not accompanied by development of the principle of participation. On the contrary, various steps in the 1970s were taken to reduce that participation.

Another important factor increasing the individual's needs for political participation has been a growing awareness of the forms of public life in other countries and the scope of freedom other people enjoy. Those experiences were a result of a great increase in the travels of Poles and their cultural contacts. It should be noted that when people compare their own situation with someone else's, they see first the most obvious aspects of the life rather than the inner political mechanisms.

All those remarks lead to the conclusion that the social order in Poland was becoming more and more inadequate in relation to the mechanisms it had set in motion itself. In other words, one might say that while providing conditions for the development and advancement of broad circles of society, the system failed to adapt its own institutions to the changed situation. It thus became a source of inner contradictions, causing deeply dysfunctional phenomena both in the sphere of economy and in the way of exercising power. The accumulation of those contradictions prepared the scene for a drama.

The Prospects for Solutions and the Dilemma

Attempts to solve the contradictions accumulated in a society in no way resemble attempts to repair a mechanism that has broken down. It would be more apt to compare the process to serious surgery on the living tissues of a social organism. This is an operation for which there are no ready-made and tested programs, no aseptic conditions, and what is most important, no team of experienced surgeons who can put the patient to sleep and then perform the necessary operation. In reality, this is a social process taking place under conditions of conflict and struggle in a situation of a grave internal and external threat. Its success is determined not only by wise ideas and good plans, but also, or perhaps mainly, by having enough strength to overcome the resistance to change.

While analyzing the possible solutions of the problems described above, one has to pay attention to their particular characteristics. I would like to mention three groups of such characteristics (without pretending to exhaust the whole list).

First, the problems that are to be solved are the essence of the dilemma. The analysis given above suggests that it would be naive to imagine a simple, long-discovered road to be followed in order to achieve the intended results. On the contrary, to cope with each of these problems, it is necessary to solve real dilemmas.

As to the reconstruction of the economy, one of the most difficult dilemmas concerns fulfilling the aspiration for justice (identified with some kind of economic egalitarianism) combined with ensuring efficient management. At the current stage of social development, efficiency requires the application of strong economic stimuli, which in effect would quickly lead to considerable economic inequality. But inequalities clash with the social feeling of justice. Sociological studies show that groups with lower incomes and a lower level of education firmly demand the leveling off of income differences—and those groups constitute the majority of society.

A number of dilemmas are linked to the question of distribution of scarce goods. To increase benefits for one group means to diminish them for other. Which groups should be privileged, and which should be the losers? To answer that no group should be privileged means to evade the issue instead of solving it, because each group with incomes above the average is privileged already. But if all groups were to have the same incomes, the economic mechanism would quickly become shaky, various factions of society would be antagonized, and the quality or availability of certain goods or services would further deteriorate.

It has been said, for instance, that the poor quality of health care services is due to the low financial standing of this professional group in society. The same is said of teachers. But an advancement of those groups at a time of economic difficulties must be followed by a relegation of other groups to the lower levels of the earnings ladder. What groups are these going to be? And to what degree should they be downgraded? What kind of advancement is and what is not justified? What criterion of justice should be applied in this case?

It is worth noting that in developed societies the relations among the situations of social groups are not the result of anyone's decisions, but are shaped by conflicts and struggles during a long process of evolution. As a result, stable rules are agreed upon by society, determining what level of incomes is just for respective groups and what services can be expected of them in return. This does not mean that such an agreement is reached once and for all. Changes in the situation of various social groups are taking place all the time. What is "agreed upon" are the main elements of the system.

One of the features of the situation in Poland after August 1980 was the questioning of hitherto accepted rules and, consequently, the demands advanced by various social groups for an improvement of their situation and a diminution of their burden: Miners asked for a five-day week; mail carriers protested against having to deliver magazines to subscribers; dock workers demanded a whole list of privileges; cultural workers wanted bigger outlays for culture, and so on.

All those demands were ostensibly addressed to the authorities. This was a mystification, because each privilege won by a given group was gained at the expense of other groups. But the centralized system of controlling social life obscured the real clash of interests and made it difficult to see the consequences that had to ensue from the demands of various professions and trades.

It must be realized that it is now necessary to work out socially acceptable rules of a just distribution of the burden and rewards for particular social groups. Conflicts will inevitably arise. What should be done to prevent these conflicts from assuming devastating proportions? How can one build the institutions that would keep these conflicts in check and help find some optimum solutions?

There are still other dilemmas connected with introducing the new economic mechanisms and eliminating the centralized ones from an economy which is not prepared for such changes—one that is heavily monopolized and hardly capable of competing in world markets.

What I have already said was meant to show that the solution of problems that the Polish economy has confronted does not consist in boldly following a selected course or in choosing between a good and a bad way out. This naive model of reforming a country, so popular in Polish society, seems to have very little in common with reality. As a matter of fact, each possible solution carries the threat of some negative consequences. Therefore the process of perfecting the economy is not just a magic jump to the realm of perfection but a time-consuming and painful search for better solutions.

Moreover, the economic dilemmas are accompanied by political ones. The latter ensue from the fact that every important change in the organization of the political system is followed by some uncontrolled effects that when they develop, may lead to a destabilization of the whole system. Normally, few people realize that a political system has a very precarious balance that can be easily upset, and when that happens, a snowballing effect follows. In this context an analogy can be made to the hormonal system in the human body. This system requires a very subtle harmony; an interference, including a therapeutic one, throws it into disarray for a long period of time.

To understand what I am saying one should look at the history of countries that experienced radical changes in the ways of exercising power, changes that were sudden instead of being anticipated by slowly maturing institutions capable of functioning under the new conditions This history abounds in prolonged internal strife, a disorganized economy, a collapse of the institutions of public life coming in the wake of a disturbance of the political equilibrium. And this is one of our dilemmas: What degree of destabilization can the ailing Polish political organism afford without risking total collapse? Those who think they have a ready answer to this are deluding themselves and others.

Second, the solving of Poland's problems is a process that takes place in a struggle. It is obvious that a social change is not inconsequential to anyone who has anything to do with it. There are people who, because of their vested interests, political motivation, or their vision of reality, are against it. There are people who want change, but not the kind that is being introduced. There are people who hope that the new situation will give them an opportunity to move up the social ladder. And, finally, there are people who, understanding nothing of what is going on, react only to the events—taking into account their direct, short-term effects instead of the future, long-range ones. When one remembers that a change in one country affects the balance of power on a wider scale, one should not be surprised that such a change evokes interest and various reactions on the part of foreign centers. Due to all those factors, the introduction of changes is, as a matter of fact, a program of struggle. The frontlines, however are not clear-cut.

It is not at all easy to distinguish those who act for the benefit of the constructive changes from those who, praising them, try to halt those changes, and those who, on the pretext of supporting changes, embark on an activity aimed at destroying the foundations on which the present form of social order in Poland is being built.

It is equally hard to qualify the opponents of changes: how to identify those who try to defend the threatened foundations, those who would like to stop the whole process, and finally those who fear that changes might further worsen already hard life?

For all these problems, one thing is certain: No social change can be accomplished without the support of major social groups, without a strong alliance of those who are ready to support it actively and fight various trends opposing it. Can one say that such an alliance has already been shaped in contemporary Poland and is strong enough to implement steadfastly and consistently a program of solving Polish problems while preserving the ability to defend the foundations of the system?

Third, the solving of the problems has to take into account the specific features of the Polish national mentality. National mentality is a product of a nation's experience, and it changes in the course of history. Such changes do not take place quickly, not in the space of one generation, at least. This means that the programs of reform must take into account the mentality of Poles as it is now. Such a statement, however, is quite ambiguous.

Above all, the definition of the mentality of a nation is ambiguous itself. One picture of that mentality was presented by Edmund Osmanczyk over thirty years ago. In an article published in the monthly *Odra*, Wladyslaw Markiewicz appears to admit that many statements made by Osmanczyk are still valid today. Also Andrzej Wasilewski, in an article published in an April 1984 issue of the weekly *Tu i Teraz*, presents an image of Poles that is very similar to that of Osmanczyk. According to those studies, Poles' thinking in terms of "sacred symbols" predominates over pragmatic thinking. There is a tendency to glorify failures instead of learning to avoid them; a lack of realism in assessing the international position of their nation and their own prospects; the perception of struggle and martyrdom as superior values, and work and efficiency as less important ones; the tendency to put the rights of an individual before those protecting the prestige of the state, giving priority to human relationships before the relationships determined by the law. And there is a heightened sensitivity about the question of national dignity and a tendency to treat certain values—freedom especially—as absolute. A community with such characteristics is not ideally suited to transform its economic and political institutions in a manner commensurate to the requirements posed by current conditions.

But is this a true description of the Polish mentality? It is hard to find a definitive answer to that. Evidence confirming such an image can be found everywhere. But one can also see different examples that do not support this view. Thus, for instance, whatever one might say about Polish recklessness, lack of realism, and the like, the phenomena connected with the introduction of martial law in Poland and reactions to it contradict that image. And this refers equally to those who have introduced martial law and those who were affected by it. Whatever one might say about the inability of Poles to do organized and effective work, one cannot forget their enterprising skills and the ability to find practical solutions in many difficult situations.

It is not the point here to multiply examples. The issue is that the mentality of a nation cannot be clearly defined. It may be dominated by some trends, but there is a potential for different trends too. Thus, depending on the circumstances, a given society may demonstrate various behaviors and attitudes. It must not be forgotten that some of those behaviors and attitudes may be dysfunctional and self-destructive. But the mentality of a nation does not have to become its doom, provided that the leaders of society are capable of taking it into account.

However, there is still another question: What does it mean to "take mentality into account"? It surely means neither encouragement nor submission to such trends that, common though they might be, threaten the interests of the state. This does not mean a submission to a nation's prejudices and stereotypes, yielding to unrealistic hopes or adjusting politics to the world of symbols rather than to realities. What this means is a construction of programs that can be understood by society and approved by the majority. The point is that it is not enough to be right in the view of history. What is needed is an ability to convince the masses of the rightness of the political line.

It is not possible to achieve understanding and approval by way of simply appealing to some highly respected value in a society, for instance, patriotism. Such a value can have a real impact on behavior only if additional conditions are met. With regard to patriotism, a feeling relating to national identity and a positive attitude to one's nation can be invoked primarily when some national interest becomes threatened by some other nation. When this condition is not fulfilled, patriotic feelings lose much of their power. Efforts to convince the nation that national interests can be threatened not only by an external enemy but also by a crisis are not likely to produce much response. What can be achieved in this way are lofty declarations but hardly any actions. To win understanding and approval for a policy they want to pursue, the authorities must see to it that its form be suited to the state of mind of the citizens, and no tricks can work here. There is nothing like the discovery of some magic key to the "soul of the nation." Any such "key" could produce temporary effects at best. What is necessary is to secure good communications between those who devise the programs and the rest of society.

Therefore, to take into account the mentality of the nation means to be constantly aware of the society's frame of mind, to analyze and consider constantly the specific perspective from which various sections of society view reality, to supervise and correct political acts always so that they are kept in tune with those perspectives.

Of course, even this directive can be simplified, trivialized and summed up in the form of a rule of avoiding actions that can irritate the society. However, avoidance creates taboo areas, encourages tactical concessions, the flattering of one or another group, and this has nothing in common with communication—it is but psychological manipulation. Moreover, psychological manipulation can bring about only short-lived effects, such as those produced by painkillers administered to a gravely sick person. They enable the patient to forget about the sickness for some time, but they do not treat it and, above all, they diminish a patient's motivation for treatment.

Success in solving our problems seems to depend on whether it will be possible in Poland to implement the principle of taking the nation's mentality into account. This implies constant and effective communication between those who organize social reality and those on whom a practical implementation of the programs depends.

Summary

The principal idea of this article is to argue that Poles shall have to face the complex and painful process of transforming the principles of their economic and political life in the current decade. There are no easy and obvious ways of implementing this process and there are no guarantees that it will succeed. On the contrary, the road leading to these changes abounds in obstacles and dangers. Perhaps the changes themselves are not inevitable. After all, history records societies that stayed "petrified" for a long period of time when the ruling class or the power elite proved unable to understand the challenge of the time. It has happened in Poland, too—eighteenth century Poland is a glaring example of that. However, to avoid the tragedy that befell nations that proved unable to carry out the changes required by the circumstances, therefore, Poles must try to understand the nature of the problems that have to be confronted. If the nation tries to avoid understanding them and to strengthen its convictions that it has followed the best routes and only the evil powers that have stopped it, Poland will be preparing for yet another failure.

PART FIVE

A Reassessment of the Polish Dilemma

The two chapters comprising the conclusion to this book reject interpretations that explain the crisis of 1980-1981 in purely political terms as insufficient to provide insight into the wider systemic crisis facing Poland. The basic dilemma confronting these two authors is how to analyze a crisis that is neither a specific event nor a sequence of events delimited by a particular time period. What they seek to fathom instead is prolonged societal conflict—the competition between those who hold power and those who do not. The very tensions that this conflict produces provide a certain stability to the current situation, one that may well be sustained indefinitely, no matter how illogical this may seem.

Rychard presents an interpretation of the Polish state that is simultaneously a critique of the whole socialist state model that has dominated Eastern Europe since the war. This is a state now in the process of disintegration. As the state becomes weaker, it is sustained more and more by circumstance than intent. Using a social systems model, Rychard emphasizes the importance of comprehending the Polish system integrally—as a mutually reinforcing set of relationships involving politics, economics, and society. His analysis emphasizes that the endeavor itself to establish totalitarian controls to shore up the system—the totalitarian mystique—has generated a new pluralism that fits neither interest group pluralism as understood in Western political science nor monolithic concepts of state and party power under socialism. In this society and polity he visualizes legitimacy as derived from a successfully functioning centrally planned economy—not from society itself. Social forces are seen as a part of what he calls "the hostile environment" assumption; this is the assumption made by those holding power that social forces must be controlled rather than permitted to express competing interests. In this society, social differences are derived more from the institutional structures imposed from above than from different constellations of interests identified with the groups themselves.

In such a setting the economy serves primarily political aims; namely—says Rychard—the striving of the ruling group to stay in power. The basic division thus is between those who hold power and those who do not. Rychard emphasizes that in this setting the dividing line within the system cuts across organizational lines: placing on one side those who manage the state and the economy, within various organizations, and on the other, those who work for these organizations, regardless of the nature of their work. It is this new institutional pluralism that the author sees as generating a pattern of class division according to who has power and who does not.

In such a world, argues Rychard, the legitimacy vacuum that has emerged itself creates certain stabilizing factors that work to maintain the wider system over time. Coercion, lack of alternatives, and mass acquiescence without according legitimacy to the authorities all can serve to prolong the existing situation indefinitely.

Pajestka, however, differs from Rychard in his assessment of the current situation. Rather than seeing a vicious circle of totalitarianism maintaining the system indefinitely, he argues that if one examines just economics and excludes the more sensitive areas of politics, certain changes are imperative if the system is to survive. He views the dichotomy between the rulers and the ruled no longer as the source of the maintenance of the present order but as the consequence of a model of the socialist state that cannot function any longer in the Polish context. He considers the gap between the state's development mission and the people's social motivation to have become so great as to make the current system of governance inoperable.

To achieve economic reform—and to him this is an imperative that cannot be avoided much longer—the excesses of the existing system must be removed. In political terms he advocates curbing statism. In economic ones he calls for an end to preoccupation with the accumulation of capital as the main instrument for economic growth, preferring to see instead improvement in working and living conditions as the vehicle for increasing productivity.

In his eyes, the sustained use of economic policy for political ends is the source of what he calls "the soft state" of the 1980s. During the 1970s what sustained the system, he writes, was the debt: the fact that money to operate the system could be obtained outside and basic decisions postponed. In such a setting, he argues, the use of coercion, which has long been one of the mechanisms for maintaining the state, is rapidly playing itself out. Thus, he arrives at the conclusion that the economic excesses of the previous generation have engendered a new reality, the only solution to which is a more limited state under socialism and the removal of state controls over important areas pertaining to the economy and society.

As a consequence, working within the context of views of Polish reality similar to those of Rychard, Pajestka arrives at very different conclusions. Rychard sees in the present the indefinite continuation of the past, perhaps under new forms but with the same old content. Pajestka sees instead the prospects of an opening because of the profundity of the crisis. He would have the authorities seize the opportunity to restructure the state, society, and the economy—without touching the commanding role occupied by the dominant political organization. By reducing the size of the state apparatus and opening up society and the economy, he believes, sufficient space could be created for independent action for the first time in forty years. Failure to do so, he concludes, will hasten the collapse of the present order.

10

Politics, the Economy, and Society: How They Interrelate

Andrzej Rychard

The purpose of this chapter is to demonstrate the relationship between the system for exercising power and the economic system and the effect of this relationship on the social structure and the main lines of division in society. The scope of this subject matter is very broad; an in-depth analysis would have to include most of the significant processes occurring within Polish society. This is more than can be accomplished within a single chapter, so I shall limit my study mainly to a description of the interrelationship among the three factors named in my title—politics, the economy and society. This means I shall leave out detailed descriptions and explanations of their internal mechanisms. Only when it is required in order to comprehend the interrelationship shall I supply a partial description of the internal structure of these systems.

I shall also limit my analysis to a certain kind of relationship between the political and economic systems. What I have in mind are those relations that exert an essential impact on the shape of the social structure, on the emergence and articulation of the interests of various groups.

As in other socialist countries, the relationship between politics and economics is of a special kind. Economic decisions are largely determined by political considerations. In turn, many political decisions and their economic consequences affect the shape of the social structure. The emergence of social differences is to a large extent a controlled rather than a spontaneous process. It depends more on political decisions than, for example, the operation of market mechanisms. This may lead to the conclusion that in such countries there is no *social* structure in the classic sense of the term and that it has been replaced by an *organizational* structure. I find this conclusion too radical. Nevertheless, it is extremely interesting to see how social structure is shaped on the basis of central-level decisions and organizational mechanisms. How are the planned processes intertwined with spontaneous ones?[1] Part of the answer to this question can be found by analyzing precisely the relations between politics and economics.

In this analysis I shall be referring to figures from empirical sociological studies, mainly ones conducted in the years 1980–1982. I think it is important to concentrate precisely on that period because it was then, during an open political and social conflict, that not only the factors "revolutionizing" the system but especially those "stabilizing" it could be easily seen at work. In other words, this was a time when it was possible to spot certain permanent mechanisms of the functioning of the system. They were pushed to the fore in the course of political discussion and the struggle for reform.

The structure of the article is the following: First I shall present the three basic theoretical conceptions that make it possible to approach the relationship between the authorities and the economy in Poland. I shall endeavor to test their usefulness by confronting these theoretical models with empirical data. The questions I will then try to answer are as follows: How aptly do these models describe the main kinds of relations between politics and economics? And how accurately do they define the main dividing lines of the conflict within society? Finally, in the third part, I shall attempt to pinpoint the main factors stabilizing the system and ensuring a certain level of integration.

The fundamental thesis underlying this analysis is the conviction that the Polish political-economic-social system is a whole that is composed of disharmonious elements. There are many levels in this disharmony, some of which I shall try to identify.

The second characteristic of this system is the coexistence of both disintegrating mechanisms (mainly conflicts) and special mechanisms of building integration and consensus. The dialectics of conflict and consensus is a natural characteristic of most societies. However, to highlight the Polish characteristics I will try to show the "Polish" mechanisms generating conflict and the unique ones ensuring integration.

Polish sociology has only recently begun to look at conflicts on a macrosocial scale as one of the more important subjects of analysis. However, in the years 1980–1982 much empirical data was collected, illustrating the main planes of the conflict, including those generated by the interdependence of politics and economics.

The Authorities and the Economy: The Possible Theoretical Approaches

The principal dilemma encountered during attempts to analyze relations between politics and economics is uncertainty about the shape of the system for exercising power and the degree to which this system determines relations in the economic field. There are two extreme positions and two matching theoretical conceptions. According to the first one, the system of power is fully centralized, with the Communist party playing the dominant role.

There is practically no differentiation within the political system, which forms a homogenous whole. A political system conceived in this manner subordinates to itself the entire sociopolitical life. This kind of thinking is most conspicuous in classical totalitarian conceptions.[2] At the other end of the scale is the position that definite differences exist in societies, both within the apparatus of power and in other subsystems. The relations among the individual subsystems of collective life are not totally determined by central political decisions, as there are also some autonomous areas. The theoretical conception corresponding with this position is that of *interest groups* as used for describing the reality of Communist countries.

The principal thesis I should like to present at this point is that the use of the principles of collective life that can be described with the help of theoretical conceptions of totalitarianism logically leads to the emergence of such unexpected results (mainly spontaneous processes) that totalitarian conceptions lose part of their explanatory value. It is therefore a peculiar "totalitarianism paradox" or "vicious circle of totalitarianism" whereby a reality that is essentially totalitarian generates its own negation. This process can be aptly illustrated by the relations between politics and economics and their social consequences (especially with regard to the attitude toward the interests of society).

To begin with, it must be said that the underground origins of the ruling political party, the war, and the early postwar conditions of establishing that rule are the factors that determine largely the methods of exercising power in Poland to this day. The term "hostile surroundings" referred, in my opinion, not only to external factors (meaning imperialists) but was probably also a token of the way in which the authorities viewed the society they ruled. In the postwar period, after a brief and timid attempt to win the backing of social forces in the process of rebuilding the country, the authorities gave up on winning that support. The program of speedy industrialization, giving priority to accumulation over consumption and to production of industrial equipment and raw materials over manufacture of consumer goods, served precisely to strengthen the power of the authorities.[3] The implementation of this program was accompanied by declarations that in the future self-denial would be rewarded by sumptuous consumption and satisfaction of ever-growing needs.

Because the authorities cannot base their actions on mechanisms of articulating interests and needs (because of "hostile surroundings") and because society has to operate somehow, institutional structures are imposed "from above." Society cannot develop structure on its own, so such a structure has to be imposed on it. In this way, social life is divided into sectors, with respective authorities being put in charge of individual parts of these sectors. This is not a metaphor but a description of reality: Social life is administered through institutional structures responsible for individual areas of human activity. All these structures are administered centrally.

However, such a method of leading a society calls for legitimization, an ideology. In that ideology the authorities cannot claim that the artificial creation of reality imposed from above is a result of their operating in hostile surroundings, that is, in a society that does not share the authorities' aims and methods of action. Such an ideology would be totally unattractive to the society. Therefore the doctrine is based on two assumptions: the identical interests of the whole society and the identity of that common interest of society with the interests of the authorities. If such assumptions are adopted—which is confirmed by the thesis propagated in the 1970s about the alleged "moral and political unity of the nation"—then it is obvious that there is no need for introducing any mechanisms facilitating the articulation of interests. If everybody, including the authorities, has identical interests, it is enough if the authorities know what their interest is. "Hierarchic representation" becomes the official form of articulating interests. It is based on the assumption that the higher one is situated in the hierarchy of government the more "general" the interests one represents.

In practice, this mechanism leads to identifying the interests of society with those of the top decisionmaking groups. This mechanism is extremely convenient for the authorities because it is based on existing institutional structures. In other words, the contrived, artificially created institutional structure is justified by the claim about the identity of interests. The elimination of pluralism is not justified by theses about "hostile surroundings" (which would be nearer to the truth) but by the assumption of the uniformity of interests. Only when a crisis erupts do the authorities find out in a painful manner that society does not share the theory of common interests.

The two theses discussed above describe the features of the system of exercising power that are essential for understanding the way the Polish economy is run. What are their consequences for the manifestation of needs and interests in economic practice? For a start I shall examine the consequences of the theory of "hostile surroundings" for economic aims.

It is obvious that the economy serves political aims, namely the striving of the ruling group to stay in power. Essentially, this was the goal (or one of them) addressed by the development of heavy industry. Such programs are pursued in accordance with political logic, that is, a logic in which the aim is more important than the costs of its pursuit. As a matter of fact, economic criteria do not matter and are replaced by an analysis of political costs and benefits, which makes it possible to launch huge investment projects that upset the economic, ecological, and social equilibrium.

However, an economy must at the same time satisfy the economic needs of society. Therefore, these needs have to be identified. I believe that this second, purely economic aim can be formulated as follows: The object is to obtain such a degree of satisfaction of needs as will guarantee "social peace." It is often a minimum level only, while the mechanisms of identification that are introduced mainly serve to satisfy the needs of those workers whose protest would threaten to disrupt sociopolitical life. Hence comes the system of privileges and inequality among individual professions and trades, which although expanded in the 1970s, has its roots back in the 1950s. This demonstrates that even strictly economic aims have some political overtones.

It turns out, however, that this mechanism of diagnosing needs does not effectively discharge its role of "pacifier of social mood." A system of consultation involving large enterprises enjoying special treatment from the authorities (in satisfying the needs of the the work force of those selected enterprises), which was designed to be both a gauge and a neutralizer of the public mood, proved inefficient. Suffice it to say that the social protest of 1980 started in large modern enterprises, whose workers were by no means at the bottom of the earnings league. It was a similar case with the earlier protests, those of 1956 and 1970.

Meeting economic goals requires, however, some measure of economic efficiency, notwithstanding the political overtones I have mentioned. My opinion is that at certain periods two principal economic goals—the maintenance of political order and the satisfaction of economic needs—can clash. A certain kind of economic reforms is a case in point. These are reforms that are part of decentralization; in other words, in the fact that some powers of the political system vis-a-vis the economy are ceded to the economy itself. This decentralization is supposed to serve efficiency: the "economic" aim of the economy. At the same time, however, decentralization clashes with the "political" aim of economic activity because it frees the economy from the strict control of the authorities. Fearing that the "decentralized" economy would get out of hand, the authorities then put brakes on the reform. In this manner, the "logic of political effects" contradicts the logic of economic effects. I therefore suspect that the search for an equilibrium between the political aim (understood as the maintenance of power) and the economic one (consisting of meeting the needs of the people) is a lasting feature of the Polish economy. For the time being, it looks as though the authorities have recognized as the optimum solution a state of equilibrium such that the economy fulfills the political aim to the maximum extent possible and the "economic" aim to the minimum extent possible so that "social peace" can still be preserved.

The theory about the social world being created from above leads to a similar contrived creation of the economy from above. The fact that the economy can be described as having been "contrived"—independent of economic laws—is also the effect of pursuing economic goals through economic moves, a process in which the logic of economic calculations clashes with the logic of the political goals.

The economy is not only purged of economic laws. It is also immune from the influence of the needs and interests of society, because the elimination of these interests and needs has become consistent with the theory about the society being a hostile environment. The elimination of economic laws and the expectations of society as the driving forces for the economy have produced unexpected consequences for the authorities themselves. The economy was to be at the disposal of the authorities thanks to its artificial creation, through the elimination of public interests and economic laws themselves. But it did not at all react to the wishes of the authorities. This leads to the next theory: The elimination of the economic rights and interests of society became the reason for a covert rivalry of interest groups.

At this point the usefulness of totalitarian or similar conceptions for describing the operation of interests in the economy becomes quite questionable. As a matter of fact, there is a "totalitarian trap," or by analogy to the vicious circle of bureaucracy, the "vicious circle of totalitarianism." Exceedingly rigid control and the elimination of the mechanisms of articulation of interests produce their own negation. Covert interest groups begin to operate—hence the popularity of conceptions of the "imperfect monism" kind. Therefore it is now necessary to refer to the next cognitive tradition, namely the conception of interest groups.

Let us therefore return to the last thesis about the elimination of a society's economic rights and interests being the reason for a covert rivalry among interest groups. It was assumed that the economy should be extremely subservient to the authorities. This goal was to be served by the creation of a whole institutional apparatus designed to exercise central control of the economy. Essentially, this apparatus does not obey economic laws, managing the economy instead through artificially set prices, values, and especially orders issued to manufacturers. At the same time, like any formalized structure, this creation becomes alienated from its master after a while. This is so because every formal structure involves a hierarchy of positions to which groups of people, with their aspirations and ambitions, are attached. The success of members of these groups in life depends on how the political authorities appraise their moves in running the economy. However, because economic laws and public expectations have been ruled out as the basis and criterion of these appraisals (e.g., the trends in investing, prices), covert bargaining becomes the only mechanism determining the correctness of the economic decisions that are adopted. From this practice stems then the well-known bargaining for funds, investment projects, and convenient prices for products, described by sociologists (especially J. Staniszkis).[4]

The economy becomes a limited-access tender: Participation is limited to the executive personnel of economic organizations, who seek maximum autonomy and minimum tasks, and the political authorities, who want to give this personnel exactly the opposite. Consumers have no say in this game. In this way, covert interest groups begin to operate, seeking to divert the flow of investment funds to their direction. The result of the competition is settled neither by economic laws (because the economy is artificial) nor by interests existing outside the political-economic establishment (because the influence of society's interests on the authorities has been eliminated, in keeping with the hostile surroundings theory). In this situation, the only way of settling rivalry among groups is by comparing the relations of individual interest groups with the system of power. In my opinion, well-placed connections are not only a method of pursuit of goals at the level of an individual (e.g., when a customer wants to buy some commodity), but they are also an institution operating at the macroeconomic level. It is possible to speak about economic-cum-political connections when examining the careers of people moving from the economy to politics.

A tender as a method of awarding contracts is not in itself bad—indeed, it is a rational method of action. However, the trouble is that first, the rules of solving disputes concerning investing or fixing prices are not openly stated; second, these criteria do not take into account economic laws or social expectations, and, third, despite all the secrecy surrounding the tender, the only valid criterion of selecting the winner is the position of representatives of individual lobbies in the system of power. Obviously enough, the functioning of the game of interests and the bidding is to some extent the result of the doctrine about the identity of the interests of all and on all issues. It is also obvious that such a method of influencing economic activity adversely affects its susceptibility to control by political authorities, as demonstrated by J. Staniszkis.[5]

A "contrived" economy thus turns against its masters: Instead of serving the interests of the authorities, it begins to serve also the interests of its own structures. Manufacturers' interest in producing expensive goods for which there is little demand in the market is not because of a lack of goodwill on the part of managerial staff but of structural solutions incorporated in the economic and financial system in which the enterprises have to operate. The desire to obtain maximum prices, maximum allocations of funds, and maximum autonomy is rational from the point of view of the managers. However, it undermines the economy's loyalty toward the authorities. Thus the contrived economy turns not only against its masters but also against the society at large. The bidding, the rivalry between economic organizations and political authorities, goes on without the participation of society. This is an interaction of two interest groups—the producers and the politicians—and it is significant that the functioning of either group does not depend in any great measure on the satisfaction of society's needs. The rules of the game that the authorities imposed on the producers, that artificial system of management, have became the basis of these producers' interests. This system was supposed to be merely a tool for implementing the loyalty of the economy to the authorities, but it started to live an independent life and engendered the interests of the managerial staff of economic organizations. This is the essence of the "totalitarian trap" paradox. The problem is that the game is contested by only two parties: the authorities and industry leaders. Individual consumers and their associations, and indeed the society, are left outside the game. However, it is very much affected by the outcome of the bargaining, for example, about the location of a factory or its future product range. Another aspect of the problem is that the authorities have never acknowledged the interests generated by the economic and financial system they created. Such interests did not fit into the doctrine. As a result, whenever the producers' response to the authorities' wishes was not prompt enough, it was attributed to ill will, whereas in reality it was a consequence of the authorities' moves.

The above description briefly demonstrates the possibility of analyzing the relationship between the authorities and the economy from the point of view of interest groups. The concept of lobbies, which has functioned for many decades in Western political science, has been applied in describing the structure of Communist societies since the 1960s. There is plenty of literature on the topic, especially on the subject of identifying and categorizing interest groups in the USSR.[6]

The way lobbies function in Western political sociology or political science and the concept of interest groups themselves, however, do not completely apply to socialist society. I should like to point to the most important aspects of interest group analysis and present their advantages and shortcomings in comparison with an ideal type of totalitarian approach.

The basic fault of totalitarian conceptions consists in the reliance on categories that are too homogeneous (the center, the party, the authorities). These in turn lead to a simplified vision of the political system and unnecessary uniformization. The corresponding failure of the interest group concept has been the assumption of an *excessive pluralism* in the system of exercising power in Communist countries. In extreme cases this may actually lead to the disappearance of any vision of a political system, which is replaced by a collection of groups with clashing interests. Political scientists appear to overestimate the differences of interest and search for too narrow interest groups.[7] As a result of such statistical compilations, which are quite common in some Western publications, little can be learned about the composition of the system as a whole.

Interest group concepts, while being of a more sociological character than totalitarian conceptions, are not free of a peculiar political science deviation either. The deviation consists in the fact that although it is argued that interest groups operate in society as well as among the ruling circles, more emphasis is put on lobbies operating in the latter milieu. However, the sociological character of interest group concepts is shown in the fact that by contrast to the ideal type of a totalitarian conception, it is not assumed that the system of authority implements its aims in a maximally effective way (e.g., through total control). In fact, the picture of the system becomes more probabilistic and more natural, as it were. But from the sociological point of view precisely it is important to point to essential shortcomings of interest groups conceptions: They usually do not contain any references either to any sociological conception of a "group" or to the concept of an "interest." The definitions are taken rather from the inventory of tools of political science and are difficult to place among sociological theories.

To summarize this part of my considerations, I should like to express the view that prior to August 1980, the conception of interest groups appeared to describe quite aptly the structure of the whole social order: The existing social bonds were mainly preserved within the formal structures of institutions. It therefore made sense to speak of managers and officials, of a political apparatus, with various levels, as well as of interest groups.

In keeping with the main stream of this line of thinking, interest groups emerge on the basis of existing institutions. Moreover, deep differences among individual branches of the economy and among organizations within the working class undercut attempts to speak of a definable class in this case.[8] It therefore appeared that the existing social structure was the aggregate of interest groups centered around formal organizations (e.g., industrial or political ones).

What happened in August 1980—in the tide of strikes that swept across practically the whole country, in the determination and prudence of the leaders of working-class actions, and most important, in the society's capacity for self-organization and integration surpassing group boundaries—was that all this made it necessary to look at the social structure differently than just from the point of view of interest groups.

Above all, there was the manifestation of solidarity, surpassing the divisions among individual industries and enterprises. Class interpretations began to emerge through which a fresh approach to structure was attempted. Such an interpretation was also suggested by events like the clear emergence of two parties to the conflict and the awareness of the different interests of these two sides.[9] The depth of the conflict, the intensity of social ties among the strikers, and especially the demand for the establishment of trade unions representing the interests of labor that are different from those of employers would dictate an interpretation in terms of a dichotomous class structure. On the one side there would be a particular "ruling class" composed of the administrators of politics and economics, that is, a group distinguishing itself by exercising political and economic authority, in other words, by its place in the *system of power* and—what appears to be no less important—occupying a privileged position in the *system of consumption*. At the other end would be the "labor class," denied the possibilities of exercising authority, which however had its own class organization from August 1980 onward: Solidarnosc should be recognized as such within this interpretation. To equate the social composition of this labor class with workers would be untrue, as is shown by the results of the Warsaw studies of the strikes.[10] Jacek Kurczewski may have been nearer the truth when he introduced the term "new middle class"—one that embraced both the better-skilled workers, "frustrated intellectuals," doctors in the national health service, and others.[11] In his view, it was this new middle class that started a social revolution. The term *middle class* implies a gradation of class structure in which there are also higher and lower classes. In my opinion, the new middle class could be interpreted within the dichotomous pattern as the most conscious section of the hired labor class.

Finally, I should like to synthesize the relationship between authority and economy (politics and economics) in each of the three approaches examined.

In the totalitarian approach, understood here in the sense of an ideal type, economics hardly exists as an autonomous force, as it is completely dominated by politics.[12] The ideal totalitarian model ignores conflicts between these forces because it assumes the absence of conflict in society in general. Any existing organizations—economic ones included—express the political interests of the ruling group. The above assumptions make up a theoretical model of ideal totalitarianism in its institutional shape. Such a picture of relations between politics and economics for obvious reasons does not fully reflect present-day reality. However, it does demonstrate the fundamental feature of this reality, that is, the application of political criteria and aims to the economy.

In spite of the numerous changes that have occurred since Stalin's times, it has been evident throughout the postwar period that the issue of political control over the economy never lost any of its topicality. This issue became especially obvious in the years 1980–1981, when there was a struggle for the relative autonomy of the economic system from the political one. The issue was probably most pronounced during the conflicts between the authorities and Solidarnosc over the powers of self-management bodies in enterprises. The contested issues were whether the self-management body should be the exclusive body authorized to select the managing director or whether this right should be limited through the influence of superior authorities.

In interest group theories, the relationship between politics and economics looks different. The assumption about a plurality of interests in a Communist society makes it imperative to acknowledge that the interests within the political and the economic system are independent of one another. In other words, there is no simple and direct primacy of politics over economics generally. Instead, there is a diversity of group interests connected with political and economic organizations. It is convenient to discuss conflicts and the search for autonomy on the part of politicians and managers of economic organizations precisely within such a theoretical framework.

The adoption of a class approach, especially one of the approaches that assume a dichotomous pattern in social structure, also produces specific consequences for the relationship between politics and economics. If the Polish situation were to be described in such terms, it is easy to notice that the class boundary would run across the economic system rather than, let us say, between the political and the economic system, as is usually assumed in interest group theories. By running across the economic system, such a boundary would also cut through economic organizations (enterprises), as the ruling class is made up of both the state and the economic administration. At the opposite pole would be hired laborers, who do not discharge managerial duties. In the case of the economy, this would be mainly workers. This division does not exhaust the problem—rather, it sketches out the two poles, without defining the social categories between which the border itself runs. However imprecise the division, it is safe to assume, however, that the border between the classes would always run across organizations.

Social Order: The Models and Practice

In this part of the chapter I shall attempt to illustrate, with empirical results from sociological studies, the theses formulated above. In particular, I shall try to answer the question about the extent to which it is possible to speak justifiably of the presence of class or group divisions in Polish society. I shall therefore concentrate on the social effects of the relationship between politics and economics that I have described. I shall be referring to studies from the years 1980–1981, with some references to analyses and observations made in 1982 and 1983.

On the basis of studies of attitudes toward the social and political situation in 1981, it is possible to identify some elementary factors influencing the attitude to the reform movement developing at that time.[13] The general conclusion is the following: Polish society was characterized by a strong polarization of interests, which divided it into two groups differing in size. On one side there was a small group displaying conservative attitudes and a reluctance toward essential changes in the system of exercising power (15–20 percent of the population). At the opposite end were all the others except for 15 percent who were undecided.[14] The attempt to identify the structural allegiances of representatives of both camps provided interesting results. It turned out that the choices corresponded to a given group's place in or proximity to the system of authority. PZPR members occupying managerial posts or PZPR members who were also members of the branch trade unions (or other permutations of these three features) tended to defend most fiercely the PZPR-dominated system of exercising power.[15] On the other side were almost all the remaining people, by no means Solidarnosc members only. This is illustrated by Table 10.1.

The evident polarization of views, demonstrated by these figures, led the authors of the study to the formulation of the above thesis about the role of proximity to the structures of authority in determining the line of social conflict. Such a structure of dichotomous interests corresponds to a vision of a society divided into distinct groups, possibly classes. The results of this study also demonstrate that the main line of the political conflict certainly did not run between individual socioprofessional groups or between the classes identified in official doctrine as characterizing Polish society, which lists workers and peasants as classes and the intelligentsia as a stratum. The most important determinant of differences in approach was the distance from the structures of power, indicated especially by the three factors: membership in the branch unions, membership in the PZPR, and the holding of a managerial position. I believe that the identification of the proponents of opposing interests is in a way tantamount to defining the "parties" to the conflict.

This, in turn, may be helpful in appraising the usefulness of the class perspective. Perhaps it might be safer to call this perspective a "dichotomous" one as it is rather difficult to describe an overwhelming majority of society as a class.

Table 10.1
The Desirable Type of Authority, According to Selected Groups

Group	Type of Government Preferred With PZPR in Leading Role (percent)	Without PZPR in Leading Role (percent)	Number
Solidarnosc members	24.5	75.5	608
Nonunion labor	30.0	70.0	624
Branch union members in managerial posts	70.3	29.7	37

Note: Based on random sample.
Source: The author's own calculations on the basis of L. Kolarska and A. Rychard, "The Influence of Industrial Organizations," Studia Socjologiczne, No. 2/77 (1980).

However, the dichotomous perspective can be enriched by approaches revealing certain internal differentiation within the two camps. There were, for example, differences of interests among narrower groups within the "world of labor" about specific political solutions and economic issues.[16] The conception of interest groups might be useful here.

The differences of interest within the hired labor class were also demonstrated in other ways. The system of economic management based on the privileged treatment of the areas or enterprises that were important from the authorities' point of view inevitably generated differences of interest between the employees of those privileged sectors and those from other sectors. This is so, notwithstanding the fact that these differences were neutralized by the need of class-wide solidarity, so spectacular during the developments of August 1980 and in the subsequent months. The results of more detailed studies carried out in industrial enterprises in autumn 1981 showed that although the main line of the conflict separated the people in managerial positions from rank-and-file employees, there were some differences of interests within the latter group, depending on the sector of the economy.[17] (In some instances, the employees of enterprises producing capital goods were more radical than workers engaged in the manufacture of consumer products.)

It is much more difficult to identify the internal divisions in the group connected with the apparatus of power. Its component parts receive a variety of labels, most frequently ones taken from the Western media: There are the "hardliners," the "moderates," and the "liberals." "Technocrats" also appear as a distinct group. This division is based on political orientation. The division is very superficial, but then its main purpose is to classify the differences occurring within the Communist political system in a way that will be easily comprehended by Western readers, perhaps at the expense of accuracy. Other classification attempts consist of associating interest groups with existing functional divisions within the political system, broadly conceived. Then there is talk about groups with ties with, for example, the administration, the military, or the security system.

The leadership of economic organizations is often distinguished as an interest group.[18] It appears that in the political structure of Communist countries these people occupy a somewhat different place than the remaining interest groups. First of all, they compete with other interest groups not so much for power as for autonomy from the political center. Besides—what appears to be the biggest distinction—there exists a permanent difference of interests between the managers of economic organizations and the groups forming the formal political center (e.g., full-time employees of the party or officials of the administrative authorities). Numerous studies have shown that these differences of interest change relatively little. The activities of economic leaders, dictated by the logic of production processes where efficiency is the supreme value, often clash with the activities of local or central-level politicians, for whom party control of the economy appears to be more important than efficiency—hence the strong pressure on autonomy and independence displayed by industry leaders in various surveys.[19]

At the root of this phenomenon lies, to some extent, the classical conflict between professional and bureaucratic values. At a time of sharp social conflict, during which the pattern of social forces undergoes polarization rather than diversification, management is automatically, as it were, classified as part of the "power elite." The studies of the strikes in Warsaw in 1980 made it possible, however, to note significant differences in the behavior of managers and of party secretaries toward the strikers. The former displayed a more pragmatic attitude while the latter were far less flexible toward the strike, refusing to negotiate or sometimes even hampering the reaching of agreement between the strikers and management.[20] In view of these differences, the authors of the surveys in question made the assumption that management is a separate interest group within the ruling class.

Thus the results of empirical studies carried out in 1980–1981 provide grounds for the hypotheses about the usefulness of a *dichotomous* perspective for describing social structures. This should be supplemented by approaches indicating a certain inner differentiation of the two opposed sections of society. Both the main line dividing the society into two parts and the lines running across these groups are to a large extent determined by the type of relationship between the system of power and the economy. The main dividing line is determined by one's position in the system of state administration and economic management, while the lines separating individual interest groups are determined by the diversity of priorities accorded to individual groups of workers (with respect to the class of hired labor) or the struggle for autonomy from the political decisionmaking centers (e.g., managers of economic organizations, who were, however, a part of the authorities).[21]

The results of the survey justify a hypothesis regarding the development of the main line of the conflict in 1980–1981 (and the subsequent period). It can be assumed that in autumn 1980 this line ran rather low in the hierarchy of economic management. This is indicated by the studies of the Warsaw strikes, which revealed that in some cases even foremen were in opposition to the strikers.[22] During the study of industrial enterprises made a year earlier, it turned out that at the enterprise level, in addition to the signs of conflict, there were the germs of consensus or tacit agreement.[23] For example, rank-and-file workers thought that enterprise managers were mainly interested in "the enterprise operating efficiently" and much less frequently believed that the managers were pursuing their own interests related to keeping their posts.[24] Although the results of the two studies quoted here are not exactly comparable, they justify the hypotheses about the line of the conflict having moved upward in the meantime and about the beginnings of acceptance at the enterprise level in the period immediately preceding the imposition of martial law. At the end of 1981, it was no longer legitimate to regard all people in managerial positions as members of the "ruling class"—this class shrank and the line of conflict now ran not so much inside industrial enterprises and other organizations as above them. This change would be the essence of this hypothesis.

The imposition of martial law may have contributed to a lowering of that border again. As a result of numerous changes in managerial posts in industry and the militarization of a part of enterprises, loyalty toward the structures of authority and the superiors may have again become indispensable for holding even the lowest managerial posts. The time of martial law and the period that followed it did not, however, remove the main axis of the conflict; at best, it prevented its open display. This hypothesis stems from the conviction that the structural reasons for the clash of interests between the dichotomous elements of society have not disappeared. Actually, martial law may have acted in two directions, so to say. On the one hand, it aggravated the conflict, confronting many people with the necessity of making often dramatic choices, while on the other, it prevented the manifestations of this conflict at a time of intensified repression.

Probably the most important thing from the structural point of view is that the dichotomy was both strengthened and weakened as a result of martial law. This paradox stems from in the fact that the dramatic nature of the December 12, 1981, decisions led to a polarization of views (intensifying the division), but at the same time the authorities took a number of decisions leading to the disintegration of "the other side" (the dissolution of the trade union set up after August 1980 was of crucial significance in this respect). The aim of these decisions was not so much to solve the conflict as to blunt its edge.

A system of diverse privileges for various branches of the economy is being reintroduced by stages, while official statements put a great deal of emphasis on a vision of society as a diversified whole, composed of groups representing conflicting interests. Although such a vision is quite novel in a Communist society (because of the abandonment of the assumption about the identity of interests of the whole society), it serves a distinct sociotechnical purpose. This may be the desire to move the border of the conflict between the authorities and society to the boundaries of society itself. In this case, society characterized by distinct marks of a class structure would again be supposed to become a kind of a federation of interest groups, which would make it possible for the authorities to gain the position of a judge settling disputes among these groups, instead of occupying the uncomfortable position of a party to the conflict. It is too early to appraise the effects of this strategy. Therefore both dichotomous and more diversified patterns would still be more suitable for describing the social effects of the relationship between the authorities and the economy.

Conflict and Acquiescence in Social Relations, in Place of a Summing-Up

Thus far this analysis has emphasized the principal lines of the conflict whose essence is the lack of legitimization of the structures of authority (cf. the attitude toward the principle of the dominant role of the PZPR in the political system). Therefore the political nature of this conflict determines the main sides involved in it: the groups connected with the system of power and those denied such power, which at the same time refuse to recognize the legitimacy of the former. This conflict is clearly manifested in economic structures. From this point of view the Polish economy is the arena in which society-wide political conflict manifests itself.

Yet in spite of this conflict, the institutional system is very stable. The main stabilizing elements are, of course, the mechanisms of coercion the state may put into operation or the particular lack of alternatives.[25] However, in addition to those mechanisms, there are some social sources of acquiescence or acceptance of the institutional status quo.

These mechanisms were especially visible at the end of 1981, which was in a way paradoxical in view of the sharp polarization of postures in the fundamental conflict. As I stated, the beginnings of acquiescence could then be spotted at the level of industrial enterprises. This was mainly manifested in the fact that rank-and-file employees perceived the interests of the directors as being devoid of conflict. The studies made in industry also indicated that the workers as a rule saw the main line of the conflict rather above the enterprise level. The factor chiefly responsible for the emergence of the germs of consensus was certainly the role of some mechanisms institutionalizing the conflict at the enterprise level (the activity of Solidarnosc, the social support for those enterprise directors who stayed in their posts throughout the "renewal" period or who replaced others as a result of social pressure).

However, one can believe that there also exist more durable sources of acquiescence, which can be seen mainly in industrial enterprises. They come from the necessity to cooperate, imposed by all the formal organizations. The workers know that the managing directors are the first element of the ruling elite, one to which they have some access, but the workers are also aware that although the managers belong to the opposite camp, they are themselves employees of the same companies and, like the workers, are interested in good economic performance.[26] This example shows how the conflict loses some of its acuteness at the lower levels of the social structure.

This type of mechanism generating acquiescence has been present virtually throughout the post–World War II period. It is the result of a situation in which the great majority of the population is dependent on the state. Although the majority does not recognize the legitimacy of the authorities' rule, some minimum amount of cooperation with their institutions is indispensable for the fulfillment of one's aims in life. The operation of this mechanism was confirmed by studies conducted in industrial enterprises in 1983 immediately after the lifting of martial law. It turned out that the management of enterprises, and especially the immediate superiors, often perform the role of "channels of articulating" workers' interests, attempting to replace the banned Solidarnosc and the not very credible new trade unions set up after its dissolution.[27] The lack of means for articulating workers' interests has been responsible for a situation in which their outlet is found in production structures (through immediate superiors). This substitution helps ease the social conflict but has an adverse impact on productivity. Social peace is thus achieved at the cost of lower efficiency.

This process is typical of all state-dominated structures. The state is not only the apparatus of power but also the institution that decides about the division of goods and satisfaction of needs. As a result, an industrial enterprise is also not only a production unit but also an institution distributing various goods and ensuring the articulation of interests.[28]

Besides the mechanisms generating the conflict, there are some that produce a certain climate of acquiescence. The conflict manifests itself mainly in the attitude toward the central political institutions. That this "political" level socialist reality is not legitimized is confirmed by the low support given to the principle of PZPR's leading role. But in addition to the political level there is the level of "daily life," in which some mechanisms of acquiescence are formed. Acquiescence would mean here a kind of a pragmatic nonideological acceptance of the existing organizational reality in one's own enterprise, university, or clinic. This would create a certain mechanism that M. Mann has termed an "institutional fitness."[29] This mechanism makes the people's careers dependent on their behavioral acceptance of the system, even though they may declare a definite dislike of that system. This behavioral factor is probably the strongest stabilizing factor in this system. The result is acquiescence without legitimization. This is at the same time an essential mechanism blurring the borderlines in the conflict.

At the outset of this chapter I wrote that I would seek to present the disharmonious elements in the relationship among the authorities, the economy, and the society. The dialectics of conflict and acquiescence is the principal manifestation of this disharmony. The peculiarity of these dialectics consists in the fact that both the conflict and the acquiescence are the outcome of a situation in which they share or participate in the structure of power. On the one hand, by subordinating to itself most areas of life, this structure breeds mutiny and reaction (at the political level), while on the other, for the same reasons, it entangles the fates and produces the interdependence of groups of people, forcing them to cooperate.

The presence of a conflict makes it possible to look at social order as a whole, bisected by a sharp political conflict, which justifies the approaches referring to class dichotomy. However, the numerous diversifying mechanisms—which also force people to cooperate—make it possible to perceive the usefulness of a more pluralistic approach, for example, that of interest groups.

It can be said that the socioinstitutional development of Poland in the period after World War II consisted in a gradual superimposition of new elements. After a totalitarian-type beginning (whose principal elements have been retained to this day) came a period of formation of group consciousness and structure, lasting until very distinct elements in the class structure (during the events of 1956, 1970, 1976, and 1980) emerged. The line of conflict became increasingly sharp, but at the same time each period generated its own mechanisms blurring that line.

Notes

1. This problem has been analyzed by W. Narojek and J. Staniszkis, among other authors. See W. Narojek, *Struktura spoleczna w doswiadczeniu jednostki* (Social Structure in the Experience of an Individual), (Warszawa: PIW, 1982), and J. Staniszkis, "Structure as the Outcome of Adaptational Processes in an Organization," in *Wierowanie w spoleczenstwie* (Leadership in Society), ed. W. Morawski (Warszawa: PWN, 1976); "The Types of Leadership Techniques in an Organization," in *Kierowanie w spoleczenstwie* (Leadership in Society), ed. W. Morawski (Warszawa: PWN, 1979), and "The Kinds of Authority," *Studia Socjologiczne*, No. 2, (Wroclaw: Ossolineum, 1973).

2. Cf. the works of C. Friedrich (1954), C. Friedrich and Z. Brzezinski (1956), L. Schapiro (1978), just to name a few classics. Complete citations are as follows C. J. Friedrich, "The Unique Character of Totalitarian Society," in *Totalitarianism*, ed. C. J. Friedrich (Cambridge, Mass.: Harvard University Press, 1954); C. J. Friedrich and Z. K. Brzezinski, *Totalitarian Dictatorship and Autocracy* (New York: Praeger, 1966); and L. Schapiro, *Totalitarianism* (London: Pall Mall Press, 1972).

3. Witold Morawski calls this a "strategy of forced industrialization." He observed that it was implemented with the assent of the society, which perceived in it an

opportunity of fulfilling its own aspirations (promotion, migration, education). However, Morawski wrote, from the mid-1960s that assent started to be gradually withdrawn. Consult W. Morawski, "Spoleczenstwo a narzucona industrializacja" (Society and the Industrialization Imposed upon It), *Kultura* (weekly), December 7, 1980.

4. See Staniszkis, "The Kinds of Authority" and "Structure as the Outcome of Adaptational Processes"

5. "Structure as the Outcome of Adaptational Processes," p. 175.

6. Cf. one of the works by H. G. Skilling and F. Griffith (eds.), *Interest Groups in Soviet Politics* (Princeton, N. J.: Princeton University Press, 1971).

7. This view is forcefully supported by the following quotation, presenting the socialist countries as fully pluralistic systems: "The various sectors of the intelligentsia exerted their influence through their institutions and associations, and through newspapers, scholarly journals, and special conferences, and in varying ways expressed the needs of broader segments of the population," R. Pethybridge, *A Key to Soviet Politics* (London: Allen & Unwin, 1962), p. 10. The author of this remark evidently overestimated the pluralism of the system. Besides, he committed an obvious error consisting in a mechanical transposition of the knowledge of professional organizations and associations operating in the West to Communist conditions. Under Communist reality, all these institutions not only represent the interests of their members but also ensure their conformism.

8. Cf. L. Kolarska and A. Rychard, "Wplyw organizacji przemyslowych na strukture spoleczenstwa socjalistycznego" (The Influence of Industrial Organizations on the Structure of Socialist Society), *Studia Socjologiczne*, No. 2/77 (1980).

9. See S. Ossowski, "Problems of Social Structure," in *Works*, Vol. 5, (Warszawa, 1968).

10. Cf. S. Rainko, "Three Interpretations," *Literatura Weekly*, No. 497 (1980). J. Drazkiewicz and A. Rychard, "Strikes in the Warsaw Region in the Summer of 1980" (a report from studies by a commission of the Polish Sociological Association), (Warszawa, 1981).

11. J. Kurczewski, "Conflict and Solidarnosc" (a paper read at a meeting of the Warsaw branch of the Polish Sociological Association, 1980).

12. In this sense, the political system would determine the economic system. In this respect, the antonym of totalitarian theories would be the theories of convergence, which rather envisage the opposite direction of the interdependence (cf. I. Sienko, *Ekonomika i polityka w teoriach sowietologow anglosaskich* (Economics and Politics in the Theories of Anglo-Saxon Sovietologists), (Warszawa: PWN, 1979), p.161.

13. I am referring here to the study *Polacy 1981: Postrzeganie kryzysu i konfliktu* (Poles 1981: The Perception of the Crisis and Conflict), W. Adamski et al., carried out in the late autumn of 1981 and covering a representative nationwide sample of adult Poles by the Institute of Philosophy and Sociology of the Polish Academy of Sciences.

14. L. Kolarska and A. Rychard, "Political Order and Economic Order," in W. Adamski et al., *Polacy 1981: Postrzeganie kryzysu i konfliktu* (Poles 1981: The Perception of the Crisis and Conflict), (Warszawa: Institute of Philosophy and Sociology of the Polish Academy of Sciences, 1982).

15. This term denotes trade unions that operated after August 1980 and were, with some oversimplification, the continuation of the pre-August unions, which usually put them at loggerheads with Solidarnosc.

16. For example, workers put more emphasis than specialists with university degrees on the need for decentralization, while the principle of the dominant role of the PZPR was equally unpopular among both groups (Kokarska and Rychard, "The Influence of Industrial Organizations").

17. The study "Gospodarka w opinii pracownikow" (The Economy as Seen by Employees), L. Kolarska, A. Rychard, and H. Sterniczuk, was conducted in the Polish Academy of Sciences' Institute of Philosophy and Sociology, Research Unit for Sociology of Organization, in 1983. It involved 39 industrial enterprises, selected nonrandomly. Within these firms, a total of 710 employees were selected by lottery as their representatives.

18. See, for example, the work of Skilling and Griffith, as well as Pethybidge. Within Skilling and Griffith, consult especially the chapter by T. Frankel and J. P. Hardt, "The Industrial Managers."

19. A. Rychard, *Reforma gospodarcza: Socjologiczna analiza zwiazkow polityki i gospodarki* (The Economic Reform: A Sociological Analysis of the Relationship between Politics and Economy), (Warszawa: Ossolineum, 1980).

20. Drazkiewicz and Rychard, "Strikes in the Warsaw Region"

21. Incidentally, these privileges were not effective in appeasing social conflicts, which is confirmed by the findings showing that the workers of the capital-equipment sector were more radical, despite enjoying rather more privileges than other groups.

22. Drazkiewicz and Rychard, "Strikes in the Warsaw Region"

23. The study "Gospodarka w opinii pracownikow."

24. "Company interests" were cited by 72.3 percent of the workers, while 27.7 percent pointed to "private interests." See A. Rychard, "The Needs and Interests in the Economy," in L. Kolarska, A. Rychard, and H. Sterniczuk, "The Economy as Seen by Employees," the report on a study of the Institute of Philosophy and Sociology of the Polish Academy of Sciences, subject 11.2: The Structure of the Changes in Polish Society (Warszawa, 1983).

25. See the articles by J. Staniszkis, already cited.

26. This is so despite all the ills in the system of management that weaken the relationship between the efficiency of the enterprise and the workers' incomes.

27. T. Zukowski, "The Studies of Workers' Self-Management Bodies" (a paper read at a meeting of the Department of Sociology of Organizations, Institute of Philosophy and Sociology of the Polish Academy of Sciences, December 1983).

28. In this way, social relations exert an influence on the economic sphere: The lack of social mechanisms of articulation of interests causes a loss of efficiency.

29. M. Mann, "The Ideology of Intellectuals and Other People in the Development of Capitalism," in L. N. Linberg et al., *Stress and Contradiction in Modern Capitalism* (Lexington, Mass.: Lexington Books, 1975).

11

Some Lessons from the Historical Experience of Poland's Development

Józef Pajestka

The continuity of the process of Poland's development was clearly disrupted in the years 1980–1982. No matter how these events are going to be appraised in the future, they will certainly be recognized as significant and as ones that shed fresh light on certain aspects of socialist evolution. It is extremely important to draw conclusions from them.

We are unlikely to be able to draw all the lessons from Poland's history that led to the events of the years 1980–1982. Too little time has passed, and there is still too much emotional involvement to allow an impartial analysis. Nevertheless, such attempts have to be made, even if they will have to be verified and supplemented in the future.

The lessons from the experience are of a multiple nature. There are lessons for politicians and for those in charge of socioeconomic policies in particular. There are also lessons not only for economics, regarding aspects of development and ways of functioning of the national economy, but also for general aspects of economic theory. I shall deal with the latter group of problems in this chapter.

The problem arises whether the experience of the Polish development process can indeed serve as a basis for more general theoretical conclusions. Is it not perhaps a bit megalomaniac to try to elevate national experience to the rank of universal significance and general theoretical theses for economics? I am as far as can be from any national megalomania, yet I cannot deny that the developments in one country may be important for other nations. However, this is not the heart of the matter.

The experience of human thought is general and universal. It is based on an appraisal of a development process that has some common features irrespective of national characteristics. What manifests itself in one country can usually be observed in other countries as well, although it need not always be equally distinct. At times some matters become more visible than others. Often the symptoms of a crisis bring to the surface that which is not so easy to see in a "normal" situation.

The same could be said about the Polish experience, and for this reason there are grounds for drawing more general conclusions from it. In fact, I believe that the Polish experience contains more universal elements, ones that apply to other socialist and nonsocialistic countries alike than is generally recognized. The analyses that have been attempted in Poland tend to interpret the developments as uniquely Polish. This leads to incorrect diagnoses and conclusions. The developments contain some specifically Polish characteristics but also fundamental issues of a broader dimension.

The process of Poland's development saw a powerful juncture between economic development and social and moral problems, which became quite pronounced during the crisis of 1980–1981. One can concludes that it is necessary to include social and moral problems in the analysis of the whole development process. In other words, economic problems should be examined in conjunction with ethical ones. This is an important conclusion from the point of view of the methodology of economics. So far, the dominant trend has been to isolate economic analysis from ethical problems. In the trends prevailing in the field of economics in Western countries, the problems of ethical aims and indeed values are weeded out. Also in Poland, not even the most prominent economists (e.g., Oskar Lange, Michal Kalecki) have touched upon social and moral problems, leaving them outside the scope of economics. At first I thought that the idea of including social and moral problems in the analysis, which is beginning to form a new movement in economic science, is quite novel. However, as I glanced through recent foreign literature, I could see that this stream of thought is displayed simultaneously by many scholars. I think it is reasonable to expect that it will receive broad support, although this will still take some time. It turns out, therefore, that the Polish point of view is not exceptional, although the Polish experience may have been more distinct.

The Polish development process has been characterized by sociopolitical conflicts that led to inevitable changes in socioeconomic policies. These changes were "extorted" through public pressure, mainly on the part of the working class. Looking at this historical experience, it is impossible to reject the impression that we are dealing here with a crisis of planning: the inability to anticipate developments, to harmonize the policy of growth with the aspirations of society, or to harmonize different policy moves. This points to the necessity of rethinking the whole concept of planning for growth.

There are many aspects of this problem, but I wish to draw special attention to one with significant implications. That one is a too narrow understanding of "planning" in the dominant theoretical approaches, limited practically to the material and economic processes of development. This narrow understanding of planning creates the danger of a lack of cohesion in development undertakings. In Poland this lack of cohesion manifested itself and led to a discrepancy between policy aims and society's aspirations and a conflict between these aims and institutional solutions.

This experience has led to a new conceptual approach to planning, which I term a conscious shaping of development processes. Its most important feature is its including the formation of material-economic processes and social aims, social and moral values, as well as institutional problems. Although the inspiration for this new theoretical approach to planning may come from Polish experience, the conclusions stemming from it are of a general nature, not necessarily directly related to that experience.

The two matters mentioned above lead to a third: the theoretical notion of socioeconomic rationality. It appears that this notion could occupy a top place in economic science. However, it has been denied that place and many economists prefer to give it up. This may be the outcome of the fate of the "principle of rational economy," which appeared to be a cornerstone of economy but later demonstrated its great limitations, especially with regard to long-range socioeconomic development. In the tradition of Poland's economic thought, it is worth considering a new approach to socioeconomic rationality, including correctness of the goals, rationality of allocation, and instrumental efficiency.

The three problems concerning new theoretical orientations have one feature in common: the reorientation of socioeconomic thought toward the future. Until now, the development of economic theory has been inspired first of all by observation of the past. I think such theory could be better justified if the shaping of theoretical thought were inspired to a greater extent by thoughts about the future. This thesis is not undermined by the assertion that there are no sources of knowledge of the future other than what is known from the past, as paradoxical as though this may sound.

Poland's Development Policy

I do not think it necessary to substantiate the statement that Poland's development policy, from the end of the 1940s to the most recent period, was oriented toward maximum technological and economic growth of the country and that this was accepted as the main strategic aim. In the country's real situation there were forces and factors supporting the goal of a high rate of economic growth. In this context I must draw special attention to the following:

1. The real strivings of broad social masses which demanded economic promotion and earnestly expected it from the state and the socialist system;
2. The aspirations of the new political forces and the political powers, professing a socialist ideology, which viewed the attainment of a high growth rate as a factor legitimizing their exercise of power;
3. The operation of the demonstration factor, that is, the influence of the example of the most developed capitalist countries on the shaping of models of standards of living and life-styles (this impact is especially strong in view of Poland's geographical situation and sociological influences).

These forces and factors can be interpreted in a way justifying the goal of rapid economic development: There was a real longing for an improvement in the material situation of society, which in turn would furnish conditions for all-round human development. This striving was intensified by the sense of dignity of the nation, which did not want to see other nations pulling ahead of it. The justification should also include, in my opinion, the aspiration of the new socialist system to prove its value in practice.

There is the important problem of parallelism in the aspirations and strivings of the political authorities and the aspirations and expectations of society. It would not be true to say that there was full parallelism in Poland, as there were also differences and conflicts. Yet in general, looking back at the period of over thirty years of the country's development, I can not reject the view that the policy of fast development corresponded to the aspirations of broad social groups and was indeed justified by these aspirations. This appraisal is not undermined by contemporary arguments about the dangers of unrestricted growth in the context of ecological limitations.

However, the actual process of the country's development led to that strategy's being questioned. This occurred, however, not through taking issue with the desirability of fast economic growth but with some of its aspects and consequences. A conflict among various social aims and social and moral values arose. This is an important conflict, one that affects the options regarding future development.

The First Phase of Development

In the first stage of the country's industrialization, the principal institutional solutions were adjusted to the aim of fast economic growth. These solutions affected the following three main lines of development strategy:

1. The growth of social accumulation—the exacting of social sacrifices with a view to ensuring a faster growth in the long run;
2. The utilization of the country's economic resources, especially manpower and production capacity, which was initially the main method of accelerating economic growth;
3. The new arrangement of economic structures, conducive to long-term growth.

The systemic and institutional instruments serving the implementation of these economic objectives had the following overriding characteristics:

1. The existence of a "firm" state, rigorously implementing the adopted development strategy through the use of political, organizational, economic, and ideological means and methods;
2. A centralized decisionmaking system, especially with regard to accumulation, allocation of means, and distribution of income.

When I observe these early institutional solutions in relatively long historical perspective today, I can think of no convincing arguments why they should be questioned as to their functionality in relation to the policy aims of the first period of industrialization and as to external determinants. I am drawing attention to the specific kind of development that is set in motion by internal factors and sociopolitical forces, which today is regarded as a desirable development strategy, one of self-reliance. In this context it is, I suppose, possible to agree about the relatively high degree of cohesion between the aims and character of growth in the difficult starting conditions, on the one hand, and the whole institutional system, on the other. It would be theoretically possible to examine different development patterns to which the above statement would not apply. I do not think, however, that the experience of other countries argues in favor of the superiority of other patterns of growth in the conditions that actually existed in Poland after World War II.

That cohesion does not mean that there were no flaws regarding the rationality of individual solutions. However, the total questioning of that cohesion and the resultant loosening of the ties between aims and methods was a further development that emerged only at a later stage. I will support this hypothesis with arguments later on. For the time being, I wish to observe that it does not confirm the widely held view that it is necessary to look to the 1940s for the sources of the present crisis. The latter view is mainly based on the appraisal of the political situation, and I am not going to challenge it on that. However, it is necessary to take into account also the socioeconomic aspects of systemic institutional solutions.

Now in retrospect, it is possible to formulate many fundamental reservations about the original institutional solutions. After all, it is a fact that they led to serious economic disproportions and sociopolitical tensions that had a negative impact on the development process. However, from a historical point of view, there are more important things to point out than the partial lack of rationality in the original system. Namely, there was an absence of an "adjusting mechanism" that would eliminate the elements which were proven to be wrong and to produce bad results. The development policy was corrected from time to time, but the changes did not affect institutional solutions. Somehow, this area was exempted from the process of learning through errors.

One problem related to the subject of irrational institutional patterns deserves special attention. It involves an area in which the distortions of rationality had a particularly negative impact and got progressively worse. What I have in mind are some features of the planning system.

The system of planning introduced in Poland in the early 1950s was based on certain doctrinal assumptions and the needs of the development strategy (particularly the three main aspects mentioned above). It was a highly centralized system of planning, nowadays referred to as the command-and-quota system, and had two remarkable features. One of them was the fact that it underestimated or plainly ignored economic criteria, with regard to both macroeconomic issues and the functioning of economic organizations. Therefore, it did not ensure the implementation of the principle of rational economy in the narrow but very important domain of cost-effectiveness analysis. The second fault was lack of appreciation of economic mechanisms and a tendency to replace them with a bureaucratic system of management. These negative features of the planning system were very easy to see in Poland. They were responsible, in an ever greater measure, for the fact that the rationality of the whole development strategy came to be questioned. The lack of an "adjusting mechanism" had particularly negative consequences.

The Second Stage

The initial conception of the development strategy evolved somewhat through the years. However, it was the changes in the real socioeconomic patterns that turned out to be crucial. Owing to these changes, more and more maladjustment and discrepancies started to appear in the original conception. In my opinion, rationality suffered first in the context of institutional solutions. In particular, the following two phenomena were present:

1. The growing discrepancy between the state's "development mission" and the aspirations of the masses that was emerging especially because of the slow improvement in economic efficiency, due to a faulty economic system;
2. The emergence of new needs of the people and new social and moral values that were blocked by existing institutional solutions.

This historical experience shows that the whole institutional pattern was not adjusted to socioeconomic needs. It produced a sociological-political existential mechanism of its own. In this way, it added to the inconsistencies and the irrationality of the entire system of influencing the processes of growth.

The conscious shaping of development processes must be complete, including both purposefulness and the economy of allocation as well as the whole institutional structure. It is impossible to ensure harmonious development if this shaping of processes of growth is limited to planning that deals only with material and economic factors. Even if that planning were ideal, it could not ensure a favorable course of growth. Moreover, experience shows that the lack of full rationality quickly leads to a degeneration in narrowly conceived economic planning.

Mounting inconsistencies in the whole system shaping socioeconomic processes slowed the country's progress and were the reason for the growing social dissatisfaction and sociopolitical conflicts emerging in Poland.

Poland's development has been characterized by sociopolitical conflicts that displayed essential controversies between the working masses and the state and political authorities on policy aims and means of pursuit. There are sufficient grounds for holding the view that these conflicts indicated the existence of an essential irrationality in the whole development process and were caused by it. However, they have been usually interpreted from the political point of view, which carries the risk of faulty diagnoses and conclusions.

The direct reason for all the conflicts was the manifest contradiction between the authorities' development mission and the strivings of society. Fulfillment of the development mission has been the common obsession of the authorities in all the socialist countries. It was justified originally by the countries'status according to Marxist thought and the ambitions of the masses. The implementation of the development mission while the economy is underdeveloped requires sacrifices on the part of society. These must be based on appropriate ethical postures deeply rooted in tradition, on strong integration of society around the common cause of development, on economic and political coercion, or a combination of the above factors. If these factors do not generate a social readiness for efforts and sacrifices, the implementation of the development mission becomes impossible. A conflict then emerges between what the authorities want and what society wants. Once such a conflict emerges, one can choose between raising the society's readiness for effort and sacrifice or reducing the development mission. If neither is done, an inconsistency between the plans of the authorities and the strivings of society emerges that is the core of a general lack of cohesion in the process of growth. This is exactly what happened in the Polish development process.

Already in the 1950s, efforts aimed at increasing the integration of society began to falter and lose their appeal to the public. This was largely due to the progressive bureaucratization of the whole state and political system. Differences in living conditions intensified and became more extreme, which is rarely conducive to sacrifice. Vertical mobility of society diminished and stratification according to the division into those who govern and those who are governed became petrified. This led to a rift between the strivings of the authorities and society. What was left was state coercion, and the whole system of management was based on it, which did not facilitate the unification of social aims and strivings.

I believe that the emergence and intensification of divergencies between the authorities' development mission and society's strivings were not perceived by our politicians. The awareness of the lack of cohesion on a fundamental issue—that of the social aims of development—seemed to be lost among those responsible for the shaping of socioeconomic processes.

The 1970s produced more discrepancies between the authorities' mission and society's aspirations. From the point of view of historical need, the development mission was less and less important as the country rose from the ruins caused by the war and made considerable progress in its industrialization effort. Efforts and sacrifices that were quite justified in the 1950s were no longer justified in the 1970s. And yet the authorities' development mission actually intensified during that period. This development mission was, to an ever greater extent, a need of the power elite itself rather than a reflection of the historical necessity of growth supported by the people.

The authorities' ambition to contribute to fast growth should not be appraised negatively. If they can release the creative powers of the nation, assist the innovative spirit, encourage rational management, and are careful to harmonize social and economic targets, everything is fine and successful efforts for fast grouth can be seen as commendable. However, if the authorities implement their plans for fast growth through new investment projects and increased outlays of labor, this effort must be matched by the readiness for sacrifice on the part of the people.

In that regard, the 1970s present a very inconsistent picture of political moves. On the one hand, politicians intensified the pursuit of their development mission, but on the other, instead of encouraging society to show readiness for work and sacrifices, they prepared it for a growth of prosperity. The state was portrayed as a benefactor of society and political enunciations focused on what the state "gave" to the people and how good it was to them instead of emphasizing that the nation's prosperity could only be improved through common effort and good work.

This inconsistency was, to a large extent, due to two factors underlying the policies of the 1970s and connected with the sociopolitical crisis of 1970. One was the thirst for economic success, which the authorities needed for political reasons, although they enjoyed a measure of social support as well. The second reason was the direct political reaction to the conflict between the sacrifices required to achieve development and the expectations of prosperity. To obtain support from society, the political authorities had to assure it that they had no plans to undercut the standard of living or to seek economic development at society's expense. They did so posing as benefactors and developing an ideology of prosperity. The political conditions and political needs of the authorities should not be ignored. It is not necessary to criticize the politicians striving to "dynamize" development and to ensure a better satisfaction of the people's needs. However, when the further course of the development process demonstrated clearly the inconsistencies of that policy and its infeasibility brought great dangers with it (which could already be seen by the middle of 1973), the politicians did not embark on the necessary course of changes. This was their biggest mistake. While failing to make the essential move, they found a "substitute," facilitated by international circumstances: Namely, they opted for heavy foreign debt. Indebtedness replaced both indispensable institutional changes and a turnabout in general development policy.

I will not try to explain here how the emergence of such inconsistencies in development policy and the exposure of the country to such a danger was possible, as the answers would call for an analysis of political processes and relations. However, I wish to draw attention to two special aspects of the situation.

The whole system of shaping development processes was narrowed down to a political exercise—the political needs involved in wielding and staying in power. In other words, politicking prevailed over political wisdom. At the same time, there was an increasingly strong tendency to view development processes in a narrowly economic or technocratic way: Technocracy, emerging under the strong influence of the bureaucratic apparatus, was beginning to predominate over strategic thinking. In my opinion, politicking and technocracy are extremely dangerous to a wise shaping of development processes. It is necessary to guard against them both institutionally (through democratic institutions) and by raising social wisdom to a higher level.

The Sources of Conflict

The clash between the development mission and society's standard-of-living aspirations has a larger dimension. It must be viewed as a conflict between insufficient progress in what is broadly understood as economic efficiency and the strivings of the masses.

From a historical and global point of view, socialist economies have shown themselves to be capable of a fast rate of economic growth. For many years, this was also true of the Polish economy. However, the socialist economic system, which proved to be very successful in making use of manpower and other economic resources as well as in achieving macroeconomic structural transformations, has turned out to be much less effective in the later stages of development when increased efficiency is improtant. Nevertheless, the system did spur broad consumer aspirations in the masses. But insufficient improvement in efficiency made it difficult to fulfill these aspirations.

It is generally believed that inadequate progress in economic efficiency is caused by faults in the functioning of the economy. The ability to attain high efficiency is a cultural factor that is shaped by a long historical process. It is necessary to look back to more distant historical periods that shaped social behavior with respect to thrift, hard work, conscientiousness, responsibility, social order, and a permanent search for more rational methods of work. While taking into account the historical reasons for inheriting low economic efficiency traits, it is nevertheless worthwhile to appraise any lengthy historical period from the point of view of the progress attained therein.

In this sense, it must be acknowledged that socialist Poland did not achieve sufficient progress in economic efficiency and the main reason for this failure were faults in the way in which the economic system functioned. However, such an observation must be understood in a very broad way, one that includes everything in the larger institutional system and the actions that affect the econimic behavior of people and determine their willingness to work hard, to save, and to introduce innovative solutions. Poland's development policy created the fundamental structural conditions conducive to a growth of efficiency, especially through the development of a complex industrial structure, a broad educational system, and research-and-development facilities. In this way, the main factors that had limited efficiency growth in prewar Poland were eliminated. However, this policy did not usher in a pattern in the larger institutional system that would favor a rapid improvement in efficiency and susceptibility to innovation.

In this context, it is necessary to decide how much progress in economic efficiency should be considered adequate. The problem is not that no progress was achieved in the Polish economy, rather that this progress was insufficient.

I do not think it is possible to give an unequivocal answer to the question about what pace of growth and improvement in efficiency is appropriate. Economics does not provide a general answer to this question nor does it even attempt to answer it.

Economists usually resort to international comparisons to determine whether the rate of growth of a given country and improvement in efficiency are high or low. (Incidentally, the two must be treated separately in very precise analyses.) Appraisals of this kind are relative, which is not to say that they have no value at all. When a given country's rate of growth is said to be high, this means high relative to other countries but does not say anything about the comparison of its development to its potential for growth nor about the way this development is appraised by the country's people.

Employing international comparisons, it cannot be denied that Poland's economy used to record a relatively fast growth rate. However, such an asssessment did not prove reliable when juxtaposed with public views and actual growth. It was reliable for the external analysis of Poland's development and the central power apparatus but not for studying the pattern of internal social relations and behavior. This proved to be an important problem for Poland that was not taken seriously enough or understood by the policymaking centers. But it must also be acknowledged that this problem was not studied and understood by the socioeconomic sciences either.

However, society was appraising the progress that was being attained in its own way. I believe that its evaluations were based on two factors:

1. The appraisal of economic efficiency and rationality from the point of view of what the people recognize as models of efficiency and rationality;
2. The social aspirations and the expectations people actually attach to progress.

It was on this basis that social conviction of an inadequate—or altogether bad—economic development of the country was built. This consciousness became a social fact with very important consequences for the development of the country and the evolution of the sociopolitical situation. This consciousness cannot be questioned as a fact, although it should be analyzed in some way.

The two reasons for society's evaluation of economic progress are each of a different kind. The former could only be questioned if it were justifiable to state that the patterns of efficiency, on the basis of which people appraise reality, are faulty or that the way in which they compare reality to model patterns is wrong. However, very little is known on this subject because of the lack of empirical studies. But in general, I do not think there are any grounds for questioning the accuracy of society's views on poor management and insufficient progress in this respect. These assessments were based on firsthand experience with the poor market situation, waste in factories, and lack of demand for innovation. They were also supported by comparisons with other countries.

Is all this to be denied by citing statistical data which demonstrate a high rate of economic growth in comparison to other countries? These figures do reflect reality with a fair measure of accuracy, although this statement must be qualified. Still there is no contradiction. The fact that a country records much better results in its development process than many other nations does not mean that it is run with sufficient efficiency. A country can be better than some and still be quite badly off. The social appraisals of poor management and poor progress cannot be undermined by statistics demonstrating a fast growth rate.

The other factor determining society's appraisal of progress is of a more complex nature. It seems doubtless that people appraise progress from the point of view of the satisfaction of their expectations and aspirations. However, these expectations may be shaped somewhat independently of the country's real economic possibilities. They are influenced by various internal and external sociological factors, and this is particularly important in the case of Poland. It is difficult to imagine a sizable, lasting disparity between aspirations and expectations, on the one hand, and real possibilities, on the other, as this would lead to enormous social frustration and, ultimately, to a painful adjustment of these expectations to harsh realities. However, for some time such discord may exist. In fact, I think this is what happened in Poland for most of the 1970s, whereas what the country experienced in 1980–1983 was the "painful adjustment of these expectations to the realities."

Socialism has released broad aspirations among the people, especially with regard to consumption. This was done through the proclamation of social promotion, social equality; through proclamations of the superiority of socialism for economic progress and the satisfaction of the people's needs. The same result was achieved through employment and educational policies and income distribution patterns. It is possible to voice reservations about various aspects of the policies implemented in these domains, but it cannot be denied that they resulted in the awakening of the broad social masses, their involvement in the process of change and development, and the growth of their aspirations.

I think the process described above deserves a decidedly positive appraisal, although some people take a different view of it. The awakening of human aspirations is a natural consequence of the striving of people for greater social justice and is also a factor strengthening the social forces

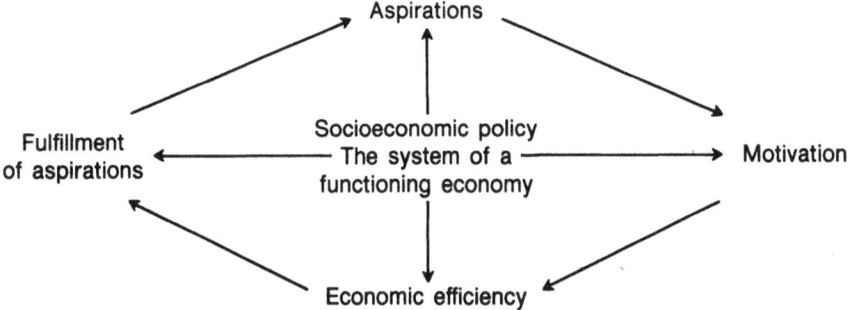

Figure 11.1 Diagram of the economic system.

of progress. This positive assessment of the awakening of broad aspirations was not the only appraisal possible. Aspirations can also have a negative effect on development processes and can themselves undergo a certain degeneration.

In order to understand the process of development of the country, it is essential to explain why a certain degeneration of aspirations occurred, leading to the emergence of too wide a gap between the aspirations and the real possibilities and, ultimately, to sociopolitical disturbances with their negative consequences for development.

The fundamental thesis that can be formulated in this context is that human aspirations exert an extremely positive influence on progress, provided they are transformed into stimuli of better work and more creative and rational activity. If that, however, is not the case, and aspirations are transformed into demands addressed toward society as a whole and the state, their influence on the process of development becomes negative. This is what I mean by the "degeneration" of aspirations. Whether or not aspirations are transformed into positive stimuli for progress depends on the arrangement of social relations in the process of production and distribution—in other words, on what is referred to as "the system of a functioning economy." The relationships existing here can be observed in Figure 11.1. Aspirations can motivate progress when their fulfillment is made conditional on activity that produces economic effects. In order to work efficiently, aspirations must shape motivations, which in turn must influence the effects. Only in this way can economic effects lead to the fulfillment of aspirations. The elementary feedback between aspirations and motivations is interrupted when the fulfillment of aspirations occurs not on the basis of real effects but, for example, as a result of the beneficial activity of the state. This feedback must operate not only on a macroeconomic scale but also with regard to all organized teams of people (e.g., enterprises) as well as individuals. Its influence is shaped by socioeconomic policy and the system of a functioning economy.

On the basis of historical experience it must be stated that socialism has released broad and strong human aspirations while failing to create sufficient motivation for progress. As a result, when economic development could no longer rely primarily on the growth of employment and on investments, its pace visibly slackened. Meanwhile, the advancement from extensive to intensive growth calls first and foremost for a strong operation of the motivation of progress. This is one of the main orientations of the economic reforms launched in various socialist countries. I think, however, that in Poland the gap between aspirations and motivations for progress was the most pronounced, even dramatic. Politicians were not able to cope with that gap because they did not tackle systemic and institutional transformations. On the contrary, they aggravated the problem by pursuing the line of the "benefactor state." This created a great inconsistency in the whole development process.

The awakening of aspirations combined with a weakening of the motivation of progress caused the aspirations to evolve into demands addressed to the state. This was complemented by the emergence of a matching social psychology consisting of the conviction that the satisfaction of the people's needs depends first of all on the state and on political decision. This kind of psychology grew particularly strong in Poland in the 1970s, affecting all socioeconomic processes. The aspirations awakened by socialism, instead of becoming a creative force for progress, degenerated and led to the upsetting of the whole socioeconomic system and great frustrations on the part of society. Although the feedback between aspirations and motivation is extremely important for the functioning of the economy in all socialist countries, in Poland its role was particularly great. This, I think, was the underlying factor in the accumulation of the huge foreign debt and economic disequilibrium.

It has already been mentioned that after the sociopolitical conflict of 1970 the state with its policies was portrayed as a benefactor. This was illustrated by wage raises awarded in the form of so-called wage regulations and the extensive development of welfare spending. The wage regulations were carried out on a national scale on the basis of central-level political decision. In time, they evolved into a systematic "giving away" of better pay. This severed the relationship between income and the results of activity and gave birth to a peculiar sociopolitical mechanism of the growth of income that replaced economic mechanisms. The new mechanism consisted of grassroot pressure for growth in income, interacting with socioinstitutional factors influencing decisions about the distribution of funds. This mechanism emerged in an uncontrolled way, but I doubt that it could have been introduced deliberately. It emerged as a result of political needs rather than strategic action.

It is necessary to draw attention to a very important problem: the operation of the sociopolitical mechanism of the struggle for higher pay in a situation when the enterprise's profitability is not the limit to which the demands may be pushed. This not only weakens the motivation to better work, it also causes demands and aspirations to grow to unrealistic dimensions. This appears to be a natural consequence of the situation in which decisions on wage increases depend on the state. Economic necessities and the resulting limits on income growth on the national scale are abstract matters, difficult for the people to understand. This creates a need for a firm state policy, strictly controlling the growth of wages. For the sake of clarity, let me add that the above remarks do not apply to sociopolitical mechanisms affecting the distribution of incomes in general but only to a situation when the suitable feedback between income and the results of work is lacking.

The analysis presented above reveals the very specific characteristics of the conflict between insufficient progress in economic efficiency and social aspirations and demands. Insufficient progress was real. However, the conflict became particularly acute when aspirations lost touch with reality. Both were a consequence of faults in the system governing the economy. These faults are of an old vintage, but in the late 1970s they were intensified.

It is hard to resist the temptation to observe that politicians did not perceive the threat of the emergence of this conflict. However, I tend to think that while pursuing narrow political objectives, they lost sight of what I call the overall rationality of the shaping of development processes.

The Unintended Consequences of the Socialist Development Model

An analysis of the country's development over a long period of history, and especially of the sociopolitical conflicts occurring in it, reveals essential inconsistencies in the whole pattern of socioeconomic processes. The irrationalities that manifested themselves could be traced back, for the most part, to the system and its institutional order. I have already expressed the view that this order did not adjust sufficiently to development needs; instead, it gave shape to social and political mechanisms of its own and evolved in a way that put it at odds with popular aspirations. This is by no means a unique development in world history. In fact, I suspect it is quite common, but that is no excuse for a country's irrationalities.

The whole system and its institutional order were not, frankly speaking, subjected to intellectual analysis and evaluation. This may have been justified in the initial period, when it was difficult to assess new socialist solutions on the basis of real-life experience. But with time, more and more experience was accumulated; yet the system was not subjected to intellectual scrutiny. To a lesser extent, this applies to scientific endeavors and to a greater extent, to political ones. It was the politicians who were unable to reflect on what was happening in the field of policy, on what determined its shape and effectiveness. In a way, this paralyzed the development of scientific analysis. After all, socioeconomic science receives a stimulus for development when it has to solve problems taken from the realm of real life.

The larger system and its institutional order must be viewed from the angle of its permanent capacity for self-improvement. This is probably the most elementary condition of rationality of the whole system shaping development processes. The absence of this self-improvement led to the emergence of the following main irrationalities in the Polish development process:

1. There was a growing disparity between the authorities' development mission and society's aspirations.

2. There was a growing disparity between the quest for faster progress and the readiness for a reconstruction of economic mechanisms in such a way as to facilitate the growth of economic efficiency. (Despite widespread public criticism and many official declarations of intention, patterns that did not encourage the observance of economic criteria stayed in force, along with ones that stifled human initiative or actually invited wasteful management.)

3. While proclaiming the desire to ensure a maximum degree of satisfaction of the people's needs, the politicians maintained systemic solutions that glaringly contradicted these claims. (The malfunctioning of the whole system of satisfying the people's needs, exemplified by the functioning of the market for goods and services, was perpetuated.)

4. The way in which the system functioned mistreated people as members of the socialist community, refusing to satisfy their need for participation, co-responsibility, and creativity. (In this way it slowed down the development of extremely important social and moral values. As a result, the whole appraisal of the correctness of the development goals from the social point of view could be questioned.)

The list given above could be much longer. Still, in my opinion it justifies the view that the principal irrationality concerned the triad incorporating the correctness of aims, the rationality of management, and the purposefulness and efficiency of systemic and institutional instruments. Therefore, the whole system could not produce fast and satisfactory progress.

It is easy to understand that the irrationalities mentioned above were perceived by society; in fact, their impact was immediate and painful. This was bound to affect strongly the society's assessments of the state of the economy and the progress that was being achieved. Even the most real achievements of the country were overshadowed by the irrationalities that directly hit the society.

I wish to draw attention to one inconsistency in the larger system and the institutional order that is particularly important from the viewpoint of the future. The emergence of the economic crisis could be clearly seen in the latter half of the 1970s. I presume that the politicians were aware of it. However, they were not capable of introducing the indispensable changes. This is connected with what I should like to term a crisis of authoritarian methods of government.

Until then, the peculiar feature of the functioning of a socialist economy was the fact that economic necessities and the requirements of progress were met with the help of the power of the state. This is what I mean by the use of authoritarian methods of government. Experience shows that the application of such methods influences social consciousness. The state claims credit for the good results of its activity, but the society also blames it for the bad or difficult aspects of its life. This makes it difficult to pursue unpopular policies, even though they are sometimes necessary. Whenever a difficult economic situation emerges, the state authorities must face the responsibility of introducing economic moves that do not enjoy public support. The authorities can, of course, do so, but this requires either a resolute resort to state power or the seeking of public support, or a combination of the two. Some solution must be found in this respect, because there can be no going away from reality. No country and no sociopolitical system is free from economic necessities.

In the actual situation that existed in Poland in the late 1970s, there was awareness of the need to change the direction of policy, but nobody had the power to do it. It was obvious that food prices had to be raised, yet the plans to raise them were abandoned in the face of public reaction (in 1976). It was widely understood that wages could not grow faster than productivity, yet there was no way to enforce this principle in practice. The same could be said of investments and budget allocations. From this, one could draw the political conclusion that the possibilities offered by the current development policy had already been exhausted and that it should have been replaced with a different one. It is more important, however, to understand how this situation was allowed to occur and what conclusions follow from it for the future.

To begin with, the authorities were neither ready for nor had confidence in the efficiency of a resolute resort to state power. Efficient application of state power in the implementation of development policy occurred in Poland in the initial period of industrialization, but in the later stages that power grew weak. Going back to my earlier arguments, I should like to formulate the theory that as the state got weaker, the gap between the development mission and social aspirations grew greater. The state's readiness to use its power with determination to implement economic necessities was undercut by the mechanisms of sociopolitical change through conflict. The use of this power threatened to set off a sociopolitical reaction that might topple the structure of political power.

Secondly, the authorities were neither ready for nor understood the need for starting a genuine dialogue with society and for seeking social approval for unpopular undertakings. They were not prepared for reforms that would change the system of authoritarian methods of government.

The possibilities of the operation of the policy were exhausted when the state could no longer use the old methods, while it lacked the ability and readiness to introduce new ones. In such circumstances, a political crisis is usually inevitable.

Lessons from the Polish Experience

It has often been argued that in the planning and development policies of socialist countries there has been too much one-sided emphasis on the development of productive forces and the growth of consumption. I do not think such a charge is unjustified in relation to Poland. By way of excuse, it can be pointed out that at a low level of economic development the satisfaction of elementary human needs is of the greatest importance, while it also requires a great deal of effort to develop production. Freedom from hunger and poverty is the foremost of all human liberties and the foremost form of justice. However, emphasis on the development of productive forces and the subordination of all systemic and institutional solutions to this goal has led to a one-sided understanding of human needs. This has become increasingly obvious as higher levels of economic development are attained.

I believe that the experience of the Polish process of development has demonstrated that at least as much emphasis should be placed on the qualitative development of humans and human relations—on freedom, justice, equality, solidarity, participation, and co-responsibility—as is put on economic growth. If there is a clash between the striving for economic development and the pursuit of the above values, the conflict should not be solved automatically to the advantage of development. Yet in the past, when there was so much emphasis on economic growth, social and moral values were assigned only a marginal role. Besides, it was easy to tolerate social demoralization and delay the evolution of positive moral values, allegedly in the interest of economic growth, but in reality because of stubborn clinging to obviously faulty systemic and institutional solutions.

This leads to an understanding of socioeconomic progress that encompasses both improving the living conditions of the population by controlling goods and services and increasing the economic rationality of action and the fulfillment of social and moral values in social relations. Only this kind of progress ensures the implementation of real human values, the satisfaction of human strivings and aspirations. People are happier when they can confirm their value through good work, when they act more wisely, contribute to the good of all, and create something new. This cannot be replaced by even the biggest supply of goods provided by the state in order to increase consumption. However, many politicians appear to be unaware of this elementary truth.

I wish to defend the theory that the crisis that erupted in Poland at the beginning of the 1980s was both a consequence of the operation of economic factors leading to a decline in management efficiency and an outcome of the poor state of affairs with regard to the people's social and moral postures. After all, these two matters are interrelated. If the process of development is not based on progress in social and moral human behavior, this undercuts economic development itself and leads to the people's dissatisfaction with themselves and with social relations in their country.

I think that the criticism of "bad socialism" that appeared and can still be heard in Poland is most pertinent with regard to the patterns of relations and methods of government that led to a degeneration of social and moral behavior. This criticism stems from the fact that people feel unhappy not only because their standard of living is lower than they think it should be, but also because they feel they are less efficient, less sensible in their social activity, less reliable, less honest, less responsible than they should be, as well as because they believe that their social environment is not sufficiently just or efficient and does not display sufficient solidarity. They blame all this on those who govern.

This is the bone of contention in the conflicts that keep reappearing in Poland. Those who govern tend to blame the economic and social failures on the negative social and moral features of the people. The argument is not totally unfounded, and it is possible to cite historical determinants that led to the demoralization of the nation and whose consequences are visible to this day. However, the governed tend to blame those who govern for the low efficiency of public activity, the negative feature of social relations, and even for their own shortcomings. In settling the dispute it is necessary to distinguish between short and long periods of time. In the short run, the governed "inherit" the qualitative, social, and moral traits of a people who do not change fast. However, in longer periods this is not so. From the point of view of the shaping of socioeconomic processes over longer periods of time, I have no doubt that the methods of government determine to a large extent the people's social and moral behavior.

To ignore that would mean to pass an incorrect judgment on the historical experience of the country. It is true that it is necessary to look for the roots of the 1980-1981 crisis in arbitrariness, irresponsibility, and lack of foresight. It is also true that these phenomena occurred against a background of the degeneration of political relations and in particular of the lack of genuine democratic institutions.

However, this truth is not complete. There is another problem as important as the ones I just mentioned: It concerns the elementary conception of government, one that does not appreciate that the most important thing from the point of view of progress is a method of government that sees effectively to the qualitative features of people and social and moral values. It is possible to limit the number of economic errors, ensure the operation of democratic institutions and of a system of social information, but all of that will not produce sufficient results unless there is progress in the social and moral attitudes of collectivities. Some people tend to think that the existence of democratic institutions and relations will deal with this problem automatically, as it were. This view can prove to be illusory, as history has shown on many occasions. Democratic institutions are not a sufficient prescription for wisdom in public matters, for foresight, or for justice. I am not looking for arguments against democracy. It is the same as with any other socioinstitutional solution. The creation of democratic institutions opens up great possibilities for wise, socially just, and prudent action, but it does not in itself guarantee that they will always operate exactly this way.

A Reassessment of the Polish Dilemma

I have previously criticized many aspects of past development policy. It is not difficult to understand that if there were foresight and prudence in that policy, it would have been possible to have avoided many very unpleasant and painful situations. I have criticized action based on "politicking" rather than political wisdom. Political wisdom means foresight and prudence.

The notion of socioeconomic rationality must include not only that which is right and comprehensible for contemporary people but must also take the future into account; this is foresight and prudence. It is difficult to define the terms with a sufficient degree of accuracy; the socioeconomic sciences take pains to decide what foresight and prudence should consist of. To accomplish this one must perceive the great limitations of the conceptions that ignore foresight and prudence (e.g., the narrowly conceived principle of the "rationality of management") and reject the simplistic, arithmetic reduction of the future to the present.

The shaping of socioeconomic processes with the future taken into account is based on the thesis of human responsibility for actions whose impact extends into the future. Should this thesis be rejected, the paradigm of a conscious shaping of socioeconomic processes would lose any meaning. Anthropologists may argue about whether people are ready for future-oriented actions and whether this readiness grows as historic processes advance. However, organized human communities must accept that readiness, and in principle they already do so. Without that there would be no continuity in the existence of nations and human civilization. The more foresight and prudence individual nations and mankind at large can show, the greater the chances of their survival and success. The disappearance of success in the process of Poland's development was the consequence of the lack of foresight and prudence. It is necessary to draw conclusions from the fact that this occurred despite the application of "planning."

The readiness to show responsibility for the future, which can be observed over the centuries, needs to be intensified in the face of the new needs that life brings with it. In my opinion, this means that the responsibility of societies and nations for future-oriented actions should be adopted as the supreme moral principle. If we were devising a fresh decalogue of basic moral standards, we should include that principle. It is a universally binding principle, but I think it is especially important for Polish society.

When I emphasize the importance of responsibility for the future, I do not mean that we should determine the goals and the ways of living of future generations. We have no moral title to do that, nor do we have sufficient intellectual premises for doing so. Future generations will themselves define the shape of life they desire. The important thing is not to deprive them of options, not to put them in an unbearable situation, in an inhuman and irreversible one—in brief, to do them no harm. These are not abstract matters. Today we can clearly see how a policy devoid of responsibility for the future has put a heavy burden on the shoulders of contemporary people. When these errors were being committed, it may have appeared that the consequences of this irresponsible approach would only come in some distant future. But an indefinite future has become the present day.

These observations, addressed to politicians, apply in a similar measure to all the sciences. Here responsibility for the future means first of all orienting theory and research toward the future.

The Implications of the Polish Case

The analysis of Polish development processes presented above leads to the fundamental conclusion that comprehensive rationality in the shaping of development processes is necessary and should encompass the correctness of the aims, economic rationality in the use of resources, and the correctness of institutional solutions. The lack of consistency with regard to these three fundamental problems leads to basic contradictions that upset the whole course of socioeconomic development.

It has been pointed out that the fundamental irrationalities that occurred in Poland's development are connected with the operation of the institutional system. I regard this as the fundamental diagnosis of the conflicts, social tensions, and lack of sufficient progress. Unless there is essential improvement in terms of overall rationality, it is hard to imagine progress that would satisfy human aspirations, harmonize the action of the authorities with the strivings of the people, keep the people satisfied about social efficiency and social order, be conducive to the growth of brotherhood and justice in human relations, and allow individuals to develop creative values and self-realization, while giving them broad opportunities to participate in shaping their life and social future.

Other alternative conceptual and research centers that have access to information and enjoy genuine independence must be established. Democracy, of great importance itself, must be supplemented with information and conceptual work. Democratic institutions do not by themselves guarantee sociopolitical wisdom. Scientific communities have a major role to play in this respect.

Looking at Poland's development in perspective, one gets the impression that the 1970s witnessed the final attempt of the state authorities to undertake on a large scale a development mission. That attempt misfired. It was undertaken because the institutional structure, designed to fulfill the development mission, was evidently capable only of reproducing that mission. The end of the decade of the 1970s testified to the fact that this kind of development mission was finally completely out of date.

The main characteristics of that development mission were the following:

1. The state and its central authorities are the chief initiating and driving force of progress. The state "imposes" development on the society and economy because the latter are not capable of producing development due

to behaviors and structures inherited from a historical process. From this follows the principal institutional thesis: the necessity of shaping the whole pattern of socioeconomic relations according to the principle of domination (by the state) and subordination (of the society and economy).

2. The main factors of economic growth are growth in the input of human labor and growth of productive assets through investments. By controlling these factors the state ensures a fast pace of economic growth.

3. The main idea of structural policy is the growth of investing potential, that is, the continuation of economic growth; consequently, priority treatment is given to the development of capital goods production.

I assume that this conception of the development mission already is part of the past. I do not see how it could be of any use in the future. It must be abandoned, together with all its components and consequences.

In my opinion, the shaping of development processes in the future should be based on the following strategic assumptions, ones that are the opposite of those mentioned above:

1. The state is not the main "driving force" of economic development. Socioeconomic development depends on people, their skills, motivations, and initiative. The state has a major role to play in organizing the processes of development and in controlling them, but the people remain the fundamental lever of progress.

2. The state must not "impose" development on people by resorting to political and economic measures. Development requires participation. The state's development aspirations should not depart from social aspirations and human abilities and readiness to implement progress.

3. The "forcing" of economic development through arbitrarily raising the rate of investment by the state is not an effective road for ensuring rapid development. The right way is to influence growth in efficiency.

4. A much closer relationship between production and human needs should be the decisive direction taken to influence the structure of production.

The above theses constitute in fact a general philosophy of the forces shaping development processes. Their applicability to the future is confirmed by observation of the past—in particular, the experience of diminishing progress in economic efficiency, the appearance of sociopolitical conflicts, and society's dissatisfaction with the progress achieved. It is also confirmed by the observation of new societal tendencies: the questioning of the omnipotence of the state, the bureaucratization of relations, and the demands for a new role for the people in socioeconomic relations. These are not completely new phenomena, but they have reappeared with greater intensity. Meeting them halfway is a necessity for the development process.

A remodeling of the institutional system is an elementary condition for this development strategy's implementation. No development philosophy can materialize so long as it is only a method of understanding processes and is not implemented in practice. This, in turn, takes effect first of all through the proper shaping of the whole institutional system. In my opinion, the fundamental issue is abandoning the all-embracing pattern of state domination and direct subordination of society and economic organizations. It is not a question of denying the state any role, but of a new type of relationship between the state apparatus, on the one hand, and society and economy, on the other.

How to Regain Economic Growth

The traditional recipe for accelerating growth or preventing its decline was raising the investment rate. This was the main method of implementing the development mission. It is worth noting that this was consistent with the economic doctrine in force in Poland and especially with widely accepted patterns of economic growth in which the rate of investment was the main instrumental variable. This line of economic reasoning did not stem from Marxist thought but rather from neoclassical theories of growth. However, I would not credit these theoretical approaches with excessive significance in shaping the strategies of economic growth. Moreover, in the socialist countries in which those growth models were not popular, policies were based on investment as the main factor of economic growth.

In the future it will be necessary to reject the theory that investments are the main means of state political influence on the rate of economic growth. This does not mean that investments become irrelevant to the processes of development or that it will never again be necessary to raise the rate of investment spending. However, it does mean that while striving to encourage fast development, the state must not arbitrarily change the rate of investment, forcing society to economize when it is not prepared to do so. This method does not promise to be sufficiently effective because economic development depends in an ever greater measure on factors more important than the volume of investments alone.

The perception of investment as the main instrument of the policy of growth dramatically impoverished state economic policy. Using such a large and easily accessible factor, this policy lost sight of other factors. It could not cope with control over scientific and technological progress, development of export specializations, or the encouragement of innovation. It was primitive about shaping organizational structures in a rational way. I believe that the emphasis on investment as the chief instrument of the growth policy was one of the main factors responsible for the degeneration of central planning.

The economic reform undertaken in Poland has initiated a major reorientation of the whole system of functioning of the economy and society. Can it be expected that the reform will accomplish its goals and do so quickly? It is not possible to give a fully unequivocal answer to this question. The reform will not automatically solve every dilemma. Those who think this view is unjustifiably skeptical should note that there are many countries in which enterprises enjoy autonomy and the market is sound, yet that do not record fast progress; in fact, they may even witness stagnation or recession.

It is paradoxical that although in Poland some economists view enterprise autonomy and market mechanisms as the key to success in every respect, in other countries economists advocate active central planning as a method of overcoming stagnation because the spontaneous operation of the market is seen as ineffective and unjust. I am not saying this in order to question the provisions of the reform—which I have regarded as indispensable for many years—but in order to point out that although they represent a fundamental breakthrough in the functioning of Poland's economy, they will not automatically guarantee fast and great progress.

While analyzing the features of economically underdeveloped countries, Gunnar Myrdal wrote that in such countries the state's ability to act is in itself an element of the "equilibrium of underdevelopment," in other words, that it is both an outcome of underdevelopment and its sustaining force. Affluent countries are not subjected to desperate political pressures on the part of impoverished masses. They can also afford to err in their policies within a wide margin. Underdeveloped countries are in a totally different situation. They lack all the "luxuries" enjoyed by the authorities of the former; most of them also lack a tradition of statehood and are burdened by an inefficient administrative apparatus. They have to take over the legacy of the past and accept responsibility for poverty, whereas they are not in a position to overcome it. In his famous formula, Myrdal observed the close relationship between a poor nation and—as he put it— a "soft state."

One can get the impression that the above observation corresponds to the situation that arose in Poland in the years 1980–1981. I have previously pointed to the emerging crisis of authoritarian methods of government— the growing inability of invoking the authority of the state for meeting economic necessities. The evolution of the socioeconomic situation in the years 1980–1981 further aggravated this crisis, narrowing down the field and the room for maneuver in state policy.

An especially significant role was played by the debt trap, which contributed to a decline in the utilization of the productive capacities and a drop in production, as well as to social pressure for greater consumption on the order of a 12 to 24 percent. Poland additionally witnessed with particular acuity sociopsychological reactions consisting of people's blaming the state for every problem. This was because the drop in consumption occurred immediately after the awakening of huge, if not unrealistic consumer aspirations (the reasons for which have already been discussed). This led to a sociopolitical evolution that further blocked the options of state activity. Eventually, the situation was characterized by severe limitations on foreign trade, an enormous lack of equilibrium in the domestic market that disrupted economic processes, and a great weakness in state action.

In this analysis, I am drawing special attention to socioeconomic factors and their institutional consequences, while leaving aside the activity of various political forces. In contrast, most Polish analysts (inside or outside

Poland) pay attention either exclusively or mostly to political matters while ignoring their socioeconomic determinants. A political analysis devoid of socioeconomic background cannot produce the proper understanding and the correct conclusions. I assume that it would be difficult to understand the political tendencies and developments of the years 1980–1982 without understanding their background—the profound socioeconomic crisis. Naturally, political phenomena are governed by their own logic and driven by their own forces to some extent, but they appear predominanty in the socioeconomic context.

I am not going to expand on the subject of whether the period of particularly weak state power that occurred was inevitable or could possibly have been avoided. Perhaps the subject will be discussed eventually, but I fear that it will be influenced to a greater extent by the political situation that exists then than by objective appraisals.

As for the near future, I can see two conclusions:

1. The period of weak state power could not and cannot continue. Unless state activities become more efficient, it will not be possible to solve the country's problems. This is not to say I anticipate that a return to arrogant methods of authoritarian rule is going to take place or that it should take place.

2. The features and trends of the period of unrest and sociopolitical frustrations, the accumulation of disadvantageous external phenomena, and weak state power should not be extrapolated into the future. The altered institutional system may produce new patterns of economic behavior, hence new efficiency features and other development trends.

The latter conclusion is particularly pertinent for the analysis I am making here. From the severe crisis of the years 1980–1982, one should not draw the conclusion that crisis tendencies are going to stay. The forecast for the country's development for the next few years should be based in a far larger measure on an appraisal of economic and human potential and of the correctness and efficiency of changes in the institutional system than on projecting into the future the tendencies that have occurred in recent years.

It is not the purpose of this chapter to present and analyze anticrisis undertakings. However, it is worth drawing attention to two matters that are important from the viewpoint of the current situation. The weighty blow caused by the decline in national income and consumption has already been "absorbed" by society and the economy. It caused a lot of pain and was accompanied by anxieties and frustrations, but that is already past. The economy will still face some dangers, but their scope is extremely small compared to what has happened already. After such a sharp decline (whose depth was hard to imagine before), a reversal of the downward trend may produce advantageous social and subsequently also economic consequences. There is a chance of a favorable feedback between systemic changes and structural transformations.

Summary

The cardinal conclusion for the future is, in my opinion, the need for a broad understanding of socioeconomic progress (as it has been formulated here) and an idea of government oriented to the qualitative features of human beings and to raising their sociomoral values. It certainly is not easy to translate this thesis into practical recommendations for social activity. However, let us note that the matter is not exactly new to history. The history of human communities and nations shows the ways of resolving this. This history demonstrates the need for "clever and just" government that cares about human virtues, the spreading of good manners, order, hard work, and the upbringing of the younger generation. It also has witnessed forms of government that definitely do not deserve such a name.

The shape of social relations determines definitely the moral postures of people in a society. This shape is in turn determined by the whole institutional system, including the functioning of the apparatus of power, political and social organizations, and the principles by which enterprises operate. The principal aim of this influence should be the shaping of human behavior. I think there are no chances of successful development in society if development addresses only material and economic problems while leaving aside moral issues, or leaving it to somebody else to fill the vacuum.

I do not suggest that state influence and actions should be eliminated. The point is that while exercising control over development processes, one cannot forget about the things that are the most important to people, including their upgrading and the proper shaping of moral postures—both traditional well-tested ones and new socialist ones, as well as those that will come in the future. It should be noted that when no attention is being paid to the shaping of moral postures, they are influenced anyway, but in an unintentional and usually bad way. This is confirmed by virtually all cases of widespread social demoralization and negative human attitudes, which are a consequence of the faulty functioning of the economy and society. This state of affairs, caused by actual socioeconomic relations, cannot be remedied by "moralizing," no matter who should be doing it.

It is worth reflecting on the reasons why the state paid so little attention to the improvement of human character and the shaping of moral values. Material products of contemporary civilization—such as cars, roads, factories, —received the greatest attention whereas human virtues, both traditional and socialist ones, were denied that kind of treatment. I get the impression that in Poland this occurred in a most pronounced form, although it might be worthwhile to verify that view.

As for development processes, the dominant style for controlling them has been one of narrow "economism" and "technocratism." To change that is, in my opinion, a vital matter for the future. The conclusions that follow from this analysis and assessment of the Polish development model also apply to the socioeconomic sciences.

Future Trends

The relationship between the state and the economy and society is one of the basic aspects of institutional patterns. With regard to that problem, I wish to formulate some controversial observations and theses concerning the directions of future evolution.

The system of socialist planning and the state authorities' role in it has been based on the predominance of macroeconomic rationality, whereas the importance of microeconomic rationality has been underestimated or ignored altogether. The state sought all-embracing rationality at a time when enterprises did not have correct information or other systemic premises or even genuine options for acting in keeping with the principle of economic rationality. History has strongly demonstrated that this was a bad state of affairs. This problem arose in Poland in the 1950s and was reflected in demands about the role of enterprises and of economic criteria. Economists are virtually unanimous on this subject.

The state fulfilled its economic management duties with the help of authoritarian methods, which meant state interference in the shaping of practically all economic processes. Experience has shown that these methods have proven to be increasingly ineffective. Their modification appears to be indispensable for raising the efficiency of state action and attaining the benefits of a planned economy.

Authoritarian methods of government replaced economic mechanisms or rendered them ineffective. The best example is the perennially faulty functioning of market mechanisms and of economic criteria related to the self-financing of enterprises. The socioeconomic impact of this situation was decidedly negative.

Centralized state management led to the suppression of social initiative and a negation of the people's role as coarchitects of progress and comanagers of the country. This produced negative economic and moral consequences.

The phenomena mentioned above led to a degeneration of centralized state planning and management, degeneration evident in the failure of the planning and management bodies to implement efficiently the strategic directions of development and to promote a general harmony of socioeconomic processes. In Polish experience, this failure has been forcefully exemplified by the cyclical character of investment drives, the periodic emergence of huge economic disequilibrium, structural disproportions leading to major disturbances in the development process, and the failure to solve crucial strategic problems (e.g., that of selecting export specializations, developing food production). In society's eyes, these phenomena have neutralized the fundamental advantages of a planned socialist economy.

It is now important to draw conclusions from this experience. In my view, these conclusions should pertain to the fundamental question of the role of the state and methods of state action in socialist society. There is no need to be afraid to formulate the question in that way as this is what the problem is really about.

Two summary theses should be formulated in a general way:

1. The socialist state is the fundamental agent involved in the conscious shaping of development processes on a national scale, bearing responsibility for the future and for safeguarding the interests of the whole society.

2. The role of the state in the direct shaping of socioeconomic processes should be very seriously limited (in comparison to the general practice of the years 1950–1980), and the exercise of these responsibilities must not undermine either the autonomy and responsibility of enterprises and the operation of economic instruments or authentic and independent activity of various public organizations, including trade unions.

The latter thesis signifies a new arrangement of socioeconomic relations. It signifies a departure from state domination, from omnipotence based on a system of hierarchic subordination, to a pattern of relations in which people acting in an organized society are the main characters and in which self-adjusting economic and socioeconomic mechanisms operate. The state retains its creative and regulatory powers with regard to these mechanisms. In other words, it establishes such mechanisms through appropriate legislation and sees to their observance with the help of suitable instruments.

I suppose that the above assertions reflect real tendencies in the evolution of the institutional system in Poland. These tendencies have been present for a number of years in public demands, scientific papers, and the attempts to reform the management system in the economy. The latest reform expresses these tendencies in a most pronounced way.

The reliance on self-adjusting mechanisms in economic management and on the autonomy of enterprises and authentic activity of public organizations definitely results in a certain spontaneity of socioeconomic processes. Some view this spontaneity as an evil because it allegedly clashes with the planned character of the economy. It is true that the clash occurs if one construes "planned character" as strict orders from above, paying no heed to the aspirations of people. However, this does not work in practice, as the Polish experience has shown. This experience clearly demonstrated the need for such a planning system in which, along with a consistent implementation of the state's development strategy, there is a large measure of flexibility in adjusting the economy to changing conditions and the utilization of new chances and possibilities and human creativity. Such a system of planning permits some spontaneity, which also engenders new human values and social trends, providing an outlet for active and creative human roles and helping to correct the designs that went wrong or were rejected by society.

Those who might not like the idea of allowing some spontaneity in adaptation and development processes should bear in mind that the kind of spontaneity that manifested itself in the sociopolitical crises that Poland has gone through is incomparably worse. The incorporation of the recommended kind of spontaneity in the planning system is a method of counteracting the eruption of great sociopolitical conflicts.

What has been said above about limiting and modifying the role of the state in shaping economic processes can be otherwise termed a departure from authoritarian methods of government. Theoretically, efficient operation of the state can be ensured either by returning to an iron-handed state implementing its socioeconomic policies through state power or by finding new methods and instruments of political action. I do not see a chance for the former option, which would in effect mean a return to the political system and economic policies of the early 1950s. This would not augur well for the solution of socioeconomic development problems in the near and more distant future. It should be obvious that the basic reason for the continued economic inefficiency and for the emergence of a succession of sociopolitical conflicts was the desire to preserve elements of that old system. Clearly, another repetition of the old alignment would not succeed. Some people think that a return to the "firm" state of the 1950s might be helpful in coping with the very difficult situation Poland has found itself in. However, experience has shown that such methods can never stimulate initiative, innovation, or efficiency. Therefore, it is necessary to take the other course.

The use of state coercion in implementing the policy of planned development could justifiably be seriously limited. Along with that, it is necessary to broaden the scope of economic coercion following from the operation of economic mechanisms and the state's legislative activity. But although the state must apply coercion, it is nevertheless essential for the state to seek genuine social support for its policies.

In a system of authoritarian rule, the state is identified with the economic management apparatus. In the organizational structure of economic management, state bodies are a component of this structure and the peak of the hierarchic system. This is very significant from the viewpoint of socioeconomic relations, although the importance of this setup is not generally appreciated.

In the system marked by a hierarchical management structure, the powers of state authorities were used for pushing through economic development. This proved to be quite effective, and without that it is doubtful that the state created by the authorities could have survived for so long. However, this effectiveness applied only to growth of the volume of production attained through a wide range of management methods, while doing little to improve efficiency. But that was not appreciated either.

It should be noted, however, that the activities of the state as a direct and fundamental element of the organizational structure of management influences certain aspects of the relations among the state, enterprises, and consumers. The state turns out to be very "soft" and "paternally permissive" toward enterprises. As producers, people are treated with forbearance, but as consumers they are forced to suffer. The alternative would be to have a system that is firm on producers, demanding from them great efforts and efficiency. But the amazing thing is that it was possible to arrive at a state that has been soft on enterprises when the system was growth oriented. I suppose this was the result of the operation of the following factors:

The domain of productive activity became heavily institutionalized, while there was no effective counterpart for consumption. As a result, the former had to predominate over the latter. The institutionalization of the productive sector directly embraced the most powerful institution of all, namely the state. In theory, the state should defend the interests of society at large and especially the interests of consumers. In reality, though, it became a constituent part of the productive domain. This meant in practice that it was defending interests that were not identical with consumer interests. Members of enterprise management often moved to central and local authority jobs and vice versa and the interests of managers and local leaders were quite similar.

The centralized decisionmaking system also played a very important role. It is difficult to imagine the state being "firm" in exacting economic efficiency and applying objective economic criteria to enterprises in a situation when these enterprises have had no say in economic decisions. The state did not keep a check on efficiency. It awarded budget subsidies to cover up wrong decisions because otherwise it would have to expose its own activity to a critical appraisal. As the state became soft—in other words, practically incapable of meeting the requirement of progress and rational management—both efficiency and consumers suffered.

I hope that the analysis I have supplied above provides a sufficient ground for drawing systemic conclusions for the future. It is necessary to move to an arrangement in socioeconomic relations characterized by firmness toward producers. Only such a pattern of relations can guarantee an improvement in economic efficiency and a dominance of consumer interests. I do not see any other way of meeting this goal except by separating state authorities from economic administration. The reforms begun in Poland "appear" to be headed in that direction. If that is so, it would be a good thing to state clearly their guiding idea.

About the Contributors

Lawrence S. Graham is professor of government and coordinator of outreach programs in the Institute of Latin American Studies at the University of Texas at Austin. Born in Daytona Beach, Florida, in 1936, he received a bachelor's degree in Spanish from Duke University (1958), a master's in Ibero-American Studies from the University of Wisconsin at Madison (1961), and a doctorate in political science from the University of Florida (1965). Long active in the Latin American field, over the past ten years his interest in the development problems of newly industrialized countries has led him into a series of research projects spanning Latin America and Europe. Grants received from the National Research Council at the National Academy of Sciences and the Calouste Gulbenkian Foundation (Lisbon) have made it possible for him to develop knowledge of southeastern as well as southwestern Europe. His publications, which include books, book chapters, and journal articles published in the United States and abroad, reflect an interest in such diverse countries as Brazil, Portugal, Mexico, Romania, Yugoslavia, and more recently, Colombia and Nicaragua.

Maria K. Ciechocińska is associate professor in the Institute of Geography and Spatial Organization at the Polish Academy of Sciences. Born in Warsaw in 1934, she received both her bachelor's degree (1956) and her doctoral degree (1963) in economics and social policy from the Central School of Planning and Statistics in Warsaw. Until 1967 she was associated with Warsaw Technical University, where she held a lectureship in sociology. She has received various grants for work abroad, from such institutions as L'Ecole des Hautes Etudes en Sciences Sociales in France, the National Academy of Sciences in the United States, and the Deutsche Forschungsgemeinschaft in West Germany. In 1980 she was a visiting professor in the Graduate School of Architecture and Urban Planning, University of California, Los Angeles. Her professional work has focused largely on regional planning and the regional aspects of social planning. To date she has published in Poland more than two hundred articles, monographs, and book chapters on applied geography, spatial planning, and regional sociology. She is also the author of seven books in Polish.

Jerzy Kruczała is professor of economics and head of postgraduate studies of tourism at the Academy of Economics in Cracow. Born in Szczekociny, Poland, in 1922, he holds a master's degree (1946) and a doctorate in economics (1948) from the Jagiellonian University (Cracow) as well as a degree of doctor habilitatus in the natural sciences (1968) from the Institute of Geography in Warsaw. (Note: the doctor habilitatus degree cited here and in subsequent biographies is a degree given in Poland after the doctorate on the basis of additional research required of a scholar before he or she may be advanced in an academic career to a level roughly equivalent to that of a tenured professor in the United States.) Besides his many publications on regional planning and regional economics in Polish, he is the author of "Regional Planning in the Cracow Voivodship," in *City and Regional Planning in Poland*, ed. Jack C. Fisher (Ithaca: Cornell University Press, 1966) and coauthor of the section on Poland in the *General Review of National and Regional Planning as a Framework for Local Planning*, prepared for selected Eastern European countries (Helsinki, 1975). He has held appointments abroad as a visiting scholar at MIT (1960), as a visiting professor at the University of Pittsburgh (1979), and as visiting professor at the Institute of International Education where he participated in a multiregional group project in 1981.

Ryszard Manteuffel-Szoege is professor emeritus at the Warsaw Agricultural University (the SGGW), former director of the Institute of Farm Economics and Management, and former deputy rector of that university. Born in Minsk Mazowiecki in 1903, he obtained a master's of science from the SGGW (1926), a doctorate in agricultural sciences from Poznan University (1948), and the degree of doctor habilitatus at the SGGW (1960). He holds honorary doctorates from four Polish and foreign universities. He headed the Polish Academy of Sciences' Committee on Farm Economics for four terms and is a full member of the academy. He is one of the most widely published scholars on farm economics in Poland and is probably the most renowned scholar in his field in his country. His papers and articles have appeared in many periodicals dealing with farm economics as well as in newspapers and magazines. He has published nearly twenty scientific books dealing with farm economics. The titles (translated into English) of the most important are *The Efficiency of Farming Investment Projects, The Economics and Organization of Work in Farming, The Economics and Management of a Farm, The Management and Running of a Farm, The Rationalization of Production in a Farm*, and *The Philosophy of Farming*.

Władysław Markiewicz is head of the Department of Sociology and Organization of Work at the University of Warsaw, editor-in-chief of the quarterly *Studia Socjologiczne*, and vicepresident of the Polish UNESCO committee. Elected a corresponding member of the Polish Academy of Sciences in 1971, he became a full member in 1976. Having held many scientific and administrative positions in the academy, he has been secretary of the academy's Social Sciences Section since 1972. Born in Ostrow Wielkopolski in 1920, he received a degree in sociology from Poznan University (1951), a doctorate in sociology from Adam Mickiewicz University in Poznan (1959), and a doctor habilitatus (1961). His publications span a wide variety of fields within sociology. His work on modern history and the social transformations of "Greater Poland" (Wielopolska) embrace the social character of the Polish uprising during World War II, the German occupation of Poland, the history of the Polish countryside, and Poland's industrialization. His publications on national sociology and the sociology of industry and work have become part of the standard bibliography on modern Poland. Additional publications deal with the social and political problems of Poland's western and northern territories, migration processes and the integration of the Polish population, and Polish-German relations. The English title of the book that perhaps best illustrates his many interests is *Sociology and Social Service* (1972).

Józef Pajestka is director of the Institute of Economic Science at the Polish Academy of Sciences and a corresponding member of the academy. Born in Milowka, Poland, in 1924, he has degrees from the Faculty of Law and the Faculty of Philosophy of the University of Warsaw, a doctorate in political economy (1959) from the same university, and a degree of doctor habilitatus (1962). His previous positions include vice chairman of the Planning Commission (1968-1978), president of the Polish Economics Society (1965-1981), and director of the Institute of Planning (1962-1972). He is also head of the editorial board of *Economista* and an adviser to the Sejm (parliament), as well as a member of the UN Committee for Development Planning since 1965, a member of the executive committee of the International Economics Association, and a member of the Club of Rome. The English language titles of works representing his publications on Polish economics are *Shaping the Development Process, The Polish Crisis 1980-1981, The Way a Socialist Economy Functions, Factors and Interrelationships in Socioeconomic Progress,* and *The Relevance of Economic Theories.*

Władysław Piwowarski is a professor at the Catholic University of Lublin, where he has been lecturing since 1974 on the sociology of religion and morality in the Theological Department, the Department of Christian Philosophy, and more recently the Department of Social Sciences. Born in Mokrzyska, Poland, in 1929, he attended the Catholic University of Lublin, receiving a doctorate in 1961. In 1967 he became an assistant professor of sociology of religion at the Catholic University and became head of the Department of Sociology in that university in 1970. In 1976-1977 he was a senior research fellow at Yale University. He has completed numerous sociological investigations on Polish religiosity and has published many books as well as some 150 articles in Polish, German, and English. The English titles of his best known works are *Rural Religiosity under Conditions of Urbanization, Urban Religiosity in Industrial Areas,* and *Popular Religiosity: Continuity and Change.* He belongs to many learned societies in Poland and abroad.

Janusz Reykowski is professor of psychology at the Polish Academy of Sciences. Born in 1929, he received his doctorate from the University of Warsaw in 1959. His primary areas of specialization are social psychology and the psychology of personality. He is director of the Department of Psychology at the academy, a member of the executive committee of the International Society of Behavioral Development, and a member of the executive committee of the European Association of Personality. He is also project director of the research program on "Personality Change as Related to Social Change." The English language titles of publications representing his scholarship are *Personality Functioning Under Psychological Stress, Experimental Psychology of Emotion, Theory of Motivation and Management, Pro-social Motivation/Pro-social Attitudes and Personality,* and *Essays on the Psychology of Social Conflict.*

Andrzej Rychard is assistant professor in the Laboratory of Organizational Sociology in the Institute of Philosophy and Sociology in the Polish Academy of Sciences. Born in Gdansk in 1951, he received a master's degree in sociology from the University of Warsaw (1974) and a doctorate from the Institute of Philosophy and Sociology (1978). His research interests center on the problems of relations between the state and the economic system and the influence these relations exert on social structure. He has conducted field research on Polish industry and is also interested in the sociology of medical institutions. His most recent research findings are contained in the book *Power and Interests in the Polish Economic System.* The English language titles of other representative publications of his are *Economic Reform: Sociological Analysis of the Relations between Politics and Economics, The Social Nature of Management*—edited with L. Kolarska and H. Sterniczuk, *The Economy in the Opinion of Employees*—coauthored with L. Kolarska and H. Sterniczuk, and *Studies in the Sociology of Disability*—edited with M. Sokolowska. He has published articles abroad in *International Studies of Management and Organization* (twice in 1980) and the *International Journal of Sociology* (also in 1980). He was a visiting fellow in the Department of Sociology at the University of Leicester (United Kingdom) in 1979 and in 1981.

Wojciech Sokolewicz is professor of constitutional law at the Institute of the State and Law in the Polish Academy of Sciences, a position he has held since 1974. Since 1970 he has been a part-time consultant to the Council of State. Born in Warsaw in 1931, he is a law graduate of the University of Warsaw (1954). He received his doctorate in the legal sciences from the same university (1964) and his doctor habilitatus in constitutional law from the Institute of the State and Law. From 1954 through 1960 he practiced law in the local administration and has worked at the Institute of the State and Law since 1963. He has been a visiting scholar at Harvard Law School (1967–1968), Columbia University Law School (1974–1975), and L'Ecole Pratique en Sciences Sociales in Paris (1965, 1970, and 1983). He is a specialist in comparative and constitutional law, especially that of the United States. Since 1984 he has been a member of the prime minister's Legislative Council; since 1983, a member of the PZPR Commission on Representative Bodies and Self-Government; and since 1982, deputy editor in chief of the journal *Panstwo i Prawo*. The English language titles of his major publications are *The Development of Democracy in the Soviet State, The Government and the Presidia of People's Councils, Representation and Administration in the System of People's Councils in Poland, U.S. Political-Legal Institutions*, and *The Constitution after the 1976 Amendments* (ed.).

Andrzej Stasiak is professor and head of the Research Center for Spatial Development at the Institute of Geography and Spatial Organization in the Polish Academy of Sciences. He is also contract professor in the socioeconomic department of the Central School of Planning and Statistics (Warsaw). Born in 1928 in Jozefow, Siedlce, Poland, he received degrees from Wroclaw University (1951), the Spatial Planning School of the Department of Architecture of Warsaw Technical University (1954), and a doctorate in the humanities from Wroclaw University (1960). Awarded the doctor habilitatus degree, he became an assistant professor at Wroclaw University in 1966, an associate professor in 1971, and professor in 1982. From 1953 to 1973 he was a researcher at what is today the Institute of Housing Management (Warsaw), where he headed the Department of Rural Development and Housing Problems (1974-1976) until he moved to the academy. His interests center around problems of urban growth and industrialization and their impact on the social structure of towns and the countryside, especially rural settlements and large urban complexes. Since 1978 he has headed the Commission for Rural Areas in the academy's Committee on Spatial Economy and Regional Planning. He was vice president of the Polish Town Planners' Association (1974-1979) and chairman of its Section on Rural Planning and its Scientific and Technical Council. He is a founding member and regional vice-chairman of the International Rural Housing Association (Caracas) and was a member of the Bureau of the International Federation for Housing and Planning at the Hague (1974-1980). English language titles of representative works are *The Development of Urban Agglomerations in Poland* and *The Projected Development of Rural Housing Construction and Its Relationship to Space*. He is coauthor and editor of *Wies Polska 2000*, parts 1 and 2.

Jerzy J. Wiatr is professor of political sociology at the University of Warsaw, a position he has held since 1969. He was chairman of the Department of Sociology (1975-1977) and dean of social sciences (1977-1980). From December 1981 through February 1984, he was director of the research institute of the Central Committee of the Polish United Workers' Party. Born in Warsaw in 1931, he graduated from the University of Warsaw in 1954, received his doctorate in sociology in 1957, and his doctor habilitatus in 1961. He has taught at Warsaw and Cracow universities as well as at the Military Political College in Warsaw. He is past president of the Polish

Political Science Association and past vice president of the International Political Science Association. Currently vice president of the Committee of Sociology in the Polish Academy of Sciences, he is vice chairman of the program committee of the International Political Science Association, and chairman of the coordinating committee of the International Stein Rokkan Archive for Comparative Studies on Leadership. His main books include *Society* (which has gone through ten editions), *Sociology of the Military*, and *Sociology of Political Relations*. His English language books are *Essays in Political Sociology*, *State of Sociology in Eastern Europe* (ed.) and *Polish Studies in the Methodology of the Social Sciences* (ed.).

Index

Absenteeism
  political, 32–33
Administration, 20, 39, 55
  people's councils, 61–62
  rural areas, 134, 142
  service centers, 168, 170–172
  See also Leadership; State
Administrative units. *See* People's councils; Service centers; Voivodships
Agrarian policy
  collectivization, 99–100
  reform, 98–99, 138, 140
  See also Agriculture
Agricultural Development Fund, 100
Agriculture, 75, 99, 148
  attitudes, 112–113
  changes, 75–76
  consumption, 109–110, 113
  development, 101–102, 113–115
  employment, 140, 141–142
  industrialization, 7, 111–113
  investment, 107–110
  modernization, 106–107
  national economy, 110, 111(tables)
  post-World War I, 137–138
  post-World War II, 95–98
  private sector, 4, 93, 98, 100–101, 113–114
  production, 96–98, 101–106, 108(table), 114–115
  public sector, 37, 79
  social change, 5–6
  structure, 78–79
  voivodships, 124–125

See also Agrarian policy; Farmland; Livestock production
AK. *See* Home Army
Armed forces, 55
Association of Friends of the USSR, 14
Autonomy, 4, 25, 34
  economic system, 204, 236
  Sejm, 42–43

Bierut, Boleslaw, 15, 17
Bloc of Democratic Parties, 17
Bobrowski, Czeslaw, 56
Boroughs. *See* Gminas
Bourgeoisie, 139(table)
Britain. *See* Great Britain
Bureaucratization, 6, 220. *See also* State

Catholic church, 1
  political associations, 9–10, 17–18, 19, 30
  political power, 28, 83–84
  social power, 69, 70, 74
  See also Catholicism
Catholicism
  attitudes, 85–89
  context, 82–84
  national religion, 84–85
  power, 81–82, 91
  practicing, 89–91
  See also Catholic church
CBOS. *See* Opinion Research Center
Censorship, 52–53

Central Industrial District (COP), 118
Centralization, 6, 242
Christian Social Association (ChSS), 9, 17
ChSS. *See* Christian Social Association
Civil servants, 56
"Code of Duties of Civil Servants, The," 56
Collectivization, 6, 99, 100. *See also* Cooperatives; Public sector; State-owned farms
Commissions, 61, 66(n33)
Committee for the Observance of Law, Public Order, and Social Discipline, 56
Committee for Youth Affairs, 56
Communist party
  World War II, 14–15
  See also Polish United Workers' party
Communist Party of Poland (KPP), 14
Constitution, 38–39
  1980-1981 crisis, 41–44
  revisions, 43–44, 65(n13)
Constitutional Tribunal, 41, 43
Consultative Economic Council, 56
Consumption, 224
  agricultural products, 109–110
  development, 229–230
Cooperatives, 100–101
Cooperatives of Farmers' Circles, 100
Cooptation, 25
COP. *See* Central Industrial District
Council of Ministers, 42, 47, 51, 67(nn 37, 38, 44)
  role, 53–57
Council of National Reconciliation, 31
Council of State, 38, 39, 42, 43, 47, 55, 66(n 29, 30, 33)
  role, 50–53
Cracow, 118, 132

Crop production, 96, 114–115. *See also* Agriculture
Cyrankiewicz, Jozef, 17, 26

Dachas, 145
Decentralization, 42, 213(n16)
Defense, 55, 67(n39)
Democratic Alliance (SD), 9, 10, 16, 17, 23(table), 30, 32, 40
  power, 18, 19
Democratization, 30
Demography. *See* Geopolitical change; Population
Development, 230, 238, 240
  economic crisis, 214–215
  goals, 233–234
  history of, 116–118
  planning, 216, 229
  plans, 118–120
  regional, 120–130
  sociopolitical system, 219–220, 227–229
  stages, 217–222
  See also Development policy; Economic development
Development policy, 216–217, 119–230, 232
  economic growth, 222–223, 241
  See also Development; Economic development

Economic development, 93–94, 139–140, 156, 215, 225–226
  consumption, 229–230
  goals, 233–234
  social advancement, 181–182
  voivodships, 128–130
  See also Development; Development policy; Economic growth; Economic policy; Economy
Economic growth, 94, 182, 216, 222, 226, 234, 235
  efficiency, 223–224
  industrialization, 7, 217
  regaining, 235–237

state, 217–218, 236
See also Economic development; Economic policy; Economy
Economic policy, 7, 26–27. *See also* Economic development
Economy, 37, 199, 208, 212(n12), 220, 224(fig.)
  agriculture, 109, 110, 111(tables), 182
  functioning, 228–229
  interest groups, 202–203, 207
  plans, 118–119
  political system, 203–204, 209
  politics, 191–192, 198–201
  public sector, 125, 126
  recession, 26–27
  reconstruction, 185, 186–187
  reform, 49–50, 60, 192
  social structure, 213(n28), 237
  society, 195–196
  and state, 196–204, 239–242
  See also Economic development; Economic growth
Education, 37, 76, 142, 177, 184, 223
  progress, 138–140
  rural areas, 137, 171–172
Elections, 17, 30, 35(n5), 50, 63
  laws, 42, 44–45, 65(nn 15, 16, 19)
  regulations, 45–46
  See also Electoral law
Electoral law, 33, 42
Employment, 78, 158
  changes in, 140–143
  industrial, 119, 123
  rural areas, 137, 138, 142–143
  voivodships, 125–126
  See also Trade unions; Working class
Entertainment, 49, 52
Environment
  threat, 127–128

Farming. *See* Agriculture
Farmland, 103, 114, 117. *See also* Agriculture

Finder, Pawel, 15
Food industry, 106. *See also* Agriculture; Food production
Food production
  animal breeding, 105–106
  farmland, 103–104
  supply, 101–103
  See also Agriculture; Livestock production
Foreign policy, 55
Forestry, 134
Forests, 127, 128
Fornalska, Malgorzata, 15
France, 17

Galicia, 137
Gdansk, 118, 140
Gdynia, 118
Geopolitical change
  post-World War II, 72–74, 140
  See also Population, relocation; Settlement patterns
Gierek, Edward, 26
GL. *See* People's Guard
Glemp, Jozef Cardinal, 83
Gminas, 58, 59, 134, 168, 170
  people's councils, 1, 60, 62
Gomulka, Wladyslaw, 15, 26
GOP. *See* Upper Silesian Industrial Basin
Government. *See* Government-in-exile; State
Government-in-exile, 14–16
Government Press Office, 57
Great Britain, 16, 17
Gromadas. See Gminas

"Hammer and Sickle" group, 14
Handicapped people, 37
Health care, 37, 142, 160, 161, 162, 177, 185
Home Army (AK), 14
Housing, 138, 160, 161, 162
  problems, 174–177
Housing Department, 176

Icon of the Czestochowa Virgin Mary, 91
Income, 166–167(figs.). *See also* Wages
Independent Self-Governed Trade Union. *See* Solidarnosc
Independent Student Union, 32
Industrialization, 7, 76, 122–123, 138, 211–212(n3)
  agriculture, 111–112
  history, 117, 119
  migration, 145–146
  recession, 26–27
  rural population, 77, 78
  state power, 197, 217, 218
  See also Industry
Industry, 37, 136, 141, 223
  historical development, 117, 118
  workers, 209–210
  See also Industrialization
Information sources, 4. *See also* Censorship; Publications
Infrastructure, 117–118, 134, 138, 139
  investments, 158–159
  See also Railroads; Social infrastructure; Transportation
Institution. *See* State
Intelligentsia, 139(table)
Interest groups, 202–203, 207

Jaroszewicz, Piotr, 26
Jaruzelski, Wojciech, 30, 31, 34, 56
July Manifesto (1944), 15

KOK. *See* National Defense Committee
KOR. *See* Workers' Defense Committee
KPP. *See* Communist Party of Poland
Krajowa Rada Narodowa. *See* National Home Council
KRN. *See* National Home Council

Labor, 208, 234
  agriculture sector, 112, 113
  political power, 206–207
  See also Labor movement; Peasantry; Trade unions; Working class
Labor Alliance, 16, 17
Labor movement, 1, 4. *See also* Labor; Solidarnosc; Trade unions
Land improvement projects, 107–108
Landowners, 239(table)
Leadership
  identification, 25–26
  party system, 24–26, 40
  promotion, 24–25
  Solidarnosc, 28–29
  See also Administration
Legislation, 57, 58, 60, 67(n39)
  agriculture, 98–99
  constitution, 65(nn 13, 15)
  elections, 65(nn 15, 16, 19)
  martial law, 43, 65(n14)
  political reform, 33–34, 42
  Sejm, 49–50, 64(n12)
  trade unions, 66(nn 28, 32)
Legitimacy, 1, 5, 20, 31, 44, 83, 192, 209, 210, 211
  ideology, 197–198
  politics, 182–183
Livestock production, 96–97, 105–106, 115
Living standards. *See* Standards of living
Lobbies. *See* Interest groups
Lodz, 132, 136

Main Office for the Control of Publications and Entertainment, 52
Martial law, 1, 29, 33, 43, 65(nn 14, 15), 208
  political parties, 31–32
Mass media, 37. *See also* Press
Mechanization
  agriculture, 106–107

Migration, 127, 138
  rural to urban, 142, 145–148, 154(n12)
  See also Geopolitical change; Rural areas; Rural-urban linkages; Settlement patterns; Urban areas; Urbanization
Mikolajczyk, Stanislaw, 14, 16, 17
Military Council of National Salvation (WRON), 31, 43, 55, 67(n40)
Militias, 59
Milk production, 97, 105
Ministries, 57, 65(n24). *See also individual ministries*
Ministry of Agriculture and Food, 100
Minorities, 72–73
Mobilization
  absenteeism, 32–33
  political, 21–24, 32
Modernization, 79, 119

National Defense Committee (KOK), 55
National Home Council (KRN), 15, 16, 17
National identity, 1, 6, 187–188
  Catholic church and, 5, 81–82
Nationalization, 37, 160
National mentality. *See* National identity
National Unity Government, 16, 17
NIK. *See* Supreme Chamber of Control
1947–1949 Three-Year Plan, 77
Nowotko, Marceli, 15

Occupation. *See* Employment
Office of Minister of Internal Affairs, 57
Office of the Council of Ministers, 56–57
Opinion Research Center (CBOS), 57

Osobka-Morawski, Edward, 15, 16

Parapolitical organizations, 22, 23
Parliament. *See* Sejm
Participation. *See* Mobilization
Party system, 13, 20, 35(n2)
  crisis, 26–31
  evolution, 14–18
  hegemony, 18–21
  leadership, 24–26
  mobilization, 21–24
  reform, 31–34
  Solidarnosc, 28–30
  structure, 9–10
  trade unions, 27–29
  See also Political system; *individual political parties*
Patriotic Movement of National Revival (PRON), 33–34, 41, 45
PAX Association, 9, 17, 30
Peasant Alliance (SL), 16, 17
Peasantry, 69, 79, 139(table)
  population, 137, 138, 140
  private ownership, 5–6
  social changes, 75, 76
  See also Labor; Migration; Working class
People's Army, 15
People's councils, 33, 38, 39, 45
  administration, 61–62
  organization, 58–59, 60–62
  role, 58–60
People's Guard (GL), 15
Petite bourgeoisie, 139
PKWN. *See* Polish Committee for National Liberation
Planning, 60, 67(n37)
  development, 216, 229
  economic growth, 221, 236
  institutional, 218–219
  See also Reform
Pluralism, 5, 19, 204, 212(n7)
  Catholic church, 84, 91
  Polish society, 4, 6–7
Policy, 120, 183, 235

goals, 232–233
socioeconomic, 215, 241
See also Agrarian policy;
Development policy; Economic
policy; Policymaking
Policymaking, 3–4, 5, 19. *See also*
Agrarian policy; Development
policy; Economic policy;
Policy
Polish Committee for National
Liberation (PKWN), 15, 16,
98
Polish Peasant Alliance (PSL), 16–17
Polish Socialist party (PPS), 15,
16, 17
Polish Socialist Youth Union
(ZSMP), 23(table), 32
Polish Union of Lay Catholics
(PZKS or ZNAK), 9–10, 17
Polish United Workers' party
(PZPR), 4, 32, 45, 64(n2)
  changes, 30–31, 42
  Council of Ministers, 53, 58
  development, 9, 17
  leadership, 25, 40
  membership, 23–24, 205,
    206(table)
  power, 18, 183, 205, 206(table),
    210
  resolution, 41–42
  role, 18–19
  Sejm, 46, 47
  Solidarnosc, 28, 36(n17)
Polish Workers' party (PPR), 14–15, 16, 17
Polish Youth Union (ZMP), 22
Politburo, 53–54
Political organizations
  membership, 22–23, 32
  See also Political parties;
    individual organizations
Political parties
  and Sejm, 46–47
  See also Party system; Political
    organizations; Political system;
    individual parties

Political system, 205
  crisis and, 230–231
  development, 219–220
  economy, 196–197, 198–201,
    203–204, 209, 212(n12)
  expectations, 224–226
  fitness, 210–211
  interest groups, 202–203
  internal orientation, 206–207
  See also Party system; Political
    organizations; Political parties
Popiel, Karol, 16
Population, 141(table)
  centers of, 117, 118, 132
  environmental threat, 127–128
  losses, 137, 140
  relocation, 6, 72–73, 94
  rural, 135–136, 137, 140–141,
    142–143, 144(map), 148–151,
    152(map), 153(map)
  suburban, 144–145
  urban, 126, 135
  voivodships, 122(table), 129–130
  See also Settlement patterns
Potsdam agreement, 72
Poultry production, 106
Power. *See* State
Poznan, 132
PPR. *See* Polish Workers' party
PPS. *See* Polish Socialist party
Press, 4. *See also* Publications
Private sector, 160, 176
  agrarian structure, 113–114
  agriculture, 4, 5–6, 98, 100, 101,
    107, 141
  See also Public sector
Productivity, 6, 229, 234, 236, 242
  agriculture, 79, 95, 96–98, 114–115
PRON. *See* Patriotic Movement of
  National Revival
Propaganda, 27, 57
  internal, 28, 164
Provinces. *See* Voivodships
PSL. *See* Polish Peasant Alliance
Publications, 37, 49, 52

Public sector, 101, 125, 126. *See also* Collectivization; Cooperatives; Private sector; State-owned farms
PZKS. *See* Polish Union of Lay Catholics
PZPR. *See* Polish United Workers' party

Radio, 4
Railroads, 117, 118
Recession, 26–27
"Reconstruction of state life" slogan, 41
Recreation, 145
Reform
  absenteeism, 32–33, 34
  economic, 49–50, 205, 235
  effects, 180–184
  political, 31–34, 205
  See also Planning
Regions. *See* Voivodships
Religion, 5
  attitudes toward, 85–89
  practice of, 89–91
  See also Catholic church; Catholicism
Resettlement
  population, 6, 69, 72
Resolution of the Ninth Extraordinary Congress of the PZPR (1981), 41
Retail trade, 37, 160
Roman Catholic church. *See* Catholic church; Catholicism
RPPS. *See* Workers' Party of Polish Socialists
Rule of law, 38, 142, 153(map), 171
Rural areas, 77, 132, 133, 134
  education, 137, 171–172
  emigration, 145–146
  farmland, 103–104
  farm structure, 78–79
  land use, 143–145
  population, 103, 135–136, 148–151, 152(map)
  religion, 85–86, 88, 89(table)
  socioeconomics, 5–6
  suburban areas, 144–145
  See also Agriculture; Farmland; Rural-urban linkages; Urban areas; Urbanization
Rural-urban linkages, 94
  history of, 131–134
  migration, 145–148
  settlement patterns, 144–145
  See also Rural areas; Suburban zones; Urban areas; Urbanization
Rural Youth Union (ZMW), 32

SD. *See* Democratic Alliance
Sejm, 38, 39, 48, 57, 98
  autonomy, 42–43
  Council of State, 50–51
  elections, 44–45, 63
  legislation, 49–50, 64(n12)
  organization, 10–11
  role, 46–47, 49–50
Self-government, 42, 63, 76
  people's councils, 58–62
  See also Self-management
Self-management, 67–68(n48), 204. *See also* Self-government
Service centers
  availability, 172–174
  distribution, 165, 168–172
  restructuring, 170–171
  See also Services
Services, 5, 6
  availability, 158, 172–174
  hierarchies, 161–163
  role, 155–156
  See also Education; Health care; Housing; Service centers; Social infrastructure
Settlement patterns
  rural-urban, 132–133
  suburban pattern, 144–145
  See also Geopolitical change; Migration; Rural areas; Rural-urban linkages; Urban areas; Urbanization

Sikorski, Wladyslaw, 14
Silesia-Dabrowa basin, 136
Six-Year Plan 1950–1955, 77, 112
SL. *See* Peasant Alliance
Social classes
　changes, 74–76
　See also Peasantry; Social structure; Working class
Social infrastructure, 170
　access, 172–174
　development, 157–159
　efficiency, 163–165
　hierarchy, 161–163
　problems, 177–178
　propaganda, 164–165
　welfare state, 159–161
　See also Education; Health care; Housing; Service centers; Services
Socialism. *See* Political system
Socialist Union of Polish Students, 23(table), 32
Social order
　models, 205–209
　See also Social structure
Social services. *See* Services
Social structure, 71, 140, 207–208, 220
　advancement, 181–182
　aspirations, 226–227
　changes, 69–70, 72–74, 76–80, 138–139, 184–189
　classes, 74–76
　crisis, 230–231
　economic growth, 223–224
　economy and, 199–200, 213(n28), 237, 239–242
　needs, 228, 231
　progress, 223–225, 226
　working class, 209–210
Society. *See* Social structure
Socioeconomic Council, 48
Socioeconomics
　change, 93–94, 140, 215, 216, 232, 234, 236–237, 238, 240, 241
Sociopolitical Committee, 54, 56

Solidarity. *See* Solidarnosc
Solidarnosc, 1, 23, 36(n17), 183, 204, 206(table)
　creation, 27–28
　dissolution, 31, 32, 49
　political activity, 28–29
Soviet Union (USSR), 16
Standards of living, 25, 145, 222, 238
　aspirations, 226–227
　rural areas, 79, 133
　voivodships, 127(table), 128(table)
　See also Education; Health care; Housing; Social structure
State, 191, 231, 238
　development, 227–229, 233–235
　economic growth, 217–218, 239–242
　economy and, 196–204, 228–229
　executive power, 53–57
　goals of, 37–38
　planning, 218–219
　power, 210, 237
　progress, 233–234
　self-government and, 58–62
　socioeconomics and, 236–237
　stability, 209, 210–211
　See also Council of Ministers; State apparatus; State organs
State apparatus, 2, 10
　system, 38–40, 63–64
　See also State; State organs
State organs
　changes, 41–43
　hierarchies, 39–40
　See also State apparatus; *individual organs*
State-owned farms, 79, 99–100, 106. *See also* Collectivization; Cooperatives; Public sector
Strikes, 26, 49, 203, 208. *See also* Solidarnosc; Trade unions
Stronnictwo Demokratyczne. *See* Democratic Alliance
Students, 91. *See also* Youth
Suburban zones, 144–145

Supreme Administrative Court, 43, 52
Supreme Chamber of Control (NIK), 39, 41, 42, 52
Supreme Court, 39, 42, 46, 52
Szczecin, 140
Szczepanski, Jan, 49

Technocracy, 6–7
Technology, 176, 216. *See also* Mechanization; Modernization
Trade unions, 53, 64(n2), 205, 212(n15)
  establishment, 27–28
  law, 33, 49, 66(nn 28, 32)
  martial law, 31–32
  participation, 22–23
  recession, 26–27
  See also Labor movement; Solidarnosc; Working class
Transportation
  employment, 141, 142(table)
  networking, 117, 118, 172–174
  rural areas, 144–145, 171
  See also Infrastructure; Railroads
Tribunal of State, 41, 43, 54

Unemployment, 138. *See also* Employment; Labor
Union of Fighters for Freedom and Democracy, 23(table)
Union of Liberation Struggle, 14
Unions. *See* Trade unions
United Peasant Alliance (ZSL), 9, 17, 23(table), 30, 32, 40
  power, 18, 19
United States, 16, 17
Upper Silesia
  industry, 117, 118
  urbanization, 136–137
Upper Silesian Industrial Basin (GOP), 144. *See also* Upper Silesia
Urban areas, 5, 117, 132
  population, 126, 135, 136(table)
  religion, 86, 87, 88, 89(table)
  See also Rural areas; Rural-urban linkages; Suburban zones; Urbanization
Urbanization, 76–77, 112, 126, 142, 154(n12)
  historical trends, 134–135, 136–137
  post-World War II, 119–120
  See also Industrialization; Migration; Rural areas; Rural-urban linkages; Suburban zones; Urban areas
USSR. *See* Soviet Union

Villages, 133–134. *See also* Rural areas; Suburban zones
Virgin Mary cult, 91
Vocational schools, 77
Voivodships, 58–59, 62, 98, 117, 148
  agriculture, 124–125
  economic development, 128–130
  employment, 125–126
  environment, 127–128
  industrialization, 119, 123–124
  standards of living, 126–127, 128(map)
  structure, 120–122

Wages, 226, 227, 229. *See also* Income; Standards of living
Warsaw, 118, 132, 136, 140, 144
Welfare, 26, 37
  infrastructure, 159–161
Welfare socialism, 26. *See also* Welfare
Wola Ludu (bulletin), 15
Wola Ludu Peasant Alliance, 15–16
Workers' Defense Committee (KOR), 27
Worker self-management. *See* Self-management
Workers' Party of Polish Socialists (RPPS), 15

Work ethic, 78
Working class, 69, 88, 139(table), 183, 213(n26)
  industry, 209-210
  role, 77-78
  See also Labor; Labor movement; Peasantry
World War II, 137-138
  party development, 14-17
Wroclaw, 118, 132, 140
WRON. *See* Military Council of National Salvation
Wyszynski, Stefan Cardinal, 83

Yalta conference (1945), 16, 72
Youth
  religious views, 86-87, 88(table), 90-91
  See also Youth organizations
Youth organizations
  participation, 22, 23-24
  See also Polish Youth Union; Youth
Yugoslavia, 16

ZMP. *See* Polish Youth Union
ZMW. *See* Rural Youth Union
ZNAK. *See* Polish Union of Lay Catholics
"Znak" Sejm Deputies' Club, 17
ZSL. *See* United Peasant Alliance
ZSMP. *See* Polish Socialist Youth Union